Books by Rudi Blesh

MODERN ART USA: MEN, REBELLION, CONQUEST, 1900–56 (*1956*)

SHINING TRUMPETS: A HISTORY OF JAZZ (*1946*)

(*with Harriet Janis*) THEY ALL PLAYED RAGTIME (*1950*)

These are Borzoi Books, published in New York by Alfred A Knopf

Modern Art USA

MEN, REBELLION, CONQUEST, 1900–1956

Rudi Blesh

MODERN ART USA

Men, Rebellion, Conquest, 1900–1956

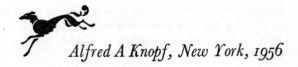

Alfred A Knopf, New York, 1956

L.C. catalog card number: 56–5779

© RUDI BLESH, *1956*

This is a BORZOI BOOK, *published by* ALFRED A. KNOPF, INC.

If you seek the kernel, then you must break the shell. And likewise if you would know the reality of nature, you must destroy the appearance, and the farther you go beyond the appearance, the nearer you will be to the essence.

MEISTER ECKHART (1260?–1327), *translated by Lyonel Feininger*

Acknowledgments

The author, for much valuable help, gratefully expresses thanks TO THE ARTISTS: Marcel Duchamp, Richard Mutt, and Rrose Sélavy; Max Weber, the late Lyonel Feininger, Abraham Walkowitz, Stuart Davis, Georgia O'Keeffe, Frederick Kiesler, Gerald Murphy, John Covert, Lucia (Mrs. Roger Wilcox), Jackson Pollock, Willem de Kooning, Mark Rothko, William Baziotes, Franz Kline, Robert Motherwell, Jimmy Ernst, Harry Holtzman, Charles Seliger, John Hultberg, and Paul Brach, AND TO: Alfred H. Barr, Jr., René d'Harnoncourt, Captain Edward Steichen, Dorothy Miller, A. Conger Goodyear, Andrew Carnduff Ritchie, Douglas MacAgy, George Heard Hamilton, Richard Griffith, and Bernard Karpel, AND TO: Holger Cahill, Henry McBride, Harris K. Prior, Francis J. Newton, Thomas B. Hess, Rue Shaw, Harriet Janis, Mrs. Dorothy Norman, Mrs. Ethel Schwabacher, Elizabeth McCausland, Leo Castelli, Jules Langsner, H. J. Allen, and Paul Ellsworth Everett, Jr., AND TO THE ART DEALERS: Marian Willard, Betty Parsons, Edith Halpert, Bertha Schaefer, Martha Jackson, Julien Levy, Pierre Matisse, Samuel Kootz, Sidney Janis, and Charles Egan, AND FINALLY TO: The Museum of Modern Art for generous permission to use as a starting point for this present book a television report prepared by the author in 1954.

Contents

Illustrations

Modern Art USA

MEN, REBELLION, CONQUEST, 1900–1956

1. *The World Stirs in Its Sleep*

"Modern," both adjective and noun, is a comparative rather than an absolute term. It is applied by definition to the just-conceived or the newly developed thing. Thus the applicability of the adjective, equally with the meaning of the noun, is forever changing fluidly as the times themselves change and as human viewpoints change with them.

Yet there is nothing equivocal or essentially vague in the term "modern" as applied to the art of the last fifty years, although in that time the concept of what art is—as well as of what *is* art—has been vastly broadened. By "modern" art in the visual fields, we understand today painting, sculpture, and allied plastic expressions that began in 1903–4 in France and soon departed basically in method and aim from all similar art as it had been known—to put it most broadly—in Europe from the beginning of the Renaissance in the fourteenth century.

Since 1904 there have been many developments, many changes, and many different schools in this modern art: Fauvism, cubism of several sorts, futurism, expressionism, neoplasticism, Dada, surrealism, and so on. They seemed startlingly new and different as they came along, and so they were. But we now can see them all as parts of the same thing: a new kind of art which expresses our times and which changes, as we do, with them.

Equally clearly, we recognize as the forerunners of modern art in the third quarter of the nineteenth century Gustave Courbet's anti-romantic realism and then that of Édouard Manet; Edgar Degas's camera viewpoint, and the light-color theorems of Claude Monet, Camille Pissarro, and the other impressionists. Each of these was, to a degree, revolutionary in its time. None, however, broke with the Renaissance idea of

art as representation of outward appearance, with the illu-
sionism of deep, perspectived space on two-dimensional canvas, with the centuries-old idea of what a picture essentially
should be.

Finally, we clearly recognize today as the immediate
forebears of modern art four gifted and remarkably individual
painters whose significant work was done in the last fifteen
years of the nineteenth century. These were the so-called post-
impressionists: Georges Seurat, Paul Gauguin, Vincent van
Gogh, and Paul Cézanne. "Post-impressionist" was a term
tossed off in 1910 by the English critic Roger Fry. Only
Seurat, with his method of painting in dots of color (*pointillisme*), was in any accurate sense an impressionist. Actually
the four men were very different in their work, and from one
or another of them can be traced the directions that modern
art, with its bewildering complexity of methods, aims, and
viewpoints, has taken. But the four were as one in the revolutionary idea they shared: that it is the artist's duty to express
himself, the artist's right to be completely of his own time.
These prerogatives, which we readily grant today, were not so
readily granted sixty years ago. From them automatically
follow the basic tenets of modern art: continually to question
all things—what is form? what is beauty? what is essential
reality? what should content be? From questions like these, so
closely allied to the questionings of the physical and mental
sciences then arising, art became and continues to become a
contemporary human expression. Art's being of its own time
is its chief justification as a serious creative pursuit, and in
retrospect is the unique value that we ascribe to each of the
great art periods of the past, and the value, as well, which
paradoxically makes each one timeless. The Roman copyists

are men without names, but Praxiteles is remembered.

These painters—the Four Titans, as they have been called—intuitively allied themselves with the scientific temper of their time. As artists they were far in advance of their time. The ideas they sowed took time to sprout—would not do so, in fact, until a new century had begun.

In the world of Seurat's paintings—as flat as a microscopic slide—matter seems porous and forms are galaxies of minute colored dots, as if the painter had a premonition of atomic structure. Like the biochemist synthesizing natural compounds in the laboratory, Seurat constructs from his minute dots the larger over-all pictorial forms of his paintings —stark, silhouetted forms that pointed the way to the relative abstraction of the early 1900's and then to the later non-objectivism or complete abstraction.

Paul Gauguin, the strange and moody stockbroker-become-artist, lived a romantic life that has been a gold mine for novelists, and in a sense his painting is vestigial romanticism. But because Gauguin looked at the South Seas through eyes that were those of both a romantic and an artist, he was the first to call our attention to primitive art and to its universal and enduring symbols. Gauguin, too, was daring in his use of color as not only a descriptive element, but as expressive in its own right. When, years later, Franz Marc came along to shock everyone with his *Blue Horse* and nudge Gelett Burgess into penning his famous quatrain about the Purple Cow, behind it all was Gauguin.

Unhappy Vincent van Gogh, tortured and yet jubilant, exploded on each canvas in an ecstasy of compulsive creation, each painting a lesson in the irrational psychology of genius which modern psychology is still struggling to explain. A third of the way into our present century, and long after Van Gogh's suicide, those tragically exultant canvases of his would travel across our land, compelling such a tribute as America has rarely paid any artist.

Paul Cézanne must be reckoned as the one of the Titans who broke with the hampering tradition of centuries so conclusively as to reorient the course of art. "The Old Man of Aix, wild, candid, irascible and good," as his friend Émile Zola described him, was the most misunderstood of all because he was the most advanced. Alone, without a guide, and purely from a deep instinct of what was wrong with painting and how it must be righted, he attacked plastic art from its very foundations: form and composition. He tore the love of the picturesque out of himself as one uproots a weed; he forced himself to see that beauty—that sacred word of art—was, like stage scenery, a deception; he looked long and hard at nature to see what was behind the way it looked. He made geometrical diagrams of the hidden structure of nature. His contemporaries, faced by his strange, seemingly fumbling paintings, were like men being shown the map of an unknown and not even guessed-at world. Cézanne was scorned as a man who did not even know how to paint; he was laughed at, but he went doggedly, obstinately on, painting in the nineteenth century pictures for the eyes of the twentieth.

These four builders of the foundations of modern art tore the tottering ancient building down and sorted out the materials from which to build the new. These basic materials were form (including line), composition, and color, and the blueprint for the rebuilding was the new way of looking at reality. And this new way, like a musical leitmotiv reasserting itself, proved to be the still more ancient one, the unspoiled and innocent vision of the primitive, the lost gift of looking at the world as if it were a new world never looked at before. Sixty years later we can look back at this revolution and see it, not as willful destruction or reckless search for the new at any cost which it once seemed, but as a brave return to the beginnings to find a new and straighter road to reality.

At the time, however, it was a different matter. Few knew it then, but all around us an old world was dying, a new one being born. Science, giving us rapid transportation and virtually instantaneous communication, was shrinking the world under our feet. The boundary lines of the nations were becoming more than ever the delible lines on a sketch map of the world as seen from twenty thousand feet in the air.

The atmosphere was uneasy; men were rubbing their eyes, trying to see this new world and to imagine what manner of role was to be theirs. Arthur Jerome Eddy, one of the earliest American champions of modern art, wrote in 1914 of the "peoples heretofore safe in their isolation" being "swept into the maelstrom," and observed that "nations which had long been sleeping, turned in their beds and stretched themselves." [1]

In 1904 not only the seeds of modern art, but dragon's teeth as well, were sprouting. Only ten years in the offing was World War I. Already under way, however, was the war to establish a contemporary and meaningful art—the art we now call modern. It was a war of esthetic ideas, and a bitter one. It was being fought in Paris, but it was a world war just the same. New and younger artists were in this war: Frenchmen, Spaniards, Romanians, Germans, Hungarians, Russians, Italians, Poles, Dutchmen, and a number of Americans living in

[1] Arthur Jerome Eddy: *Cubists and Post-Impressionism* (Chicago, 1914).

France. Their war was not for, but against, boundaries, for universality, for a world language of art that would be affirmative. They were in advance of the scientific and political happenings that in time would bleach out those lines on the sketch map, fainter and fainter, in the hope one day of making one world.

Across the Atlantic, in majestic insularity, America too was stirring in her sleep. What would happen when this new art crossed the sea to invade and disturb the smug isolation of her dream?

2. *Home Life on the Other Side of the Moon*

The general isolation of America at the beginning of the twentieth century is difficult to imagine today, when we are potentially involved by events in almost any corner of the globe. Politically and culturally, this country lived in a virtual vacuum frequently called provincialism. The term is historically inaccurate, for when America *was* a province (in other words, still a British colony), it was far more receptive to cultural ideas from abroad than it was as a free and sovereign nation almost two centuries later.

In 1750 American architects were building after the latest Georgian modes; American cabinetmakers were working in the latest "modern" style of Thomas Chippendale; American composers were adapting the advanced contrapuntal and scalar innovations that the great baroque musicians had left as their legacy to the world; and American painters were following the newest concepts of Gainsborough. It was no one-way line, either, like calf at udder: the American scene, the wonder of the great, green new continent, the magic myth of the Noble Redskin, was firing the imaginations of Europeans. So, too, were the deeds of our frontiersmen, the courage of whose daily lives—it might have been foreseen—would inevitably make a free nation of us. We did not just import culture in design books; we participated creatively, altered, extended, adapted. The Georgian house in Virginia or New England became unmistakably an American house. In John Singleton Copley, Gainsborough found a strength and forthrightness he never knew.

And it should never be forgotten that these forefathers of ours had broad, humane, elastic minds. In this same eighteenth century they were absorbing the new philosophy of Jean Jacques Rousseau to such effect that they would start building a new nation around the cornerstone of his premise that "all men are created free." Long before the American artist, the American political man would be free. The former soon would enter a long, strange slavery. His rights as a useful member of society would be denied him, and, unaccountably, he would not rebel. His fellows in Europe, too, would be similarly disfranchised, artistically speaking, but some of them would rebel. For a long three quarters of a century the American artist would join no rebellions. A newly preoccupied society had kicked him upstairs: he became a man on a pedestal. The useful artist who had done our portraits and decorated our walls and painted our tavern signs would become lost up there. Unaccustomed to heroic bronze posturing, he would become instead an entertainer and the graven pedestal a stage.

For society had found a new preoccupation. In America it became an obsession. Early in the nineteenth century we, like Europe, plunged into an age of invention, laying the groundwork for the technology and industry that, step by step, have shrunk the limits of the world. Soon our portraits were being made by a little box fitted with a lens. That was more practical than painting them, and soon *any* painting came to look insignificant alongside Eli Whitney's newly invented cotton gin. One day the little *Clermont* steamed painfully up the Hudson; almost the next—so compressed and inevitable seems the process in our long view today—the *Great Western* was crossing the Atlantic; one day came the first finger tap on telegraph key, and on the next the transatlantic cable was being laid; one day Stephenson's *Rocket* jerked haltingly over its wooden rails, and the next, long trains of cars behind powerful locomotives were roaring over networks of rails that crisscrossed America, the British Isles, and Europe. And men of that century, like the spiritual descendants of Leonardo that they were, dreamed of machines that would fly.

But with each step that brought the continents nearer to each other, America seemed to pull more and more into her shell. By her own choice, or through her preoccupation, she became a political and cultural recluse. Not only did we no longer know what was happening in art and philosophy abroad—we did not want to know. With each development in communication we communicated less in a real sense with our neighbors. With each speed-up in transportation, more of us traveled, and traveled less in the sense of adventure. We crowded the museums and fell in love with the past—all naturally enough because with us art was already in the past. Over all those years, it may be believed, not one Innocent Abroad set foot in the studio of Ingres, Delacroix, or Courbet.

By the 1880's—or even before—our painting had become a ritual, a topical exercise, of literal landscape washed clean of all except the pretty (and perhaps a nymph or two), of photographic genre subjects, and of discreetly draped figures whose allowable nudity was in direct proportion to the nobility and abstraction of the allegory they were supposed to represent. Truth, or Freedom, or the Spirit of Humanity could, in extreme cases, cavort over a canvas as if in the Garden of Eden. Eve herself, however, was likely to wear more clothes than the modern woman could comfortably carry for summer street wear. Eve, we knew, was human and had sinned; Truth and her sisters, by definition, could not. Mary Magdalene, though a sinner, was a glorious exception: history had recorded that in a few days, or a week at most, she would repent. With redemption so near, it was permissible to show her in sin.

The rule governing subjects of cruelty and violence was simple: they must be historical. The longer ago it happened, the more cruel and violent the action could be. And it was even better if it was some trifling incident—like annihilation— forced on a weaker race by a stronger (and hence nobler) race. Like Rome liquidating Carthage. Napoleon was a good subject any time. He lent himself to big canvases, and no one could look nobler amid scenes of carnage.

It was all very tidy. No one could possibly be offended except those rare souls who are offended when the censor removes every possible source of offense. It was Victoria's age, the great age of Duty. Art had its Duty: to entertain us in lighter moments, and in more solemn ones to instruct us by antiseptic precept. It was never to challenge, never to question why; art was not even to do, it was merely to die. Die it very nearly did. By 1900 in America it lay moribund under an oxygen tent in the hospital called the Academy. It is now, on the whole—that sort of art—much a thing of the past. At least, it is not the only kind recognized as art. Its lovely presence, however, lingers on like the Cheshire Cat in the mechanical smiles of our television salesmen and the annual Miss Something-or-Other.

There was, it is true, a minor uprising or two. In 1878 a band of young American painters led by Frank Duveneck of Cincinnati came back from Munich and gave affront to respectability by an exhibition of their work at the American Galleries in New York. Their outlawry consisted, essentially, in rediscovering the "realism" and the untamed brushwork of Frans Hals, who had died over two centuries before.

And, of course, from the vast output of the century some names have emerged: certain of the Hudson River School of landscape painters, as also Winslow Homer, George Inness, Thomas Eakins, and Albert Pinkham Ryder. Homer and the Hudson River men were not rebels: they were men like Thoreau afflicted by nostalgia for an America vanishing all around them. They produced landscapes unsullied by factories, tracts over which the primeval magic still hung. Their poetry is that of regret. The realism of Eakins may be considered a revolutionary thing in its time. Yet it effected no revolution, and with equal justice may be seen as another continuation of a past when the artist had been a man of honor in this country. His portraits and the celebrated *Gross Clinic* are honestly observed painting without frills. They are part and parcel of the portraits by Copley and our eighteenth-century "limners," the itinerant, unashamed peddlers of their craft. There is in them all the same angularity of arrested motion; the style is different, the spirit the same. Ryder was a mystic. The mystic's art is of all time and no time, starts no schools, effects no revolutions.

Only five years after Duveneck came home, there was a second and last crisis in the reign of the Academy. Durand-Ruel showed the work of the French impressionists in New York. The Academy shook, but only with rage. The show came down, and everyone went back to sleep. Twenty years later, in 1903, long after impressionism had been absorbed in France in a continuing revolution, it was still being debated in America. It was the twentieth century by then, but, as far as art was concerned, we had not been told. We were where we seemed to want to be, quiet on the other side of the moon.

In 1904 real art revolt broke out in France, one phase of the general awakening of the civilized world to a new age. Its social concomitant was a strong feeling of unrest on the part of people everywhere, a dim awareness of forces in conflict, a vague and nameless feeling of anticipation the world over. Anticipation of what? No one quite knew.

Despite our isolation, we could not escape these feelings. We were not immune. So here, too, art revolt began. Our established Academy, symbol here as in France of the tyrannical *status quo*, began to come under attack. From the turn of the century to the outbreak of the First World War in Europe, rebellious American artists faced a choice: they fought it out at home or they went to the larger battlefield in Paris. For once the escapists were right. The stay-at-homes did not get very far. Fight tradition as they might, they simply did not know how to go on from there. They were in an isolation ward. During the first, fast-moving, exciting years of the new art in Paris, not a word about it, not a reproduction of a painting, appeared in an American magazine or newspaper of note.

In cosmopolitan Paris, however, there was only tradition to combat, and this in a milieu where the artist was accepted as an important unit of society. As a result, the few Americans who migrated to the Left Bank of the Seine were the ones who, in the upshot, turned the tide for modern art in this country.

Chief stay-at-home rebel was the American painter and teacher Robert Henri. In 1904, Cincinnati-born Henri was thirty-nine years old and had had a bellyful of the Academy and its works. He had gone to Paris, all right, but had come home too early. Having studied at the Pennsylvania Academy and found it too academic, he had gone on to the Académie Julian in Paris. There, too, he writhed against the restraint and the narrowness of vision. He looked around him and came up with the best he could find—Courbet, Manet, and Whistler— and became what was then called a realist.

Robert Henri was a born fighter. He would have gone great if he had stayed in France only a few years more. As it was, however, Henri wasted his energies fighting, not for modernism at all, but for its prerequisites. On these he had to waste his energies precisely because he was in an America that was thirty years behind the times. He fought Cézanne's battle all over again, and Van Gogh's—for the right of the artist to paint as he wished.

Henri waged his fight exactly as he always began a painting, "as though he were going into battle." [1] He was a great propagandist, a man of enormous personal magnetism. He immediately got on the academic blacklist, condemned as "The Bad Boy of American Art." That brought volunteers to his side. They called themselves The Eight, and their members, besides Henri, were John Sloan, William Glackens, Everett Shinn, George Luks, Ernest Lawson, Maurice Prendergast, and Arthur B. Davies. They have been called a school, but they were not. No two of them painted alike or with the same aims. They shared a dangerous dissatisfaction.

After all the fat years, the Academy sensed a threat. Here was "a dangerous unaccustomed mingling of art and life"; [2] the rebels were dubbed a "revolutionary black gang"; and the realistic "slum" paintings of some of the younger American painters were contemptuously designated "Ash Can Pictures." These men had had the temerity to choose, without clearing it with the powers, subject matter that they saw with their own eyes.

Like a manufacturer in control of all the distributors, the Academy and its followers had the upper hand. Their product

[1] Nathaniel Pousette-Dart: *Robert Henri* (New York, 1922).

[2] Helen Appleton Read: Introduction to the catalogue of the Whitney exhibit "New York Realists 1900–1914" (1937).

was accepted; dealers vied for it; and the Academy had its own gallery. No one would show The Eight. Henri, it is true, could get a medal in 1904 at the Art Institute of Chicago, Lawson one the same year at the St. Louis Exposition, but these were only bribes of expediency. The Eight had to have a show—a barrage-like big show—or they were not a going concern. In Paris, the revolutionaries—Matisse, Picasso, Braque, and the rest—were meeting the same difficulties by taking over the traditional *salon d'automne*. There was nothing here comparable to the *salon* that The Eight could seize.

While The Eight waited for a chance, three unknown young painters—Arnold Friedman, Glenn Coleman, and Jules Golz—showed how it could be done if you were willing to dispense with style. In 1908 these three youngsters got really worked up. Over dinners of cheap spaghetti in Greenwich Village, and stirred by the fumes of red wine, they worried the question "What to do about the Academy?" To them it was simple: give an independent exhibition. And they did. So far as is known, it was the first independent show ever held in America.

Many years later Friedman was to comment: "When three men, without funds, not extraordinarily energetic, having no special flair for invention or initiative, could have been so spurred into action, some slight understanding can be gained of the utter hopelessness, the void, or, better, the blank stone wall which confronted young painters of the time." [3]

The three young men found two possible locations for a show. Both were the opposite of well-lighted de-luxe galleries. One on 57th Street—now the center of Manhattan's art-dealer galleries—was then felt to be too far uptown. The

[3] From unpublished ms by Friedman in Museum of Modern Art Library.

second was a large double loft in bad repair on 42nd Street facing Bryant Park, behind the New York Public Library. This was chosen. Word got around among the young painters, and in rushed a group of twelve joiners, who included George Bellows, Guy Pène du Bois, Edward Hopper, Rockwell Kent, and Carl Sprinchorn. Bellows took over the decoration and installation, making adroit and inexpensive use of muslin and calcimine to create a gallery. In March 1908 the show opened.

"Was it a success?" Friedman himself posed the question many years later. "None of us," he observed in retrospect, "had delusions of greatness . . . but all hopefully believed that the gesture of initiative . . . would receive attention."

"Was it a success?"

No, he seems to answer. "The reviewers," he relates, "treated it merely as another point to cover and the show without flourish passed into limbo. . . .

"You see," Friedman concluded, "we were all too young to . . . understand that the pioneering spirit is applauded only in retrospect."

Friedman was a modest man. He was a postman. Stuart Davis says that Friedman in his spare time had studied with Robert Henri. Although the show got no critical applause, three young men had shown that, with an empty loft and the will, it could be done. Unrest had come out into the open.

That same year there was another indication of the serious plight of unknown or divergent artists in America. The first free outdoor art show—come one, come all—occurred in Washington Square in Greenwich Village. As is well known, these shows have continued ever since, a colorful feature of New York life.

The august Metropolitan Museum of Art was having no

part of anything contemporary, even a good hot quarrel. Later that same year, through its Director, Sir Purdon Clark, it commented officially on the deplorable disquiet felt everywhere: "I," he said, "dislike unrest."

Clark was J. Pierpont Morgan's man, the man for the job. He resisted not only the twentieth century, but the nineteenth, eighteenth, and a goodly part of the seventeenth as well. He held in effective leash his brilliant young countryman Roger Fry, Curator of Paintings, who had dangerous ideas about contemporary American art and even those terrible things which had happened in France twenty-five years before. Like a colonial governor standing off his soldiery from the pretty native girls, Sir Purdon's solid, stolid, British bulk stood between the public and anything contemporary.

"Impressionism" was a naughty word in the sacred precincts. It could stay in France as a part of that outlandish tongue. Fortunately for America, we had a few daring collectors who felt otherwise. Already, for nearly twenty years, Mrs. Potter Palmer of Chicago, undeterred by the laughter of her friends, had been collecting impressionist work, often buying direct from the studios of Monet, Pissarro, and other leaders of the movement in France. It was said that behind her back in society circles in the Windy City she was sometimes called Mrs. "Potty" Palmer, but years later her bequest of plein-air masterpieces would make the Art Institute of Chicago one of the greatest repositories in the world of this important early revolutionary work. Not that the Art Institute had anything to do with it at the time: it was like the Metropolitan.

Then there was that unspeakable Cézanne, a man who didn't even bother to cover all of his canvas with paint. In the East before 1910, the wealthy collector H. O. Havemeyer added five great Cézanne pictures to his Courbets, Degases, Goyas, and El Grecos. Twenty-odd years later these would enrich the Metropolitan, regardless of what it thought then or has thought since of Cézanne. What got into Havemeyer? There is a strong suspicion that young Roger Fry found his ear.

The Metropolitan had had a glorious opportunity way back in 1905 to become the first museum in the world to show the new art. That was the year when Fry joined the staff. J. P. Morgan had heard of Fry's brilliance, but not of his up-to-date tendencies. Fry, however, at first rebuffed the great Morgan's offer of a job. "Get him," was Morgan's order. Fry was got.

That first year, Roger Fry was the lion of the "Four Hundred." As Virginia Woolf has written, "He was feted . . . was astonished by the luxury of millionaires." On one occasion he traveled in the international banker's private car "tacked on to the end of a private express. It was snowing and a log fire was lit in the car, which was 'fitted up like a private house in the grandest style.' " [4]

Between glasses of champagne, the new Curator's job was made clear to him. Already he could observe that the Metropolitan had more funds at its disposal than any other gallery in the world, but was not interested in the works of contemporary Americans in any style, much less modern. Nevertheless, he found "more and more nice people . . . very keen to help the new ideas at the Museum." [5]

By the second year, Fry was no longer traveling in Morgan's palatial private car. He had been, as he said,

[4] Virginia Woolf: *Roger Fry, A Biography* (London, 1940).
[5] Ibid.

"moved out of the lion's cage into the smaller carnivora."

Now he should have been able to get to work, but his purchases of advanced art were blocked. In 1910 he finally tangled directly with Morgan, and was dismissed. Fry returned to England. He took his integrity with him. Shortly before his dismissal he had commented: "I have not yet learned not to say what I think. But I'm not in a hurry to mend it."

That very autumn he put on the first exhibit of modern art that England had ever seen. The show at the Grafton Gallery in London, which ranged from Manet to Cézanne to Picasso, was a sensation and a scandal that foretold the reception that the first large show of modern art would have in America three years later.

Despite the hubbub in England, Roger Fry's show had small immediate effect on English art. It would be two decades before modernism would take root on the snug little isle. In America, when the big show finally came, it was a far different thing. Fry had found "far more enthusiasm for art in America than in England." [6] The seed in American soil sprouted right away, as though cubism were a native genus.

In that same eventful year of 1910, The Eight got their independent show. They had been battling with increased determination ever since Friedman and his friends had turned the trick two years before. They had pointed to that earlier show as an example and finally prevailed upon a New York dealer to give them a small show in 1908. This was William Macbeth, whose gallery was then at 450 Fifth Avenue. Finally, in 1910, came the big independent show of The Eight in midtown Manhattan. It set the critics warring with one another

[6] Ibid.

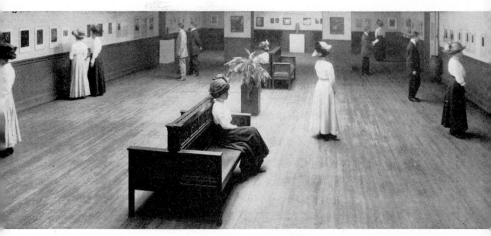

Modern photography at the Newark Museum, 1911—show hung by Max Weber.

John Cotton Dana, c. 1924.

The Armory Show, New York, 1913. Extreme left: Derain Fauve. Left foreground: five Brancusi sculptures. Center middleground: Lehmbruck Kneeling Woman. Rear wall, left of Lehmbruck: two Rouaults and other Fauves. Right middleground: Maillol nude (relief).

and almost brought mass apoplexy to the academicians. But it left the public strangely unmoved.

Why?

Because it was a time for revolution, not for mere revolt. The Eight did not go far enough. They left the last word with the Academy by granting the decisive point: *the purpose of art is the representation of natural appearances.* As long as that point stood, there was no real revolution. The argument of The Eight with the Academy was little more than a dispute on parliamentary procedure while the same old meeting went on. It was a quibble on two relatively minor points: first, subject matter (Do we paint glamorous creatures or washerwomen? Sylvan landscapes or factory dumps?); second, comparative realism (Do we try to beat the camera at its own game, or do we broaden our brushstrokes a wee bit and use a little heavier paint?).

Actually, except as a proof of freedom, it mattered little which side won. There was no effectiveness to our anger. We had no program. We had lived alone too long; the woods had grown over the paths. There was a new path somewhere, and a lot of shouting over that far hill, but we just could not get there.

Nevertheless, there was a lot of courage in it all. Henri, the "Bad Boy," was a brave boy. One wonders after all these years about his painting. Strangely enough, there are no traces there of all that fighting long ago. His pictures look tame; one asks: "How did they offend anyone?" It is difficult to see that they once were a challenge, to imagine Henri as a prophet of progess in art.

It was Robert Henri the remarkable man, the individual and the individualist, and not his paintings, that once counted.

In his own time "the aura of Henri's personality and the ideals he was battling for . . . lent them a radicalism that they did not in actuality possess. . . . Henri's radicalism was largely a matter of point of view. He did not introduce startling new esthetic formulas." [7]

Henri nevertheless did something that, belated as it may have been, had to be done: he reasserted the rights of the individual in art. He asserted them without, in a way, exercising them as an artist. He fought for others, though he himself would have been the last to think so. He softened up the opposition, prepared the way. The Bad Boy found life at home stifling, but he was not prepared to run away.

But the revolution was to come. It was already in the mind of another man, one of the most remarkable and intuitive individualists this country has ever known. Almost ironically—because it was the camera that had spelled the death of copyist art—he was a photographer and not a painter at all. He plotted to overthrow the tyranny of outworn tradition in a small attic room in a Manhattan business building.

The little attic was at 291 Fifth Avenue, and the man was Alfred Stieglitz.

[7] Helen Appleton Read: *Robert Henri* (New York, 1931).

Paris in 1904—or at least the Montmartre section, where the artists lived—was still truly Bohemia as Henri Murger had described it a full generation before. There the well-to-do could live in a de-luxe furnished apartment (one with plumbing) or a luxurious heated studio of great size for five francs (then $1.25) a day, while the poor artist—like Max Weber, who came from America in 1905—could find a ground-floor studio in which to work and live at $20 a year.

As Elizabeth McCausland has observed, "No student ever had to starve; Parisians were full of trust. . . . The baker would be leaving rolls and milk at the door every morning." [1] It was village life in a city. Paris, not unlike New York, was a series of districts, each with the sense of a self-contained neighborhood. For all their sharpness and frugality in money matters, the French, being affectionate, are capable of the most amiable lenience. The familiar story of the artist who exchanges drawings and paintings for meals and wine at the corner *bistro* is more than a romantic tale. It happened then; it even happens today; and many of the artists most famous today knew the time when they held body and soul together by such apparently inequitable barter.

The restaurant-keepers of course held on to the unnegotiable canvases. After all, they were art; they were real paintings done on real canvas by a real artist—"I knew him. He lived only three doors from here." Suddenly the artist was famous. He had long since gone away. Dealers were knocking at the restaurant-keeper's door. He would take his sudden good fortune in the same calm way in which he had given the meals with no prospect of cash. No one would ever know if he had been astute or only remarkably lucky.

[1] Elizabeth McCausland: *A. H. Maurer* (New York, 1951).

To the middle-class French, the artist, even in rags, rated somehow a notch or two above the prosperous doctor or lawyer. Like the cathedral-builders, he was a craftsman of a craft not chained to practical ends. Through the peculiar workings of the Latin mind, even the cubist, whose work was certainly a horror, inherited that medieval honor. And yet, to the practical French, he was also a man, with a man's need to work, to be sheltered from the rain, to eat a little food and drink a little wine, to be sad, to be gay, to hate, and to be in love.

Here was the Bohemia where the international art called modern began, where its ideas germinated and grew, where its first crucial battles were fought. From everywhere came the discontented, wanting to be free of history. As modernism began to grow, the roster became more and more international: Matisse, Léger, Braque, Derain, Dufy, Rouault, Delaunay, and the brothers Duchamp, all of France; Picasso, Gargallo, Gris, and Miro of Spain; Brancusi of Romania; Modigliani, Chirico, Boccioni, Carra, and Severini of Italy; Mondrian of Holland; and Chagall and Soutine of Russia. All of this was in Paris. It was the focus, though the ferment was going on elsewhere—in the Germanic countries and in Italy, as well as in Russia.

The Americans who came to Paris settled gratefully into this lively, sympathetic world as though they were coming home. Revolution was scarcely their first thought. Alfred Maurer, who came from New York in 1897, became the wit and mustached dandy among the Americans in the Quarter; Edward Steichen, who came from Milwaukee in 1901, palette in one hand and camera in the other, immediately sought out Rodin, his epoch ended, to photograph him in the deserted monastery that was his studio.

Soon a small-scale exodus from America was beginning. Like the Hebrews fleeing Egypt, the cream of the crop of young American artists began coming one by one to Bohemia on the Seine. Walter Pach came in 1904 and finally, in 1910, settled for three years. Wry, lean John Marin arrived in 1905, as did Arthur B. Carles. Morgan Russell and Abraham Walkowitz landed one year later, followed in 1907 by Stanton Macdonald-Wright and Patrick Henry Bruce. By 1912, Russell and Macdonald-Wright would have founded the first international modern-art movement ever initiated by American artists.

And still they came: Arthur G. Dove, Joseph Stella, Marsden Hartley, and Charles Sheeler. Only one is known to have found Paris not to his liking. And that was Jacob Epstein. Walkowitz was a boyhood friend of Epstein on the lower East Side of Manhattan, where the Epstein family ran a bakery on Hester Street. Walkowitz tells how the young sculptor, Epstein, made a "fortune"—$400—suddenly in 1902 by illustrating a book called *Spirit of the Ghetto*, and immediately took off by cattle boat. After a few months in Paris he crossed the channel to England, where he has remained ever since, frightening the English with his sculptures until at length they have knighted him.

Walkowitz met the sculptor's brother, Dr. Sidney Epstein, who remained in America, shortly after the 1954 Honors List of the new queen was made public.

"Well," Walkowitz said, "I see Jake is Sir Jake now."

"Pfui," said Dr. Epstein. "Jake was knighted at 102 Hester Street."

From 1903 the whole American art colony centered

around the fabulous Steins and their two apartments. The Steins were from San Francisco. First to come had been Michael Stein, retired businessman, and his wife, Sarah. They took quarters in the rue Madame. Then came Michael's younger brother, Leo, "amateur painter, philosopher, and, in the best sense of the word, esthete. . . . Early in 1903 he settled . . . at 27 rue de Fleurus, where he was joined shortly by his younger sister Gertrude." [2]

The Steins were to prove an advance guard more advanced than any as yet among even the French, public and critics alike. Leo, in particular, followed much the same steps that the young French rebels-to-be, Matisse especially, had taken: he discovered Cézanne, whom Matisse was to call "*le père de nous tous*" [3]—the father of us all; then Van Gogh and Gauguin. Soon the Steins were to discover and to embrace the still newer, still more revolutionary painters then just beginning their careers.

Meanwhile, everyone gathered at the Steins'. By 1905, Henri Matisse was already an honor guest at the salon of Leo and Gertrude. Leo had just bought his highly controversial painting *Woman with the Hat* from the Autumn Salon of that year. Although modernism was in its infancy, Matisse was already a man of thirty-six, securely married and sedately bearded, his appearance of a mild bourgeois so contradictory of his violent painting. "At the rue de Fleurus, on Saturday evenings, Matisse met Germans, Englishmen, Poles, Russians, Scandinavians, Spaniards and, of course, Americans. They were critics, painters, sculptors, writers, collectors, society people, businessmen, musicians, museum people, art historians

[2] Alfred H. Barr, Jr.: *Matisse: His Art and His Public* (New York, 1951).
[3] Ibid.

—and most of them had come to see the paintings, the Cézannes and Renoirs at first, then after 1905 the Matisses and,
a little later, the Picassos." [4]

The talk was endless, much of it witty, some of it profound. The pictures spoke, too—silently—settling many an
argument with the finality of things accomplished and beyond
argument. As two cubist painters wrote only a little later,
"The picture which only surrenders itself slowly seems always
to wait until we interrogate it, as though it reserved an infinity
of replies to an infinity of questions." [5]

The American artists, though not in the inmost councils
of revolt, nevertheless could not hold back from joining. The
air was electric with young enthusiasm. Maurer had already
quit the Académie Julian in disgust after a few weeks in its
ateliers; Steichen did likewise; and then Weber, too, came to
Julian's to find Walkowitz there. In the life class of this world-
famous *académie*, revolt was already almost out in the open. In
a dozen languages the students all around Weber were saying:
"What nonsense is all this? What are we doing here?" Weber
and Walkowitz quit the academy, too—a real act of courage,
for they had saved for years just for the opportunity to attend
it, and where did you go from there?

Everyone knew a war was going on. You could feel it
everywhere. But it was still underground. Where and how to
enlist? And with whom? Maurer, Steichen, Weber, Walkowitz, and all of the lot, separately, haunted the Luxembourg
and the Louvre, hoping to find guidance among the masterpieces of the past.

Then suddenly it was the end of 1905 and the *salon*

---

[4] Ibid.
[5] Albert Gleizes and Jean Metzinger: *Du Cubisme* (Paris, 1912).

d'automne was open with a great memorial display of Van Gogh
and the new work of the younger men: the mordant melancholy and the fierce questionings of Picasso's Blue Period
canvases and the lurid, writhing landscapes of Matisse, Derain,
Vlaminck, and the others of their group.

Pandemonium broke out. In all the pigmented fury of its
exploded landscapes, its tortured, distorted nudes, its brutal
destruction of the neat, the sweet, and the pretty, the sheer
effrontery struck everyone full in the face. Academicians and
critics were offended and furious; the public was stunned.
Someone wrote or said: "*Les fauves!*" and the chant was taken
up: "Wild beasts! Wild beasts!" And of all the wild beasts,
everyone agreed, Matisse was king. The room where the most
horrid of his pictures hung was even called the "central cage."

That painting was the painting that Leo Stein eventually
bought, the unbelievable portrait of the artist's wife: *Woman
with the Hat*. There were those who claimed, half in derision
and half in anger, that it could be heard roaring from the street
outside. It was deliberately brutal, ugly with a purpose, an
incredible patchwork of smears and blotches of violent color
applied with a fiendish crudity. The face leered out like an
obscene mask of crimson, carmine, orange, yellow, livid
greens, and blue.

In the presence of this picture, the loud, contentious
arguments at Leo and Gertrude Stein's suddenly seemed only
peaceful philosophic discussions, an unhurried acceptance,
teacup in hand, of progress step by easy step. It was this
moment when Leo Stein showed what he was made of. Over
forty years later he said of the *Woman with the Hat*: "It was
. . . a thing brilliant and powerful, but the nastiest smear of
paint I have ever seen. . . . I would have snatched it at once

if I had not needed a few days to get over the unpleasantness of the putting on of the paint." [6] Then Leo bought it, his first Matisse, took it home, and hung it. The apartment he shared with Gertrude was no longer even in a slight degree an ivory tower: it was a powder heap.

Autumn after autumn the annual Matisse sensation followed *Woman with the Hat* to the walls of the rue de Fleurus apartment. Next year the *Woman* was joined by the vast (almost nine feet long) *Joy of Life*, now the prize Matisse of the Barnes Foundation at Merion, Pennsylvania. This seemingly shameless bacchanal created a greater shock than had the *Woman with the Hat*: "Even Matisse's new champion was shaken. The first time Leo Stein went to the *Indépendants* he was with Maurice Sterne. They looked at the *Joy of Life* together. Sterne recalls that they both disliked it at first, Stein only a little less intensely than Sterne. Stein returned again and again to study it. After several weeks he announced to Sterne that the big painting was the most important done in our time and proceeded to buy it though his funds, as always, were limited." [7] Thirty-five years later Stein's judgment would be confirmed. The Museum of Modern Art's Alfred H. Barr, Jr., author of the definitive book on Matisse, characterized the *Joy of Life* as "a magnificent act of courage, a prime monument in the history of modern painting, and what is equally important still a delight to the eye." [8]

The *Joy of Life* actually, but only by slow degrees, became a "delight to the eye." We know how sorely it offended everyone, even the brave man who bought it. And yet this is turning the whole matter around. As Virginia Woolf once wrote,

[6] Leo Stein: *Appreciation: Painting* (New York, 1947).
[7] Barr: op. cit.
[8] Barr: op. cit.

"Pictures do not change. People change."

But in those days it was no delight; it was plain agony. The world had been rudely slapped in the face. Or, rather, only one cheek caught the blow. America had not even heard about modern art. It was Edward Steichen who saw to that matter. Habitually he returned to America each year for the winter months. On each visit he renewed his acquaintance with photographer Alfred Stieglitz in New York. Brimming with the news of what was happening, Steichen went to work on Stieglitz. He had an idea in mind.

Steichen knew that his friend was a modernist at heart. He had shown it in his fight to have the camera accepted as a machine, to discredit the arty photographs that tried to look like paintings. This, Steichen knew, was the sign of an advanced point of view. His tales of revolt in Paris silenced for once the incessant and eloquent talker Stieglitz. The older man was spellbound; his imagination was fired. This was Steichen's moment.

"Find a small gallery," he urged.

Stieglitz was cagy. He pretended not to understand. "There's not enough good photography to show," he said.

"Show modern paintings and drawings, too," Steichen said.

Stieglitz was almost, but not quite, ready for this. He did find the gallery, and small it was, a fifteen-foot-square attic at 291 Fifth Avenue which was reached by an elevator that somewhat later an American art critic called "the smallest elevator in the world." Then Stieglitz proceeded to show photography there. He called it The Photo-Secession Galleries, but to everyone it became "291." At about this point, Steichen hustled him off to Europe. During a short stay he met the Steins and some of the new artists—and that did it.

Meanwhile, following the earthquake and fire in San Francisco in 1906, the Michael Steins made a quick trip home. The first Matisse works to reach America came with Sarah. They are described by Barr as "a drawing of a reclining nude leaning on one arm and an oil of a model standing before a screen." All of Sarah's friends in San Francisco—Alice B. Toklas included—saw them. She showed them in New York, too, and a painter and fashionable picture-framer by the name of George F. Of commissioned Mrs. Stein to choose a Matisse for him upon her return to Paris. The painting, *Nude in a Wood*, arrived in due course, the first Matisse to be owned in America. It is still in Of's possession.

At the same time the great collection of Dr. Claribel and Miss Etta Cone, now the prize of the Baltimore Museum of Art, was just being started. The Cone sisters were cousins of the Steins, and while Etta was the house guest of Michael and Sarah in Paris later in 1906, she bought Matisse's *The Yellow Jug* from Leo and Gertrude; she brought it home with her that same year. Even though *Nude in a Wood* and *The Yellow Jug* were seen by relatively few people, infiltration had begun. America already was being infected by what an academic critic was soon to call "the bacillus of the Matisse craze." [9]

In the winter of 1907–8, Stieglitz began to show art at 291. Steichen brought over a group of Rodin's wash drawings of nudes. These are typical sculptor's sketches emphasizing plasticity, attitude, and volume rather than more conventional pictorial qualities. Rodin was to be the curtain-raiser for Matisse, and the choice was canny. The drawings had certain modern attributes: a freedom of spirit, some of the new realism

[9] Arthur Hoeber in the *New York Globe*, April 1909.

of emphasis through physical distortion, and a total unconcern with formal beauty or the picturesque, classic pose. Rodin, then near seventy but still combative, lion-maned, and noble, was, in the public mind, the greatest living figure of art. There was something a little like Michelangelo about him. His battles with Philistine opinion were already historic; the memory of the French official rejection of his notorious statue of Balzac late in the nineteenth century was still fresh.[1]

Rodin was a tartar; his drawings were unknown in America; it was going to be fun to see what the critics did with them. They were thrown into real confusion and had quite a time of it trying to balance off the lines they saw as scrawling and the sheer vitality of them, the accepted idea of Rodin as the heroic hewer of marble and these "nude women in attitudes . . . not for public exhibition." [2]

Matisse came next: watercolors, prints, and drawings. No *salon d'automne*, to be sure, this couple of dozen small pictures matted and hung in a tiny attic still unknown to the general public. But the two dozen served very well. The voice of the critics was babel. Here was something new for which no glib, ready-made phrases were available. It was an issue no one could straddle; each man had to stand up and be counted. The vote was No! by a large majority, with only a few dissenting. James Gibbons Huneker, though forced to describe the Matisse line as "swirling and strong . . . virile and masterly," was yet appalled by these documents of "the female animal in all her shame and horror," documents that he called "memoranda of the gutter and the brothel." No acceptance but bristled with contradictory "buts." The monthly *The Scrip*,

[1] A version of the Balzac bronze was acquired by the Museum of Modern Art in 1955.

[2] W. B. McCormick in the *Press*, April 1909.

like the *New York Sun*'s Huneker, held a hand over one horrified eye while looking at this "great artist," for the great
artist was at the same time all too decadent in his "physical
distortion" and "malevolent" in his presentation of "nude
[women] so vulgarized . . . as to suggest . . . the abnormal."

Perhaps women—not Matisse's women, to be sure—were
more innocent in that day. At least, it took a woman of the
press to catch the essential innocence and childlikeness that we
all see nowadays in the Matisse vision. Elizabeth Luther Cary
of the *New York Times* praised these "little views [that] have a
charm like . . . snatches of song in the open air. . . ."

Steichen kept up his trips back and forth across the
Atlantic as the messenger boy of modern art. So for the next
few years Stieglitz's 291 became the tiny peephole through
which America could look at the rest of the art world. Despite
the critics, 291 immediately attracted a growing avant-garde
who filled the place at all hours with argument and discussion,
Stieglitz always at its center. Remote from Paris, the attic
became a kind of Manhattan salon not unlike Leo and
Gertrude Stein's apartment.

The leading New York dealers refused to follow Stieglitz's
example, but a small dealer or two, as always, began to think:
"What do I have to lose?" The same year Stieglitz showed
Matisse, young Walkowitz came back penniless from Paris. He
carted his drawings and paintings from gallery to gallery until
he finally found Julius Haas, a picture-framer whose shop was
on Madison Avenue near 59th Street. He had some large
basement storerooms. Walkowitz, prowling around, discovered them.

"If I show that stuff, I'll lose all my clients," Haas complained. One week later, Walkowitz having cleaned out the storerooms, his paintings went on public exhibition. There is no record that Haas lost any clients or, for that matter, gained any. In any event, nothing was sold from the show. "A success of disesteem," Walkowitz calls it. He had gone to every newspaper office and made sure that the critics would come. "What a roasting!" Walkowitz says.

Good old Elizabeth Cary, however, though bewildered, was inclined to be sympathetic. Her heart, though she did not know it, belonged to modern art. And then there was contentious young Guy Pène du Bois, painter as well as writer. He let out a hungry yelp of joy. "A wild beast like the Fauves," he exulted, "has arrived at the Haas gallery!"

A year later Max Weber returned from Paris, broke too, and with work even more radically modern than that of his friend Walkowitz. Walkowitz promptly collared Haas and got a show for his friend. "The critics liked him as well as they liked me," says Walkowitz, "but Robert Henri actually bought one of Weber's things. Haas never really believed it happened."

Weber had moved into the Brooklyn home of his orthodox Jewish parents, where, as Walkowitz says, "He didn't dare unroll a nude canvas even though she was all cubist bevels." So Weber moved in with Walkowitz for a while in the tiny, airless Manhattan room where the latter made a meager living painting signs. Weber stayed at home painting on pieces of cardboard which he picked up in the streets. Soon both the young men were being shown at Stieglitz's 291.

Stieglitz, though international-minded, had a strong American bent that would intensify as the years went by. Soon he gave the first American shows of the pictures that Alfred

Maurer and John Marin were doing in Paris. He began at that time to assemble his famous stable of native painters. And then, a year later in 1910, he opened his second Matisse show. The critics, for the most part, had now settled into two opposing camps—where, for that matter, they and their descendants have been ever since.

National Academician Arthur Hoeber was one of the chief spokesmen for what was already being called the reactionaries. He described Matisse's new work as "insolent . . . foolish . . . graceless." [3]

Huneker was inclined to be cautious. He was the leading critic of the day; his reputation was at stake; and he seemed to sense something momentous happening. He fenced with the Matisse problem, writing: "At his worst he shocks; at his best his art is as attractive as art can be." He then touted the little show as "more instructive and moving than a century of academy shows," and ended with a word of advice: "If you can't swallow Matisse go . . . and look at Kenyon Cox's mural . . . for the public library of Winona, Minnesota . . . Heaven knows *it* is soothing." Cox was a National Academician, a painter of noble, draped, allegorical attitudes. Cox, too, loved to rush into rather purple-prose denunciations of the new art.

Frank Jewett Mather, Jr., of the *New York Evening Post*, wrote: "A Matisse drawing belongs in the great tradition of art that has envisaged the human form in terms of energy and counterpoise." And some, like Townsend of *American Art News*, were still "frankly at sea." Townsend stated that at the earlier Matisse show his soul had been sickened, that at the present one he looked on with complacence. He strongly inferred that

[3] Arthur Hoeber in the *New York Globe*, February 1910.

he was caught in the well-known series of reactions to vice: first pity, then condone, and then embrace.

Stieglitz gloried in his new role. He showed less and less photography. After each show of modern art, his magazine *Camera Work* [4] featured the hostile reviews over the few favorable ones. Show after show, the "unterrified virtuoso of 291" kept hammering away like a boxer trying to keep his opponent off balance. He opened his 1911 season with a show of the Paris work of Max Weber. Weber at the moment was like an ambassador from the King of the Fauves, as he had studied in Matisse's first and only art class, which had been organized in 1907 by Sarah Stein and a young German artist, Hans Purrman.

The name-droppers had their chance. Poor little Max was only a home-town boy from the Delancey Street neighborhood (came anything good out of Samaria?), and the critics fixed him, but good. Roger Fry had singled him out as the most promising young American painter he had seen, but that opinion cut no ice. One scribe saw Weber's solid, serious cubist works as "emanations . . . from . . . an insane asylum"; another called them "insane obsession"; a third said loftily: "His work . . . is only a bore." [5]

Max Weber might treasure the one lone voice that had praised him as "an ambitious young painter . . . worthy of attention and study," [6] but his goose was cooked anyway. Struggle as he might, he never again could get back to Paris.

[4] The *Camera Work* reproductions, particularly of photography, have probably never been excelled. Stieglitz himself had once worked in his father's engraving plant. The *Camera Work* plates were made and printed in Germany.

[5] The three quotations are, respectively: Hoeber in the *New York Globe*, January 1911; J. Edgar Chamberlin in the *New York Evening Mail*, January 1911; Royal Cortissoz in the *New York Tribune*, January 1911.

[6] Harrington in the *New York Herald*, January 1911.

One of the finest draftsmen we have produced, he could not even get a teaching job in the public schools. Not cubism barred him, but his accent!

Two months later Cézanne, too, got the brush-off. At 291 the Master of Aix, already five years dead, got his first American showing. The once-enigma, now god of the modernists, was a nobody here. "He never really arrived," wrote one critic, who termed the now almost priceless watercolors "pale memoranda" and thus spoke for all. Then in April came the formidable Picasso. *He* was a name: the ogre who lived in the castle, and none had seen his face. Now here were the faceless faces of his cubist drawings.

The long war of nerves at 291 was beginning to have its effect. A few writers were irreconcilable, like one who again leveled the charge of insanity: "emanations of a disordered mind . . . gibberings of a lunatic," but most were uneasily beginning to glimpse method in this new madness. It was time for the cover-up. One cleared his throat and began: "The obvious, though difficult course is to study this Parisianized Spaniard seriously . . . to get the occult message he has to convey," and then in senatorial bass tones spoke of "something doing of large import for the future." Another, complaining of the "discordant sound" of Picasso's drawings, acknowledged that "it is a sound . . . apt to precede revolution." [7]

The charge of madness, actually, was becoming a joke. One B. P. Stephenson, in the *New York Evening Post*, quoted Stieglitz's physician brother as saying: "Why, these fellows are suffering from paresis and I will bring a noted alienist to

[7] The three quotations are, respectively: Hoeber in the *New York Globe;* Tyrell in the *New York Evening World;* Elizabeth Luther Cary in the *New York Times;* all April 1911.

prove it." The writer continued: "It may be our own brains are 'out of gear.' At latest advices the alienist had not arrived —'too busy looking after other sane persons,' as Stieglitz remarked."

Huneker took the firmest stand of all on cubism and Picasso. "No dim hint of indecision here," he wrote. "The lines are pyramidal. Tremendous power is in them." This observation of cubism could stand unaltered today.

In the five years up to 1912, Stieglitz shoved a lot of unfamiliar fare down America's throat: forerunners Manet (1910), Cézanne (1910 and 1911), Renoir (1910), Rodin (1908 and 1910), and Toulouse-Lautrec (1909 and 1910); European moderns Matisse (1908, 1910, 1912) and Picasso (1911); and American moderns Maurer and Marin (1909), Weber (1911), and Walkowitz (1912). Stieglitz pioneered in photography, then in art and even in literature. In 1912 he published Gertrude Stein's articles on Picasso and Matisse. He looked them over in manuscript and unashamedly admitted that he didn't in the least know what she was talking about. But then, he conceded, he didn't really know what her subjects' paintings were all about, either. But Miss Stein wrote as they painted, so it was authentic: one could sense value before the text was deciphered.

Gertrude Stein's stream-of-consciousness prose stunned American literati, but Hutchins Hapgood, at least, though finding it "impossible to state" what her writings said ("they say nothing"), found her articles "intensely human," suggesting "a complete and single mood, in which ideas, feelings, sensations, tendencies of the nerves, of hope, of imagination are indissolubly combined."

Aided by Steichen, Stieglitz kept gaily and stubbornly on

in that little attic room which Marianne Moore remembers as "an American Acropolis . . . with a stove in it," hanging these "paintings seemingly without commercial value . . . with respect, with sensitiveness and with intelligence." [8] Then, in 1917, 291 was no more; the building at that address was torn down. Stieglitz had two subsequent places, An American Place the better known of the two. But already in 1917 the great pioneering days of 291 were over and it had become mainly the propaganda center for a selected group of American modernists. Alfred Stieglitz had an early role. He filled it admirably. But the situations of modern art change as swiftly as modern times. Stieglitz could have grasped a new role, but he did not recognize it when it came.

291, in any event, has never been forgotten. Many people still can summon to memory the little room, in its center "Stieglitz in a deep chair, people around him . . . his head poised as if it were the prototype of all cameras, recording with uncanny sensitiveness all that is visible and much that is not." Many still "can re-enact . . . the . . . bewilderment, wonder, and thrilling discovery that attended [Stieglitz's] introduction of modern art in America." 291, to be sure, was "merely the tiniest outpost of the European artistic radicals, a gallery into which scarcely a dozen people could crowd at a time," yet the American painter Marsden Hartley would observe that "this little room has become . . . an enormous room." [9]

---

[8] The two quotations are, respectively: Marianne Moore in *Stieglitz Memorial Portfolio* (New York, 1947); Paul Strand in *America and Alfred Stieglitz* (New York, 1934).

[9] The four quotations are, respectively: Jean Toomer in *America and Alfred Stieglitz*, op. cit.; Henry Clifford and Carl Zigrosser: foreword to catalogue of Philadelphia Museum of Art Exhibit "History of an American" (1944); Russell

An enormous room indeed, all America, too big even for Stieglitz to host. By 1912, in fact, the attic plot was hatched, the mass rebellion was inevitable. Stieglitz could not see it, but others did. The Academy, even then, ensured that the attack would come as a complete surprise, for the Academy slept on while critics vainly sounded the warning: "Wake up, American painters!"

The attack, a full-scale revolt, would be the greatest show of contemporary art in all history. It would be a decisive event in many respects and a scandal of vast proportions. It would make modern art headline material. It would be the world-famous Armory Show of 1913 in New York.

Lynes: "Whirlwind on Twenty-Sixth Street," *Harper's Magazine,* June 1954; Marsden Hartley in *Stieglitz Memorial Portfolio,* op. cit.

4. *Rebellion in an Armory*

It all started quietly enough.

In 1911, Walt Kuhn, an American painter and caricaturist, met with two painters, Jerome Myers and Elmer MacRae. Kuhn proposed a large show of progressive American art, together with "a few of the radical things from abroad to create additional interest." [1] What was meant by "progressive" was far from the Fauvism of Maurer, the cubism of Weber and Marin, and the Matisse-like free drawing of Walkowitz, all of them by that time home in America. The word meant to Kuhn and the other two the impressionism of men like Ernest Lawson, Maurice Prendergast, and Childe Hassam and the "realism" of Henri, Bellows, and the Ash Can painters.

Myers and MacRae agreed with Kuhn; they prepared a list of artists and approached them. The response was good, and an organization called the Association of American Painters and Sculptors was set up, with painter J. Alden Weir as president, sculptor Gutzon Borglum as vice-president, and Kuhn as secretary. The original membership of about twenty-five included old warriors like Henri, Glackens, and Sloan of The Eight and somewhat younger men like Bellows and Jo Davidson. It was not a particularly young group, however (Kuhn was thirty-one, Weir, fifty-nine); nor was it remarkably insurgent.

Enthusiasm rode high until the difficulties of arranging and financing a large show were encountered. Weir then resigned, and in 1912, with the project almost abandoned, Arthur B. Davies was persuaded by Kuhn to take hold. Davies, one of The Eight, was a recluse, a mystic of sorts—all in all,

[1] This and all succeeding quotations by Kuhn are from his twenty-eight-page pamphlet *The Story of the Armory Show* (privately printed, New York, 1938).

an unlikely choice to push a progressive show. Ash-Canner Jerome Myers described him as "the one artist in America who had little to do with his contemporaries, who had vast influence with the wealthiest women, who painted unicorns and maidens under moonlight." [2]

Davies almost morbidly disliked crowds. No artists knew where his studio was, his real friends being outside the art world. Fostering—or living—a legend of the rapt artist, he belonged in spirit to the nineteenth-century pre-Raphaelite world of Burne-Jones and Dante Gabriel Rossetti.

Overnight, this shy Arthur B. Davies changed. He took command, suddenly revealing executive powers and an autocratic will, and somewhere in his thin, elegant body found the energy of a dynamo. More astonishing still, this man who harked back to early Italian art as his personal ideal, calmly announced that the "few radical things from abroad" would become instead the core of the show. Even Kuhn was surprised, while the others in the Association could not trust their ears. Before a mouth could be opened in protest, Davies was on his way like a dainty steamroller. He promptly collared his rich friends and raised the needed financial support.

Enthusiasm rode high again. Kuhn dashed around New York, searching for a place to hold the show. Someone made the inspired suggestion that an armory be hired: some of these huge, tax-exempt structures that dot Manhattan Island like Tudor castles and Florentine palaces were rented out for public tennis. Why not for art? So Kuhn switched to armories, and finally found the place at 26th Street and Lexington Avenue, the almost brand-new (1904) and almost

[2] This and all succeeding quotations by Myers are from his book *Artist in Manhattan* (New York, 1940).

city-block-square home of the 69th—the "Fighting Irish"—
Regiment of the New York National Guard. Colonel Conley,
in command, named a rental that Kuhn later recalled as
$5,500 for one month, of which $1,500 was to be paid as
deposit, the rest before the show opened. In the late spring
or early summer of 1912, Kuhn reserved the Armory for the
month from February 15 to March 15, 1913. The legal ar-
rangements were handled by John Quinn, prominent lawyer,
art-collector, and friend of Davies.

When the committee was selecting American work for
the show, Kuhn overconfidently went off to Nova Scotia to
paint. He had barely set up his easel when he was ordered to
fold it up again. Davies had now expanded his plan to a
mammoth full-scale showing of all the revolutionary movements current abroad. Davies sent Kuhn a catalogue of the
Sonderbund ("Secessionist Group") exhibition of modern art
then on view in Germany, enclosing steamship passage for
Europe. Kuhn glanced at the closing-date on the catalogue
and ran for the train. He arrived in Cologne the very day the
Sonderbund closed, but succeeded in seeing most of the exhibits
as they were being crated. Then he was off for Paris with way-
stops.

Meanwhile, at home, George Bellows, who had arranged
the settings for the independent shows of 1908 and 1910, set
to work under Davies's guidance, planning a series of eighteen
rooms to be created by burlap partitions in the vast empty
Armory hall. Before the show was hung, Davies had personally
executed drawings of each of the seventy-two walls in his
immaculate draftsmanship, showing where each painting
would be displayed. Society women were busy cornering
greenery and potted palms to give the Armory that lived-in

look and, what is more, they were footing the bills.

Then suddenly they all awoke to the problem of getting foreign paintings and sculpture through the American tariff wall. At that time a heavy duty was levied on all works of art less than twenty years old. If they were brought in under bond, shown, and shipped back, the chief method of defraying the huge costs of the show—sales—would be relinquished. With shipping-costs, insurance, salaries of stenographers and ticket girls, and the rental balance of $4,000 still to be faced, bonding of the works was rejected.

In a sense, America herself solved the problem of duties. We were beginning to catch up with the world, responding somewhat to world-wide currents. That fall of 1912, inter-national-minded Woodrow Wilson was elected President, a chief plank of his platform being the lowering of tariffs and the encouragement of world commerce.

The obstacle seemed insuperable until John Quinn, a Democrat high in his party's councils, came to the rescue.

"I will get the tariff on paintings removed," he promised Davies.

"In time for the show?" Davies asked incredulously.

"Precisely," said Quinn. He made good his promise.

Later Quinn revealed his strategy. He had gone straight to the Senate committee that was considering the new tariff legislation.

"Why are you aiding the millionaires and discriminating against those of moderate means?" he demanded bluntly.

The senators were flabbergasted. "This duty is aimed at the rich," one solon expostulated.

"If it is," Quinn retorted, "then you'd better improve your aim. Millionaires buy old masters. Under your age re-

striction, they come in duty-free. People like me can afford
only paintings by young artists. And you soak *us*."

That settled it.

In Europe, Walt Kuhn raced from Cologne to The
Hague, where he visited the aged French painter Odilon
Redon, whose mystical work was already known in America.
He promised an entire room at the exhibition to Redon, en-
trained for a short stay at Munich, and then left for Paris.

There he seems to have grasped for the first time the size
of his task. "One night in my hotel," he wrote later, "the
magnitude and importance of the whole thing came over me."
He cabled Davies, who immediately sailed to join him. Together they saw one of the American exiles, Walter Pach, who
showed them around the studios.

Here were no "pale memoranda" in an attic, but the
most vivid and astonishing paintings and sculpture within
memory. The three men were intoxicated with excitement.
They forgot sleep; day and night they met artists, borrowed
from them, and even wheedled masterpieces from Ambroise
Vollard, dealer and perennial friend of art rebels. Vollard,
who had befriended the impressionists and had been almost
the only one to whom Cézanne could sell a painting, ended
by becoming enthusiastic for this daring show in the New
World. With his approval gained, every collector's door was
open.

In one studio Pach introduced Davies and Kuhn to a
twenty-six-year-old artist and to a painting less than two
years old which, though they could not know it, would assure
an overwhelming success to the exhibit. The artist was a
sensitive, highly intelligent Frenchman by the name of Marcel
Duchamp. The painting bore the tantalizing title *Nu descendant*

un escalier (*Nude Descending a Staircase*). This painting would set America on its ears; would bewilder, enrage, or amuse millions of people. The *Nude* would become a scandal that would put *September Morn* in the shade, a profitable scandal that would put the Armory Show's precarious finances well into the black.

Weeks and then months went by while Davies and Kuhn stayed on. It was near the end of November, with the show due to open in less than three months, when they sailed for home, Pach staying in Paris to see to the crating and shipping.

The returning president and secretary of the Association of American Painters and Sculptors knew by now that they were unleashing a revolution. The symbol of the American Revolution must have been in the front of their minds, because the lapel button they designed for the show, as well as the catalogue, bore over the motto: *The New Spirit,* the Pine Tree symbol of early Revolutionary days.

By mid-January the partitions had been installed, catalogues and tickets were ready, the American works were being installed, and Pach had cabled that the foreign exhibits were on a French ship at sea. They were over the hump. Everyone relaxed.

Then gigantic winter gales hit the Atlantic. The ship was reported delayed one day, then two days, then a week—she had no radio. One morning, rumors circulated that she was lost at sea, and Davies and Kuhn were almost thinking of suicide. Finally she limped in, badly battered and two weeks overdue. The watchers on the dock cheered as the precious crates were unloaded and rushed through customs with Quinn's ever-present help. Horse-drawn vans lumbered uptown to the Armory. A score of volunteers worked under

Davies's direction for twenty-four hours without rest, and the Armory Show opened for an evening preview two days late. Society and all in the know had been alerted and had been sharing the weeks of anxiety. The outpouring of guests was vast. Lexington Avenue and the side streets in the vicinity were jammed with taxis, hansom cabs, limousines, and private carriages.

Although the catalogue lists about a thousand items, nearer sixteen hundred were actually shown, hundreds of American paintings and sculptures having arrived too late to be catalogued. During the first week they were still being installed. As reports from abroad had told how the "few radical things" had become a "core" and then had kept on growing, the American committee had striven to balance things until, finally, nearly every known native artist had been invited. But in vain. In the end, only half of the galleries held American art.

Davies's idea, it was revealed, had been historical as well as radical. The center galleries, which held the foreign art, had their own core: three of the four "fathers of modernism," Cézanne, Van Gogh, and Gauguin, were honored by separate rooms, as was Redon, thus making good Kuhn's promise to the aged artist. Within this core was a still earlier one: "revolutionary" paintings by Ingres, Delacroix, Corot, Daumier, Puvis de Chavannes, and the impressionists Renoir and Monet.

Then, finally, came the veritable modernists: Matisse and the Fauves, Picasso and Braque and their cubist group, Léger, Picabia, Kandinsky—all the great new names. The sole exceptions were Boccioni, Severini, and the other Italian futurists, absent because their paintings were on exhibit in

Europe; however, Joseph Stella, the Italian-born American futurist, was nobly represented.

In the peripheral galleries hung the American work, the most radical of it—except for Stella and one or two others— pale and ineffectual, even its freshest paint badly dated. It was an omnibus collection, all-representative, including Glackens and the rest of The Eight, Edward Hopper, George Bellows, Bernard Karfiol, and Stuart Davis, the last to become one of our leading abstract painters only a few years later. In the welter, Albert Ryder shone with the timeless validity of the true mystic.

But the opening-night crowds pedaled through the outer rooms to get at the foreign moderns without delay. In scope and magnitude, that inner core was the work of Arthur B. Davies alone. Its historical emphasis (including current history) proved that his insistence on a full contemporary showing was no unaccountable vagary of Davies the artist, but the thesis of Davies the unsuspected scholar. He had stolen a march on time, setting the pattern for today's great retrospective exhibitions of modern art.

It was a gala night even though President-elect Woodrow Wilson, the Governor of New York State, and the Mayor of New York City, having been duly invited, had sent polite regrets. Artists, critics, society folk—some four thousand of them—crowded the Armory. Quinn gave the opening speech. "It is the most complete art exhibition," he announced, "that has been held anywhere in the world during the last quarter of a century."

As he finished speaking, the regimental band started its repertoire of marches, waltzes, Irish jigs, and ragtime from the balcony, and the guests began to move around. The exhibit rooms were large, but somehow, jerry-built as they were in the vast brick cavern, seemed small and unreal. Bellows had built them of light scantlings over which burlap was stretched, almost as if each flat were a stretched canvas awaiting the brush. The partitions ran up only to the height of rather high-ceilinged rooms—and at the top carried no ceilings. Far above the crowds the great empty vault loomed and echoed in darkness. It was unreal—a stage setting for some strange play being given a *première* in perpetual night at the edge of the world. The visitors felt the undercurrents and crowded instinctively together. Through the American rooms they surged, and on into the foreign section. At last in the cubist room in the southwest section, a dead-end corner, the nameless feeling found its proper setting; it was released in one loud, concerted gasp. There and then the cubist room was christened the Chamber of Horrors, the Dime Museum become the Grand Guignol.

The previewers were stunned; the babble of excited voices seemed angry and disturbed. Then the waves of sound smoothed out and it became a different sound. As Steichen remembers it today, "It was an uproar and one phrase above all stuck out: 'Do you mean to stand there and tell me . . . !!!' You heard it repeated over and over—gruff male and shrill female. It was pure, primordial amazement."

Walter Pach and Francis Picabia, the latter a leading Paris modernist, were explaining the art to all who would listen. People stared; the cubist pictures stared back in their faceless monumentality. Here and there laughter broke out.

Next day came the gray dawn of the public opening. The press came back for a second look, as if to make sure it had not all been a bad dream. The public came not at all.

Despite all the advance publicity, including the drama of the delayed ship, not a soul appeared. The reporters and critics walked around the empty rooms, open notebooks in hand; the air was acrid with the stench of flashlight powder. In the first editions of the evening papers came the opening trickle of what was soon to be a deluge. Reporters, critics, cartoonists, and editorial writers all had their innings; it was front-page stuff—the landing of H. G. Wells's Martians could hardly have been given more space. Some presidential elections have aroused less controversy.

And yet Davies, strangely, had hoped to avoid controversy. "The Association has embarked on no propaganda," he had written in the catalogue. The Association, he went on, "proposes to enter in no controversy. [Let] the intelligent . . . judge for themselves by themselves." He relied on intelligence. But this new art was heady stuff that upset the intelligence, awakened the most unruly emotions.

The Society (or Association—Davies used the names interchangeably), had acquiesced while he strongheadedly led the way. Thus, he was encouraged to write: "This . . . Association . . . is composed of persons of varying tastes and predilections . . . agreed on one thing: that the time has arrived for giving the public a chance to see for themselves the results of new influences at work in other countries."

Just how agreed they were, time would tell. Newspaper opinion of all shades and degrees was an explosive mixture. The leader against all this "wrong-headed nonsense" was Royal Cortissoz of the *New York Tribune*, master of the insulting adjective. Through a long writing career Cortissoz would remain implacably hostile to every form of modernism. In 1944, closing his career at the age of seventy-five, he would still be an embattled rear guard of the nineteenth century. At the Armory Show he fulminated at the sight of "misguided experimentalists wallowing in error" and producing "some of the most stupidly ugly pictures in the world and . . . sculpture to match. . . ."

The *Times* echoed Cortissoz: "The Armory Show is pathological . . . hideous!" And so went the consensus, with some notable exceptions. Young Henry McBride, who had newly replaced the retired Huneker on the *Sun*, had his first big chance. McBride today is still the fiery and poetic champion of new art that he became on that occasion. With undiminished enthusiasm he recalls his first glimpse of the Armory Show as "Enchanting—as enchanting as black magic and as shocking. But," he adds with twentieth-century wisdom, "to be shocked says well for the power of any painting."

Art critics have to be serious; reporters sometimes can choose where they stand; cartoonists have to be funny. Laughter won by a vote of two to one. The Third Estate's guffaws echoed up and down Manhattan Island. A slapstick hoax, they decided—irresponsible artists having fun with the public. There was no Mark Twain or Artemus Ward around to lead the chorus, but the hearty laughter was as thoroughly American as Keystone comedies and the Sunday funny papers. It was warm, not bitter, laughter, more uninformed than Philistine. Stuart Davis today credits this "healthy laughter" with having ensured the ultimate popular success of modern art in America.

"If Americans begin by fighting you, look out," Davis says. "They'll never give up. If the whole thing is too damned serious, look out. They'll never believe it. But make 'em laugh to begin with, and you're in."

But only the press was laughing, not the public: its indifference was truly colossal. Expenses mounted; salaries became pressing; the great show looked like a great flop. Davies, Kuhn, and Pach were despondent. Conservative members of the Society were beginning to say: "We told you so," blaming it all on cubism, which, they claimed, was keeping New York's five million lovers of art away.

Ten whole days—a third of the exhibition period—had passed. Then, suddenly and unaccountably, one bright, cold morning an army of citizenry stood at the gates, jammed the stairs under the great arch, backed up like flood waters on the wide sidewalks from 25th Street to 26th. Here was New York: "Actors, musicians, butlers, and shop girls . . . the exquisite, the vulgar from all walks of life," as Walt Kuhn said, crowding in to see what all the shouting was about. School children by the hundreds were shepherded by indignant art teachers through the maze of "vulgar, lawless and profane" works of art. Commoners peered and jeered. Celebrities cashed in. Enrico Caruso, then at his peak, entertained the crowds by drawing caricatures of the pictures and tossing them in the air while people grabbed them.

Day by day, on through the show, the crowds swelled. Finally, the price of morning admission was raised from twenty-five cents to one dollar so that serious students could get near the pictures. More than one hundred thousand people came in those remaining weeks to see curiosities that outshone the dime museums. The reactions were emphatic. Some people were worried, as though trying to remember a forgotten word or wrestling with an insoluble puzzle. A few were angry: a good friend had betrayed them. All the rest laughed uproariously. The volume of laughter matched the

Marcel Duchamp with Nude Descending a Staircase,
Sidney Janis Gallery, New York, 1956.

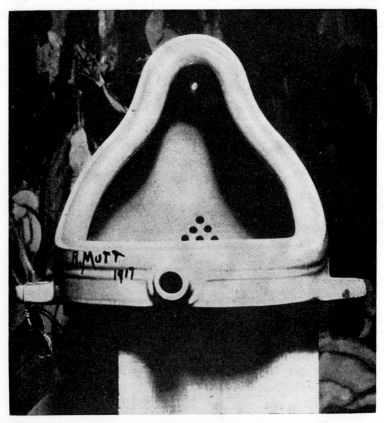

Fountain *by* R. Mutt *(Marcel Duchamp)*.
"To any innocent eye how pleasant is its chaste simplicity."
Louise Norton (Varese), in Blind Man, *1917*.

volume of the crowds, which, incidentally, set a world record for art-attendance which would stand for nearly a quarter of a century.[3]

Gutzon Borglum, no modernist, who had resigned from the Society before the show, was powerfully impressed by the laughter. He wrote in the *New York Evening Post*: "People laugh at things that are different and that they don't understand. Give 'em a thousand such things and they get tired of laughing: they begin to see the real point . . . to understand that all art has not got to be like the things they were brought up on."

Most of the people came to see one painting, the surprise hit and scandal of the show, the painting by an almost unknown young French artist which bore the fascinating title *Nude Descending a Staircase*. There was infinite promise of lovely things in that title, but thereafter—only frustration. Was it a jigsaw puzzle assembled by an idiot? It became a game to try to find her, this daring gal flaunting downstairs in the raw, a game that New Yorkers played and the newspapers and cartoonists played up. Soon the whole country was playing it, studying the halftones in their local papers. Prizes went unclaimed: no one could find her. Hidden she remained, more modest in the bareness of her sober brown cubist planes than in a department-storeful of clothes.

Her room was mobbed every day. People formed queues, waiting for thirty, even forty, minutes just to stand momentarily in her presence, venting their shocked gasps of disbelief, their rage, or their raucous laughter before giving way to the next in line, already elbowing and shoving for their turn.

[3] In 1935 the Museum of Modern Art, in its sixth year and in much smaller quarters than at present, would draw 123,309 people to see its Van Gogh Retrospective.

In less than four weeks Marcel Duchamp's *Nude Descending a Staircase* became the most famous "woman" painting in America. To this day it remains so, sharing the honor with only one other painting, the *Arrangement in Black and Grey* more commonly known as "Whistler's Mother."

The very first day of the show a dazed reporter had attempted to describe the *Nude* as "a fearful explosion in a lumber yard." [4] Almost everyone, in fact, saw the painting with its chastely painted overlapping planes of brown and gray—representations of mass in motion so abstract as to approximate geometry—as an explosion or an aftermath of strewn wreckage. Julian Street called it an "explosion in a shingle factory," and *American Art News* inventoried it as "leather, tin, and broken violins." Duchamp's cubist-futurist canvas became a symbol, not only of the Armory Show, but of modern art itself. Modern art was, indeed, a chain of explosions. The Armory Show was one in that chain, one whose repercussions are still felt today. Frank Crowninshield commented years later on the phenomenon: "The commotion which it everywhere created was difficult to account for, since Duchamp, a serious, modest and extremely intellectual man had . . . certainly been free of any attempt at hoax or guile." [5]

Meanwhile, a great voice boomed out, one that carried authority. Theodore Roosevelt, who, by running for president on an independent ticket, had defeated William Howard Taft and assured the victory of Woodrow Wilson, declined to attend Wilson's inauguration on March 4, 1913—his privilege as an ex-president. He chose, instead, to see the Armory

[4] Unknown reporter in the *New York World*, February 17, 1913.
[5] Frank Crowninshield in *Vogue*, September 15, 1940.

SEEING NEW YORK WITH A CUBIST

The Rude Descending a Staircase
(Rush Hour at the Subway)

New York Evening SUN, *March 20, 1913*

Show on that day. Walt Kuhn and Davies showed T.R. around, and he wrote his impressions for *Outlook* magazine in prose that, as always, carried a punch.

Teddy Roosevelt reacted bitterly against the cubists, and yet saw clearly that freedom for the artist, like freedom for any man, was right and good. He commended the "real value in . . . such an exhibition," and applauded the fact that "there was one note entirely missing . . . and that was the note of the commonplace.

"There was not a touch," he reported, "of simpering, self-satisfied conventionality . . . no stunting or dwarfing, no requirement that a man whose gifts lay in new directions should measure up or down to stereotyped and fossilized standards.

"It is vitally necessary," said Teddy, "to move forward and to shake off the dead hand of the reactionaries."

The Armory Show closed on the eve of St. Patrick's Day, 1913. "It was the wildest, maddest, most intensely excited crowd . . . I have witnessed," wrote Jerome Myers. It was the biggest crowd of all, too. From dusty subway-riders to the cream of society, all came, as though to say farewell to a friend. Reporters elbowed through the throngs, and suddenly the Fighting Irish band burst into a Sousa march. It was late at night when the last visitors straggled out. The band was beckoned down from the balcony, and the artists and their girls, as if in Montmartre, fell in behind, marching from room to room. Then outdoors to the pavements, a carnival let loose on gray Lexington Avenue. Back in again—and from behind Bellows's burlap walls came champagne. Corks popped and the band went into a waltz. As the couples whirled around the floor, deliriously gay, toasts were offered and drunk amid cheers.

"To the Academy!" shouted an artist derisively.

John Quinn smiled. "No, no," he said. "Don't you remember Captain John Philip of the *Texas*? When his guns sank a Spanish ship at Santiago, he said: 'Don't cheer, boys, the poor devils are dying.' "

All through the night the band played without pay. The Irish regiment, from Colonel Conley down to the last private, was vastly impressed by the success of the show. Not to mention John Quinn, special ornament of the Sons of Erin. Stuart Davis, at least, was not particularly surprised at this. He had previously, as a joke, taken his favorite Irish bartender from Newark to see the famous *Nude* on her staircase. Completely oblivious of the laughter all around, the Irishman took his time. He studied the picture carefully from every angle, and then said to all who cared to listen: "Paint like an angel, he can, that fellow!"

From New York the show went to the Art Institute of
Chicago. The Windy City's attendance matched Manhattan's; her behavior was quite Midwestern in its lack of inhi-
bition. Art students burned a Matisse painting as well as
Walter Pach—both, fortunately, in effigy. The local politi-
cians seized the opportunity to wage a short-lived campaign
against vice and immorality in art. They had scanned in advance the titles in the catalogue. One state senator stormed in
with the press at his heels, demanding to be shown an obscure
painting called *Prostitution* by an unknown American painter.
It was a terrible letdown: *Prostitution* showed only a sad woman
looking out of a window. A big official delegation came to
demand that the *Nude Descending a Staircase* be torn from the
wall. They, like everyone else, were totally unable "to make
out either the lady or the stairway."

Finally, by invitation of the Copley Society, the exhibition went on to Boston. Boston behaved most admirably like
Boston: not shocked, not scandalized, not amused, not even
interested. The Armory Show could have gone on for years.
Pach records that "a dozen other cities applied for the show
in vain." [1] The paintings borrowed from abroad had to be
returned—all except the considerable number that had been
sold.

With all the laughter, all the scoffing, the Armory Show
was over. Yet because of it America would never be the same
again. Stieglitz had opened the door an inch; this blast had
blown it clear off its hinges. America had joined the world.
The show cleared the way for independent shows that the
public would support; it pointed to the need, soon to come,

[1] Walter Pach: *Queer Thing, Painting* (New York, 1938).

for a museum to show contemporary art no matter how controversial. The public had evidenced no apathy: "cubistic," "futuristic," and "modernistic" were now household words, as was touchingly shown by Tin Pan Alley's tribute: *That Futuristic Rag*.

Important to the museums yet to come was the beginning, then and a little later, of the great private collections like those of Lillie P. Bliss, Stephen C. Clark, Arthur Jerome Eddy, Albert C. Barnes, John Quinn, and Walter and Louise Arensberg. These pioneer collectors started a trend so strong that by mid-century America would own a lion's share of the masterpieces of modern art.

Eddy, a successful Chicago businessman, bought the most "difficult" and controversial of the cubist work; in 1914 he wrote the first book on cubism to appear in America; the major part of his collection eventually enriched the Art Institute of Chicago. Quinn had been a collector for years, but his modern acquisitions began with purchases totaling more than $3,000—at the low prices then current—from the Armory Show. When eventually dispersed by sale after his death in the mid-twenties, the Quinn modern collection numbered over two thousand items, many of major importance.

The first picture sold from the Armory Show was Redon's *Silence*. It went to Miss Bliss, and with it she became a collector. Her famous collection, which went as a bequest in 1931 to the Museum of Modern Art, eventually included many priceless works by Rousseau, Cézanne, Van Gogh, Braque, and Picasso.

Dr. Barnes, as is well known, created, patented, and made a huge fortune from the antiseptic called Argyrol. He then began amassing almost incredible quantities of important paintings. Primarily interested in the late nineteenth century, he gathered Renoirs, Cézannes, and Seurats, to which he added Rousseaus, Matisses, and early Picassos. His taste never included cubism or the still more abstract developments that followed.

Irascible and headstrong, Barnes was embroiled in continual controversy. Infuriated at the bad reception of his first exhibitions in Philadelphia in the 1920's, he set up his Foundation on a large country estate at Merion, Pennsylvania, and proceeded to run it like a baronial museum. By admitting a trickle of students under the most rigorous conditions, he secured the tax-exempt status of an educational institution. Other visitors were rare; they had to apply humbly for written invitations; even armed with these, they were often turned away at the doorstep. After Barnes's sudden death in 1951, court action was brought to open the Foundation's doors to the public, but a decision that smacked of the peculiar largely confirmed its policy of exclusion.

Barnes fortunately was atypical of his class. It has come to be accepted by wealthy amateurs that the great collections they alone can afford eventually will be opened to the public view. This has come to be the chief prestige, as well as one of the deepest satisfactions, of the rich collector. The tendency has even been reflected in recent income-tax provisions greatly liberalizing exemptions for such gifts. In 1955 the exemption was raised to thirty per cent of total income, allowable at the time the gift is announced, though the donor may retain it until his death.

Walter and Louise Arensberg ended up with a large historical collection, strongly personalized in its selection, that included the largest single group of the sparse work of Marcel

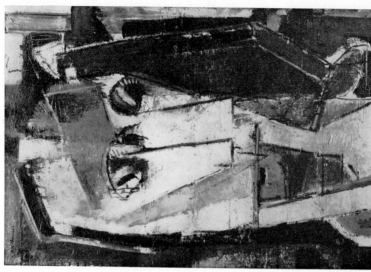

Heads, 1931–2, by Alfred Maurer.
Oil on canvas, 30″ x 19¾″. Collection: Bertha Schaefer.

Synchromy in Blue, 1916, by Stanton Macdonald-Wright.
Oil on canvas, 26″ x 20″. Collection: Janis.

Brooklyn Bridge, *1917–18, by Joseph Stella.*
Oil and lithographic crayon on bedsheet, 84" by 76".
Collection: Yale University Art Gallery.

Joseph Stella and Marcel Duchamp, New York, 1920.

Duchamp. For a long time the Arensbergs could not snare the prize Duchamp, the *Nude Descending a Staircase*. In spite of all the hullabaloo, it went unsold in New York, and it seemed that it would not be sold in Chicago. At the last moment a San Francisco art dealer, the late Frederic C. Torrey, bought it for the asking price of $350.[2] Torrey took it to San Francisco and strove manfully to bring about a modern movement on the Pacific Coast. A rather noted connoisseur of etchings and Japanese prints, he fell in love with the thorny *Nude* and, through her, with modernism. He even visited France in order to meet Duchamp, and the two became fast friends.

Late in the very year of the Armory Show, Torrey was trying to proselytize in Portland, Oregon. In the 22nd Annual Report of the Portland Art Museum, 1913, we find the following note: "November 24, the post-impressionistic exhibition lent by Mr. Frederic C. Torrey, of San Francisco, opened. This was an important collection, consisting of the painting the *Nude Descending a Staircase*, by Marcel Duchamp, and about one hundred prints, original lithographs in color, and photographs of paintings and drawings, forming a most interesting series of examples of the works of El Greco, Courbet, Manet, Cézanne, Van Gogh, Gauguin, Renoir, Maurice Denis, Matisse and Picasso."

Torrey finally gave up the unequal battle and went back to etchings. He hung the *Nude* on the stair landing of his big redwood house in Berkeley. Torrey's onetime business partner, H. J. Allen (later California State Director of the WPA Art Project), writes "how unacceptable it was to his clients and how they regarded it as an amusing stunt. This caused him to obscure it in his house. And that when he sold it, he hung

[2] The Philadelphia Museum of Art now has the *Nude* insured for $50,000.

a photo-facsimile on the stair landing where it had hung and no one noticed the difference. . . . I know Fred sold it with the understanding there would be no public announcement. He disliked parting with it." It is not clear, actually, just who bought it from Torrey. Daniel Catton Rich, director of the Art Institute of Chicago, wrote that the *Nude* was once in Jerome Eddy's collection, while Walter Pach has said that he himself negotiated the sale between Torrey and Arensberg a few years following the Armory Show.[3]

On the world scene of modern art, the Armory Show, while of vast import to America, was only one event. The year 1913, as Sidney Janis has pointed out, was a climactic year. All of the elements of modern art as we now know it were already here, actually or potentially. The Matisse style of free expressive drawing and color was well established, and so was its antithesis, cubism, with its almost scientific geometry of form-analysis. Well developed, too, was futurism, "replete with scientific attitudes, [having] emerged from the neo-impressionist breaking of light and the cubist breaking of form. Adding kinetics," as Janis writes, "it utilized pictorially the progression and velocity of movement, dynamic tensions, lines of force and other concepts." [4] Dadaism was already implicit in the ironic paintings of Picabia and those of Duchamp which immediately followed the *Nude*.

In 1913, too, the German expressionist Vassily Kandinsky was painting his non-representational *Improvisations*, which

[3] The Rich statement appears in his foreword to the Art Institute of Chicago catalogue of the Eddy Collection: "Eddy at one time owned the 'Nude Descending a Staircase,' but this famous picture—the irritation spot of the Armory Show—passed into other hands at his death." Walter Pach's statement was recently made in a conversation as reported by Harriet Janis.

[4] Sidney Janis: *Abstract and Surrealist Art in America* (New York, 1944).

are among the earliest completely abstract paintings. Swirling things of free color, they seem, in retrospect, stream-of-consciousness symphonies intuitively created without conscious control. Hardly ten years later—an awareness of Freud having intervened—the surrealists would be using such automatic techniques.

It has been remarked that whatever you look for in the past you can find. The *Improvisations* had been foretold eighty or more years earlier. It was Joseph Mallord William Turner who for about a dozen years early in the nineteenth century painted fantasies of color and light from which natural appearances had almost completely disappeared. Like every great art rebel since, Turner was called mad. Some even suggested that he be locked up in Bedlam. Just after the middle of the century, Turner's work greatly influenced the founding of impressionism when it was seen at the Tate Gallery in London by Claude Monet. Monet, however, never wanted to be so abstract as Turner had been. The Kandinsky of the *Improvisations*, however, is like the English "madman" come to life again.

"Other . . . precursors of surrealism," says Janis, "were Chirico, whose inner eye first registered the oblique light of his arcaded silent cities in 1911 [and] Chagall who in the same year began to paint Russian folklore in a phantasmagoric and weightless world."

This was 1913, year of climax. With the next year would come war, to end once and for all the hold of the nineteenth century, to usher in, for better or worse, a new world, a new time. Art, which heralded it all, would suffer in the holocaust. Great artists would die in the fighting. None of those who survived or did not fight would go untouched. Modern art would be interrupted, but not extinguished. No one knows, however, how much it was changed.

So far as America was concerned, the Armory Show was a curtain-raiser, not a final event. It posed questions, did not solve them. The dissensions forgotten during work on the show now burst out more violently than ever. Now the rebels had weapons, and the conservatives had felt their strength. American art, like that of Europe, was irrevocably split from top to bottom.

The very success of the Armory Show was a sore spot. Over three hundred works of art were sold, almost all of them foreign. Right then and there came the emphasis on "imported art." Local reputations were diminished—almost demolished. It was too late a lesson, too bitter a pill. Most of the members resigned. Then the Association itself dissolved.

Jerome Myers, one of the unhappy instigators of the show, summed up the feeling then general among the majority of American artists. America, he said, had become a colony, art-wise: "Our land of opportunity was thrown open to foreign art, unrestricted and triumphant."

Outpost it actually was at that moment. Colony it did not need to become, though for three decades it would seemingly be just that. In 1913 we had greatly talented modern artists of our own: Alfred Maurer, Max Weber, John Marin, Stanton Macdonald-Wright, and a goodly number of others. Almost immediately, too, new talents would spring up. But, with some of us looking at Paris and the rest of us looking at the past, we paid them no mind. Highly ironic became the hopeful dedication of the Armory Show: "To the American Artists of the Future."

Despite Quinn's exultant words on the closing night, the

Academy was not dead. It never dies. It is more than a group of artists; it is the whole Loyal Opposition—all those who compulsively and unaccountably look backward as the world moves on. Generation by generation, it arises to oppose the new and the vital and the timely. The wars of art must be fought over and over. And then over again.

Among all the heated comment at the time, that of disinterested observers makes the most sense. Theodore Roosevelt instinctively went to the core of the issue: freedom. Others, like a writer in *Current Opinion*, sensed historical importances. "Whatever our feeling," he wrote, "we can hardly escape a sense of the vital significance of the exhibition." Then, recalling the early hostility toward impressionism, he reflected: "Is it utterly extravagant to prophesy that some of the works of Cézanne, Gauguin, Van Gogh, Matisse and Picasso may become historic?" [5]

Above all, however, was the great roar of laughter at the first glimpse of modern art. It is easily tabbed as raucous Philistinism, but it was more than that. Jerome Eddy wrote that "the cubist pictures . . . attracted throngs because they were strange, but the throngs would never have gazed as they did unless behind the outward strangeness there had been an inner seriousness of purpose.

" 'Those fellows are trying to say something,' was . . . often . . . heard.

"The papers would say, 'They are simply making fun of the public,' but the public, generally speaking, did not feel that way.

"A goodly section of the public made fun of the pictures, but very few people honestly felt the pictures made fun of the

[5] *Current Opinion*, Spring 1913.

public—*if anything they were rather too serious.*" [6]

Eddy was the type of man on whom the Armory Show made its deepest impression. An old man when cubism came, he was flexible enough to embrace it. Author of *Recollections and Impressions of James A. McNeill Whistler*—Whistler had once painted his portrait—he was ready in 1913 to write the first American book on cubism. This was only one year after the publication in Paris of the famous *Du Cubisme* by the painters Gleizes and Metzinger.

"The new, however good, is always strange," Eddy wrote, "the old, however bad, is never strange." He was humorously contemptuous of the closed mind. "The same ladies and gentlemen," he predicted, "who shook their heads at Monet in 1890, shook their heads at the cubists in 1913. If they live another quarter of a century they will once more shake their heads at the new art of that day—for such is life." Surrealism, when it came, made a good prophet of Eddy.

Twenty-five years after the Armory Show, Walt Kuhn, whose part had been so large, summed up his feelings about it. "We naïve artists," he wrote, "we wanted to see what was going on in the world of art . . . wanted to open up the mind of the public.

"Did we do it? We did more than that.

"The Armory Show affected the whole culture of America. Business caught on immediately. . . . The outer appearance of industry absorbed the lesson like a sponge. Drabness, awkwardness began to disappear from American life, and color and grace stepped in. . . . The decorative elements of Matisse and the cubists were immediately taken on as models of a brighter, more lively America. Brancusi went into every-

[6] Arthur Jerome Eddy: *Cubists and Post-Impressionism* (Chicago, 1914).

thing from milliners' dummies to streamline trains.

"The exhibition affected every phase of American life—the apparel of men and women, the stage, automobiles, airplanes, furniture, interior decorations, beauty parlors, advertising and printing in its various departments, plumbing, hardware—everything from the modernistic designs of gas pumps and added color of beach umbrellas and bathing suits, down to the merchandise of the dime store."

The effect, indeed, has been as Kuhn observed, and was more immediate than he indicated. While the Armory Show was still on, Paul Poiret was brought from Paris to design "cubist" fabrics; "futuristic cretonnes" were displayed on Fifth Avenue; and Wanamaker's in New York announced that "at last the modern spirit is developing in the realm of women's dress." [7]

"Many great exhibitions since then," Kuhn continued, "could not have appeared without it. The Museum of Modern Art in New York would never have been possible."

At the Armory Show's end, Kuhn recalled, "one of the conservative critics said with good humor, 'Men, it was a bully show, but don't do it again.'

"We did not have to do it again," Kuhn observed with a pioneer's pride. "It kept right on going, and is going better than ever today."

[7] Advertisement in the *New York Evening Sun*, March 13, 1913.

6. *Independents' Day*

Within a year after the Armory Show a number of galleries in New York, some of them new, were handling modern art and, despite the war in Europe, were getting pictures in. Attendance and sales at the Show had encouraged private enterprise; removal of the art tariff had made it practicable. Soon the list was long: Knoedler, Macbeth, and Montross, the Modern Gallery, de Zayas, Bourgeois, and Daniel, as well as others, were supplying the new collectors, large and small.

By 1915, Matisse was being given a one-man show at the Montross Gallery; cubist, futurist, and expressionist work was coming in, as were the new collage paintings of Picasso and Braque, with their trade labels and scraps of newspaper pasted on the canvas in serious experimental design, intellectual art that disclaimed the ivory tower, claimed kinship with the man on the street and his real yet changing world.

In all of this the American modernist had little part. Nearly all of the expatriates were now back home, forced by war to leave Paris, but eager, anyway, to carry on here. The emphasis unfortunately, but perhaps inevitably, imposed by the Armory Show persisted. Dealers made slight effort to propagandize and, if necessary, subsidize the domestic product when the imported sold more easily and at higher prices. Stieglitz, commendably, concentrated more and more on Americans of talent, supporting several by drawing accounts with no due date. But his resources were limited and, while an admirable propagandist, he was not the most effective of salesmen. Even in propaganda he thought in terms of the small intellectual circle that is often long on enthusiasm and short on buying-power. It was a time for idealism sharpened by realism. It is the fashion today to malign the dealers—

harpies of the arts, they have been called. But the dealer is a force; he is an indispensable factor in the artist's existence in a money world. Compel the artist to be his own salesman and you get the commercial artist or the defeated one. There are exceptions to the rule, of course: Picasso is one.

It is one thing for the artist to be poor in Paris and another in New York. There was no real Bohemia to be found in Manhattan. Within two years the American modernist was in a bad way. Nevertheless, he was far from despair. If the dealers refused him, they must be brought around: there was always the possibility of the large group show. The Academy was no longer the whole works; the big freeze-out was over. So again and even more generally the idea of the independent show was in the air.

In 1916 came the Forum Exhibition of Modern American Painters. Organized by Willard Huntington Wright (S. S. Van Dine), brother of Macdonald-Wright, the Forum Exhibition was on display during March at the Anderson Galleries in New York. Seventeen painters and sculptors were shown, including Thomas H. Benton, Arthur G. Dove, Macdonald-Wright, Marsden Hartley, Marin, Maurer, Man Ray, Charles Sheeler, Walkowitz, and William and Marguerite Zorach. Synchromism, founded in Paris several years earlier by Macdonald-Wright and Morgan Russell, was featured at the Forum. Notable omissions were cubist Weber and futurist Stella. Also in 1916 came Philadelphia's first modern exhibition. It was assembled by Morton L. Schamberg, painter of machine abstractions, and was presented at the McClees Gallery.

That same year the Society of Independent Artists, Inc.,

was formed. The new organization filled the void left by the break-up of the Association of American Painters and Sculptors after the Armory Show. Old wounds seemed to heal as modernists and semi-modernists of the pattern of The Eight joined hands. Directors included advanced painters like Stella, Marin, Man Ray, and John Covert, and more conservative men like Bellows, Prendergast, Rockwell Kent, and Charles W. Hawthorne. Walter Arensberg was managing director. A surprising name on the board was that of Marcel Duchamp, who had moved to New York.

The backing of wealth and social prestige, first evident at the Armory Show, became even more evident when the new Society held a remarkable first show. It was sponsored by glittering names, among them Archer M. Huntington, and the Mmes Philip M. Lydig, William K. Vanderbilt, and Harry Payne Whitney. Another was Miss Katherine Dreier, herself a painter, who would soon found a pioneer museum for modern art.

Contemporary art, however, rather than modern alone, was the keynote of this and all successive shows by the Independent Society. Granted that by then all American artists were pretty much in the same boat, this boat became more crowded than even the *Mayflower*. The Society's object, said the first catalogue, was to make certain that whatever artists of all schools sent would be hung, and that all would have an equal opportunity. It would be a sort of annual State of the Union speech on American art. Well, it was.

All the artists agreed on the idea: no jury, no prizes. No less an aristocrat of painting than Ingres had formulated that democratic doctrine around the middle of the nineteenth century. "A jury, however formulated," Ingres had said, "will always work badly. The need of our time is for unlimited admission. . . . I consider unjust and immoral any restriction tending to prevent a man from living from the product of his work."

In 1884 the Société des Artistes Indépendants of Paris had adopted as its keystone policy Ingres's idea of no juries. The added idea of no prizes had been advanced as late as 1912 by Renoir. The American Independents was modeled after the Société. From Marcel Duchamp came the final democratic formula: hanging of the works alphabetically by the artists' names. His, too, was the witty, almost Dada, idea of determining the letter to begin with by an annual drawing of lots. He was pushing it to the limit. As we shall see, Duchamp was about to test some rather definite ideas about it all. In any event, the Society followed his suggestions, and the placing of the phenomenal 2,007 entries of the first Independent Society show began with the letter R.

Determined to show everybody, the Society set the easiest of admission requirements: acceptance of its principles, an initiation fee of one dollar, annual dues of five dollars. All exhibitors were *ipso facto* members; all had a vote on directors and policy. By 1917, after a few months of existence, the Society numbered twelve hundred members.

The first show ran from March 6 to April 10, 1916, at the Grand Central Palace on Lexington Avenue at 46th Street. It attracted over twenty thousand visitors; forty-five works of art were sold. Although the Independent shows continued on into the 1940's, the ambitious original program was never fully realized. This program, rather remarkably prefiguring (and, in fact, going beyond) that of the Museum of Modern Art (which would not be founded until twelve years later), was to have included, besides painting, drawing, prints, and sculpture, presentations of literature, music, drama, and the motion picture.

Henry McBride has described the great excitement of the opening night: "Everybody ran about in a rapture discovering things. The Bastille had fallen, the doors were open, and Democracy, for a very slight entrance fee, was supplying its own art. There was an especial enthusiasm for everything that had hitherto been suppressed. A picture by a George Somebody of Boston, who had adorned his Venus with real jewels and who also asked an enormous price for his work—or possibly for the jewels—ran Mr. Eilshemius a close second as a sensation." [1]

Louis Eilshemius, eccentric, painter, poet, dramatist "second only to Shakespeare," and scientist, was the five-day wonder of the first Independent. Marcel Duchamp, who was the first to take his work seriously, later arranged a one-man Eilshemius show at the Katherine Dreier museum. The discovery of an Eilshemius was an unexpected bonus from the Independent Show.

According to John Covert, Marcel Duchamp and he rounded up the guarantors in advance—twelve of them at $1,000 each—to make the first Independent possible. "From the sales," Covert recalls, "each got $50 back. One was sore about it but Marcel silenced him.

" 'You got two miles of pictures for your $950,' said Duchamp. He knew what he was talking about. He and I

---

[1] George E. Lothrop, now unremembered, was a remarkable primitive painter who showed in the early Independents. The quotation is from Henry McBride: "The Discovery of Louis Eilshemius," *The Arts*, December 1926. McBride had forgotten the real title: *God's Girl* (see No. 65, illustrated, in the Independents catalogue).

had measured them by pacing it off."

As for Duchamp himself, a founder and director of the Society, he was not represented in the show for reasons that we shall see. However, there was a strong foreign representation that first year, including fifteen of the leaders: Brancusi, Braque, Delaunay, Derain, Duchamp-Villon, Dufy, Gris, Matisse, Metzinger, Picabia, Picasso, Severini, Signac, Jacques Villon, and Vlaminck.

The absence of a work by Marcel Duchamp was actually a culmination of events and, strangely enough, of a lack of events. The internationally famous painter of the *Nude Descending a Staircase* had not put a brush to a canvas for several years. It was not that his creativeness had ceased, but that it had found other channels. He had been counted on as a headliner. Perhaps he would come up with another sensation like the *Nude*. Although he was rumored to be inactive, all except his intimates nevertheless expected him to produce a masterpiece painted in secret. When a little later his cessation of orthodox work became a certainty, it was both a shocking disappointment and an enigma to his contemporaries. It is still both today.

With Marcel Duchamp one is never through with enigmas. His celebrated *Nude* baffled a whole generation; he himself remains a greater enigma. One thing is crystal clear about the urbane, coolly detached Duchamp: he is one of the outstanding intellectuals of our time. He is also a paradox within himself. A professed and dedicated nihilist throughout all his maturity, he has yet, at various times, been impelled to justify himself in the eyes of the world. He painted, obviously, before he gave up painting; painted a short series of pictures that have ripened into prime masterpieces. Ye Compleat Nihilist would never have painted at all. Turning from painting, he took up chess and moved quickly into near-championship class. A few triumphs, and he gave up all public playing. Ye Compleat Nihilist would never have played at all. Such a contradiction would not bother Duchamp. "Complete nihilism," he would say, "is clearly impossible: Nothing is Something."

And Duchamp glories in these paradoxes. About it all there is the slightest odor of sophistry, gay and subtly disarming, but sophistry still, for he conceals the real answers within himself. Others must speculate. Some think that he came to feel that the purity and philosophical non-involvement of his cerebrations would be compromised or subtly flawed by their utilization in exterior activity. That is one extreme, the precious one. The other is the belief that, once having proved by an external Q.E.D. that he could do a given thing, Duchamp would give it up like a perversely brilliant child breaking the toys he masters so quickly. At either extreme there was that need first to do it.

There is more: a gentle destructiveness disguised as an acceptance of destruction by nature. There was, for example, the *Unhappy Ready-made* that he constructed in Europe during 1922–3: a geometry book that Duchamp had mastered as a child was opened and held in the air by taut strings tied through holes in its four corners and then stretched and fastened like guy wires. This was out-of-doors on a balcony in the home near Paris of his sister, Suzanne Duchamp, also a painter. Through the long winter the book hung there, its pages turned or torn out by the fingers of the wind, its printed lore of theorems and equations slowly dissolving in the rain and sleet.

"How sad it looks," Marcel said when he returned in the spring to mark its ruin.

Again, the speculations. A brilliant prank? Then why remembered through a busy winter? Or did Duchamp himself hang there in effigy, suspended through the winter of his disbelief? A paralyzing disbelief in education and dogma, in truth and knowledge of the truth, in the institutions of man and then in man. And I, too, Duchamp may have thought, am a man.

Then there is the famous big picture on glass, *La mariée mise à nu par ses célibataires, même* or *The Bride Stripped Bare by Her Bachelors, Even.* Duchamp worked intermittently for eight years, from 1915 to 1923, on the glass, which is generally called "The Large Glass." It is no doubt true that at this point the clarity of his ideas seemed to him to reject the gross opacity of canvas and paint. For it was Duchamp's intention that *The Bride* should not hang passively on a wall, but should stand in the open to be walked around, looked at and through. She was not to be half-imprisoned, but to be truly the bride of space and time.

Yet fragile canvas often survives when plate glass is shattered. Duchamp, Covert says, spoke often of this possibility while working on it. Finally, without accident, the nine-foot-tall glass was completed. Katherine Dreier bought it. Four years later came the inevitable: *The Bride*, as Duchamp must have foreseen, was ravished. Coming back to Miss Dreier's from a Brooklyn Museum exhibition, it split into a maze of cracks; it arrived in hundreds of pieces.

Thereupon Duchamp, who had knowingly worked all along with fate, set to work again. Like the great symbol of our bivalent age which he is, he patiently reassembled the ruin, sandwiching it between clear sheets of plate glass. As if to say "This is ruin's gestation," he finished the restoration in nine months. *The Bride* stands today, Duchamp's generally recognized masterpiece, in the Philadelphia Museum, the gift of Miss Dreier, looking somewhat like a vast etching-plate that its maker had canceled with slashes of the burin. In all the time since then—Duchamp was sixty-nine in 1956—he has never made an orthodox picture.

Marcel Duchamp is a man wholly and without question of our time, balancing a destructive nihilism against an innate creativeness, a creativeness that flows like a spring—dammed here, breaking through there. The material, Freudians tell us, of neurosis, and yet Duchamp manages this with calm equanimity and the air of an Eastern contemplative.

"Problems?" he will ask with a quiet smile. "There are no problems; problems are inventions of the mind." And there he would let the matter stand. Yet he is constantly being asked why he gave up painting. His carefully reasoned, ironic explanations have only deepened the mystery. He sometimes seems to imply—remotely and obliquely, to be sure—that no one quite understands his paintings. Picasso does not trouble to conceal this kind of impatience, an impatience with stupidity. Picasso fairly breathes contempt, but if it exists in Duchamp at all, it is as a sort of concealed quiet despair. Part of the measure of the difference between these two men, both great artists, is to be found in the fact that Picasso is a very rich man today, Duchamp a poor one who could have waxed rich on his early success.

With this picture of Duchamp, man and artist, in mind, it is clear why by 1915 he would be busy with Francis Picabia

Interior with Men, *1919, by Max Weber.*
Tempera on canvas, 22" x 18".
Collection: Wright Ludington.

Vocalization, c. *1919, by John K. Covert.*
Oil and wooden dowels nailed to composition board.
Collection: Yale University Art Gallery.

Watch, *by Gerald Murphy. Oil, 72" x 72".*

Gerald Murphy and Pablo Picasso on the beach at Cap d'Antibes, 1925.

and Man Ray making the beginnings of Dada in America—
that ironic, contemptuous rejection of esthetic values as so
many empty clichés, that horselaugh at the respectable and
the revered. So we find Duchamp making an extraordinary
gesture as a contributor to the big first Independent Show of
1917. He had long been fascinated by the esthetic qualities
that he discovered in certain commercial and industrial
objects, and equally fascinated by the implied disparagement
of conventional art. He chose such an object as his sole entry
in the exhibition. It was a "ready-made"—what French
artists call *un objet tout fait*—an item of bathroom plumbing
entitled *Fontaine*, or *Fountain*, which he signed with a pseudonym, R. [Richard] Mutt. The title in French indicates
that this object was Duchamp's—or Richard Mutt's—own
particular fable. The pseudonym, on the other hand, indicates both the universality of the object and the anonymity
of its creator. For this was long before the day of publicized
industrial designers, and Mutt, of course, was half of the
famous cartoon team of Mutt and Jeff. Or perhaps Duchamp
cherished and hoped to preserve the anonymity of industrial
designers: Richard Mott was a well-known manufacturer of
bathroom fixtures.

It was a slap in the face of the Society; more, it put their
whole wide-ranging democratic program on trial. Their courage did not match that of Duchamp; there were violent
protests—particularly, Duchamp recalls, from George Bellows, "portraitist," as he says, "of bloody prize fighters."
Finally, in a futile compromise, the Independents "accepted"
the *Fountain*, but hung it out of sight in a space behind a
partition to which there was no public access. It was not listed

in the official catalogue. The *Fountain* was a thing of gleaming white porcelain; its lines were Brancusi-like in their purity; it was a urinal.

The urinal was a *cause célèbre* in a closet: shielded from the public and the press, it embroiled the whole Independent group. It was a controversy the more malignant because all silence on one side. Those who got slapped were mutely well-bred: one did not discuss functional plumbing, much less functions—least of all, the functions of an artist. Duchamp, having spoken in the act of submitting his *Fountain*, said no more. Others, however, spoke out for him. The little Dada magazine *Blind Man*, in its first and only issue, included Stieglitz's photograph of the urinal, a prose ode by Louise Norton Varese to its "chaste simplicity and calm curves," and a poem to Richard Mutt composed by the American painter Charles Demuth.

Duchamp was thereupon through with the Independents. He found no independence of thought among them; he could only question art and artists the more. Unquestionably he had chosen an object certain of rejection; knowing the answer in advance, he had made sure that the Independents themselves pronounced it. So he had gone through all the prescribed motions: first accepting at its face value the basic premise of the Independent program, "Art by Everyone for Everyone," and then selecting and submitting an esthetic object made by non-artists (i.e., Everyone) for everyone—or, at least, for the *male* everyone.

R. Mutt's *Fountain* was the sixty-four-dollar question: Art by Everyone for Everyone? Embattled prudism had just said: "NO!" We still ask it, however, and answer it: "Why, sure, everyone can be an artist," as children trace televised drawings on paper held over the screen of the home receiving-set and their elders paint *Davy Crockett's Last Fight* in pre-mixed colors that they apply to numbered sections on canvases bought at the dime store. Seldom, however, does a mind as aristocratic as that of Marcel Duchamp pose the question in terms as final as a urinal. A lesser man would have whispered it with a perfume vial or a shiny percolator.

Duchamp tells how Walter Arensberg, hearing of the incident, went to the Independent Show and asked to see "the *Fountain* by R. Mutt." Attendants called officials. The officials said that they had never heard of it.

"I know better than that," said Arensberg. His next remark stunned his fellow officials. "I want to buy it," he said calmly.

Still it could not be found. Thereupon Duchamp and Man Ray, poking around, discovered the offending object behind the partition. They called to Arensberg, who took out his checkbook and announced that he would buy it sight unseen.

"Fill in the amount yourselves," he said, and then required the urinal to be brought out and carried in plain view through the crowded galleries. His Duchamp collection, eventually the most extensive in the world, was richer by one item. At the door, while Duchamp and Man Ray stood by, holding the new acquisition as though it were a marble Aphrodite, Arensberg turned and in his quiet voice tendered his resignation from the Society of Independent Artists.

For a number of years after this, Duchamp chose and exhibited on various occasions a series of ready-mades, among them an Underwood typewriter cover, a clothes hanger, a rack for drying milk bottles, a bird cage filled with sugar lumps fashioned of marble with a thermometer in their midst (more accurately described, perhaps, as a construction),[2] and a shovel which, in a take-off of Art Appreciation, he described as of "exquisite lines, balance, and symmetry" and titled *In Advance of the Broken Arm.*[3]

The Independent Shows kept on for many years, but there never was another like the first. The total number of entries dropped sharply—to 845 in 1918, the next year to 647. The foreign entries decreased, and in a few years disappeared altogether; so did most of the works of the American vanguard. "Art by Everyone for Everyone" became the reign of the reactionary and the mediocre, a new academy or the academy in a new guise, it matters little which. Never at any one time are there enough great artists; never at any one time are there few enough poor ones.

Nevertheless, the huge Independent catch-alls showed up clearly the most urgent need of the time: a public forum for great modern art which would have room for the new and the experimental in the changing continuum of contemporary expression. The established American museums were not ready for the vast, expensive, and specialized task. The Art Institute of Chicago held back; the Philadelphia Museum stayed in the nineteenth century; the Boston Fine Arts hibernated with the Brahmins; and the Metropolitan, as though still ruled by Sir Purdon Clark, even hid from view the fine Cézanne that, yielding to pressure in 1913, it had bought from the Armory Show. Here and there, important museums like

[2] In the Arensberg Collection at the Philadelphia Museum of Art, titled *Why Not Sneeze?* and signed with the pseudonym Rrose Sélavy.

[3] Duchamp submitted the shovel, the typewriter cover, and the clothes hanger to the Bourgeois Gallery in New York.

the Brooklyn or smaller and more provincial ones like the Newark were attempting to break the ice. The former flexed its muscles with the first museum show, in America at least, of African Negro sculpture as art, not as ethnology. The Newark Museum started much earlier. In 1913, under the guidance of its founder, John Cotton Dana, it was far and away the most progressive museum in the country. That Armory year, showing Max Weber's most advanced cubist work, it led the way as the first American museum to show a modernist, American or otherwise.

John Cotton Dana deserves a large place in any American history of art. He was a librarian, not a curator, by profession. His was no bookworm's mind, however, but an almost completely unprejudiced organ of perception. He was no "confused" liberal, but one of the original American species of liberal. The Museum grew in 1909 out of art rooms that Dana had started in 1902 in the Newark Library. He worked with the public schools and with all interested clubs and groups. On extremely modest funds, as he had done many years earlier with the Denver Library, he sent the public schools photographic reproductions of the most advanced art then current, meanwhile throwing the art rooms open for lectures and meetings. Figures show the extent of his accomplishment: from 1902 to 1909, over five hundred different local groups—school, art, and museum supervisors, architects, art classes, women's clubs, art, musical, and literary groups—held 3,664 meetings in the rooms. This is an average of ten every week, with a total attendance of 112,200. In the same period, the art rooms put on fifty-six exhibitions with a total attendance of 266,000, all of this in a relatively small community.

If Dana's showing in 1912 of the art in industry of the German *Werkbund* seems advanced—as it was—what can one say of his acceptance in 1889, in so many words, of the machine in art? A follower of the famous English designer William Morris and sharer of Morris's concern "that the greater part of the people have no share of art," and disturbed, too, by the death of handicraft, Dana had had the vision to foresee the alliance that would come decades later between the artist-designer and industry. Twenty years later, and well into the twentieth century, Elbert Hubbard and his Roycrofters would be cutting type, printing and illuminating books by hand, binding them in floppy leather; and over the country his followers would be burning designs with hot implements in wood and, through a score of such activities, trying in vain to keep handicraft alive. Dana had accepted facts even before they had finally become facts.

Dana had a clear idea of the museum as an educative force. Within the limits of the resources available, he made the Newark Museum such a force. His sense of history included history in the making. He had every right to point, as he fearlessly pointed, to the "idle folly" of the rich Metropolitan Museum, "that they decline to buy, but what is far more reprehensible, even to display, the work of contemporary artists."

Holger Cahill, who worked with Dana during somewhat later years, truly says that he "guided American museums toward greater service to the community." And in those days they sorely needed guidance. Dana pioneered many things in America: visual aids in art education (first in Denver, later in Newark: thousands of cards of art and design sent to the schools), circulating exhibitions, industrial art shows, contemporary architecture, and other things. But greatest of all was the almost incredible openmindedness that impelled him to show advanced art that he frankly neither liked nor understood: he simply refused to censor current history.

From 1909 to 1920, however, Dana and the Newark Museum stuck it out alone. No other American museum, large or small, would join his vanguard. Most of our museums actually were ill-suited physically and temperamentally for this new task. They were designed as repositories of the wealth of the past. You could take your time with the past and, on the whole, avoid costly mistakes. The past would wait for you to make up your mind. But not this fast, fast present. Science, indeed the whole world, was racing ahead. And with art, today's "ism" trod on the heels of yesterday's. You could not confine that sort of thing in a bank vault. What you needed was something more along the lines of a landing-field for new ideas. At least, that was one of the things that you needed.

In those years, the problems that beset the modern artist even in France were especially severe and complex in America. Possibly no museums, even ones devoted exclusively to modern art, could have solved them all. In retrospect, at the middle of our modern century, it is clear that none of them did. And there is little evidence that they even sensed some of the graver problems.

Pioneer Alfred Stieglitz, who passed up the chance to put on the big curtain-raiser, did see the dual role of the champion of modern art in this country, which, put in its simplest form, has always been that of getting the American modernist accepted along with modern art. This has not been so simple as it sounds, for a dozen reasons, all familiar: the never dying allure of the imported, the snobbery of the culture-climber, the perpetual distrust of our own artistic abilities which contrasts so strongly with our abiding faith in our mechanical and material abilities—and on down the list.

The modern-art problem in this country, then, was a double problem and a difficult one, but there is no reason to believe it could not have been solved. On the whole, we concentrated on half of the problem, choosing to propagandize the international art that came from France, in the belief—if we thought about it at all—that the American artist would benefit, too.

A modern museum, and then another, came on the scene. They stubbornly and gallantly waged the fight for public acceptance of modern art. And won it, in the main, for Paris, which did not even have a public museum for modern art until many years after ours had been established. It was our collectors, too, who, more than any others, raised and raised again the prices on the Picassos, the Matisses, the Braques, and the rest.

There have been some long, hard years for some remarkably fine American artists. A real Dark Age. It is only today, forty-three years after the Armory Show, which so brilliantly introduced the New Vision and was so hopefully dedicated "To the American Artists of the Future," that the last of the darkness is beginning to lift.

Société Anonyme's International Exhibition at the Brooklyn Museum, November 19, 1926, to January 1, 1927. Seen through Marcel Duchamp's "Large Glass" are two Mondrians and a Léger. The "Large Glass" was broken right after this exhibition.

...ge Heard Hamilton, ...Katherine S. Dreier, ...d Marcel Duchamp, New Haven, 1945.

Midi, by Stuart Davis. Oil, 28" x 36".
Collection: Wadsworth Athenaeum, Hartford, Connecticut.

*Stuart Davis signing 8' x 35' mural for Drake University,
Des Moines, Iowa, 1955.*

7. *Dada and Despair*

By 1920, despite the giant shove of the Armory Show and the nudges of the Forum and the Independent exhibitions, native modernism was dying out. This period, from about 1910 to about 1925, has been called "the first wave of abstract art in America," [1] as indeed it was. Some critics have concluded, as one of them puts it, that our modern pioneers of modern art had only a "superficial understanding, no matter how enthusiastic, . . . [of the] abstract art in Paris," and that therefore, "as soon as the surprise faded most of them abandoned it." [2] The early work of these pioneers stands as the most effective of all rebuttals of such an opinion, which shows little general understanding of that period in American art history.

Neglected by dealers, ignored by museums, passed over by collectors, unknown by the public, ridiculed and pressured by more conventional, more successful, fellow painters, the advanced artists in America lived in a cold and hostile climate. Even worse, they lived apart even from one another. Here the easy café life of Paris—the stimulating argument, the fruitful discussion—seemingly could not exist. Our sidewalks are reserved for walking. And let artists, ragged-poor anyway, try sitting overtime at a table with a waiter waving the check and newer comers staring holes in their backs! Not "surprise" fades in such a climate—bit by bit will fades, and enthusiasm, and vision.

So, by the early 1920's, the brightest of our native talents were in a near-fatal position. Max Weber and Alfred Maurer

---

[1] Andrew Carnduff Ritchie: *Abstract Painting and Sculpture in America* (New York, 1951). Published in connection with the exhibition of the same name at the Museum of Modern Art.

[2] Thomas B. Hess: *Abstract Painting, Background and American phase* (New York, 1951).

were in virtual destitution, unable to raise steerage funds to return to Paris, dependent upon crumbs for support. Maurer could not even borrow the little money needed to bring over all the brilliant work he had left in Paris in his studio: it eventually disappeared, and the few surviving pictures were picked up years later in secondhand stores in France. Weber painted on paper and cardboard, and no one bought his pictures, anyway. When he could not buy paint, he drew with charcoal and crayon and fought on.

Maurer, who had won a fifteen-hundred-dollar Carnegie prize in 1901 for conventional painting and had then deserted it all to follow the new star, was even more sorely hit than Weber. The onetime wit and dandy of Montmartre became a tortured and obsessed man, a sunken-eyed scarecrow driven by a demon. In his last decade Alfred Maurer alternated between fits of madness and lucid periods when he painted pictures that are strangely haunting. Some are cubist still-lifes, architectural and yet transparent, as if materialized by a spiritualist medium. In others he seemed to return to his earlier portraits, but his hand could no longer paint, as it once had painted, like Whistler's. Staring-eyed heads fill the canvas, side by side like a movie film run amok. In 1931 he hanged himself. This was the man who, like Max Weber, had had full fellowship with the young revolutionaries in Paris, had rubbed elbows with Matisse, Picasso, and Braque.

As for Weber today, whatever late plaudits and fame have come and may come to him, they will all be, in one sense, too little and too late. They will never quite fill the empty years, the years when in final despair he gave up the most advanced phases of his work. The strong but more figurative work that followed represents the investment of a large part of Weber's maturity. It is no more than natural that in public statements he is moved to defend it as a step of progress over his cubist period. But when he shows a visitor around his house, Max Weber returns to his cubist pictures again and again. His volubility ceases, he gazes at them, into them, affectionately and yet almost as if they had been painted by someone else in another time.

It is true that in Paris immediately after World War I there was a temporary return on the part of many to highly representational painting, best exemplified by Picasso's Classic Period figure paintings. Cubism and abstraction appeared to have run their courses. Actually, they had paused, as one might say, to get their bearings again, to try to recapture the spirit of what Chirico called "the subtle and fertile pre-war years." In America there was not a pause but a cessation as, one by one, most of our early modernists gave up the unequal struggle.

There was Stanton Macdonald-Wright, who with Morgan Russell founded in 1912 the style known as synchromism. It is treated today as little more than a historical oddity, but it was the only independent modern art movement launched by Americans in the pre-war years, and it compelled enough interest and respect to be given three separate exhibitions in 1913, only one year after its launching. These were at Munich; in Paris, at Bernheim-Jeune; and in New York, at the Carroll Gallery. Earlier the same year, synchromist canvases had been shown at the Salon des Indépendants as well as at the Armory Show. Developing out of cubism into explorations of pure color, synchromism and Robert Delaunay's orphism were parallel movements. Synchromism, in particular, using high-pitched hues, exploited the advancing and receding qualities, respectively, of warm and cool colors to fill with abstract, prismatic movement the shallow space that the cubists had discovered. On the basis of comparative accomplishment, synchromism deserves the same respect as orphism, interest in which has recently awakened.

Synchromism flourished until 1916, at which time Macdonald-Wright returned to America. Russell remained in Paris through two world wars, not to return until thirty years later. With its two leaders separated, the movement died. Russell, returning to representational painting in the general pause or lull that followed the Armistice in Paris, never found his way back to abstract work.

Back in America the other half of the creative partnership, Macdonald-Wright, saw synchromism briefly glorified in 1916 at the Forum Exhibition, but then began to run into the same difficulties that all the modernists were facing at home. By 1920 he had given up abstract work, and then for years he veered uncertainly like a migratory bird lost from the flock. Synchromism, it seemed, had had its brief day and would remain a direction never to be fully explored. As late as 1944 Macdonald-Wright could state: "Synchromism was the first movement to adumbrate the use of formal color in abstract design. My aims were to compose in depth by means of the natural three-dimensional extensions of the chromatic gamut." And could add with unfathomable regret: "I still feel that a related color design is the characteristic expression of our age." [3]

It now appears, however, that the last chapter on Stanton

[3] Quoted by Sidney Janis in *Abstract and Surrealist Art in America* (New York, 1944).

Macdonald-Wright and synchromism may yet have to be written. In 1956, at a one-man show at the Los Angeles County Museum, Wright is suddenly found to have re-embraced his own synchromism. At the age of sixty-six he exposes a group of forceful canvases that are simultaneously youthful and mature, full of what Jules Langsner, writing in *Art News*, calls "lyrical freshness and vitality."

In the long years after 1916 Macdonald-Wright seems to have wandered far, not only on the earth but in the uncharted space of metaphysics—finding himself at last in Zen Buddhism. From such extremes as administering the WPA Art Project in his region to the mastering of the Chinese and Japanese languages and from ten years of professorship in Oriental art at the University of California at Los Angeles to lectures in Japan about modern art, he searched for the lost thing.

At last, as Langsner writes, "on his return from Japan in 1953 . . . Wright experienced an astonishing metamorphosis." Perhaps there is something to be said for—rather than against—escapism. Or, at least, for the circuitous route. Fleeing America, Macdonald-Wright found America and himself as well. There is no mapping of private roads—the enigmatic wanderings that bring men home again at last.

But it is a long way and a lonely way and possible only for some. The 1920's in America were a dreadful time when the American artists back from Paris were slapped in the face by arrogant disbelief, when even faith like stone was eaten away, grain by grain, by the muddy, stale water of the mundane. It was the Main Street of Sinclair Lewis for a while. And then America, slowly awakening to modern art, saw Paris instead of international art, and our internationalists were passed by simply because, like prophets, they had come home.

It was all too easy, simply and literally, to starve. By the mid-1920's, sick of poverty, Joseph Stella, for example, went into decorative figure painting. His masterpiece, the *Brooklyn Bridge* of 1917–18, was done in paint, eked out by cheap crayon, on a bed sheet! And yet Stella, alone and in America, had continued futurism for years after the war in Europe had destroyed its international leader, Umberto Boccioni, and brought the movement substantially to an end. Among all the achievements of futurism, Stella's view of the futurists' elected material—force, movement, light, and sound in the twentieth-century world—was the most natural, the least affected. Whereas the futurists in Milan were celebrating the industrialization just then beginning to transform the Renaissance cities of Italy, Stella was brought up in an America already heavily industrialized. Even before 1909 he was executing drawings of factories. His point of view was contemporary and not, like that of the Italian futurists, essentially romantic.

The early modern work of men like Weber, Maurer, Macdonald-Wright, and Stella greatly needs to be set into the proper perspective in an international sense. This will require a complete re-evaluation, impartial and neither pro-American nor pro-European. In the process some names unknown today are likely to emerge. One of these might well be that of John Covert, born in 1882 in Pittsburgh, who was an organizer of the Independent Show of 1917. He exhibited then and at several successive shows. Then he and his work disappeared. Marcel Duchamp, years later, would write of him in terms he would not use lightly: "Among the young American painters who, in 1915, joined forces with the pioneers of the new art movements, John Covert was an outstanding figure from the beginning. Instead of following and adopting one of the new expressions, he found his personal form in a combination of painting and sculptured reliefs made of superimposed planes. If this technique, as such, showed Covert's imagination, far more important was the direction given to the material by his idea: the unrolling of interwoven surfaces. The same process was used later in several institutes of mathematics to illustrate the non-Euclidean geometries." Duchamp classified Covert's work as "an American interpretation of . . . new esthetic needs." [4]

Covert used plywood, stretched string, thumbtacks, and other materials not usually associated with painting. His first relief constructions coincide in point of time with the first works of the Russian constructivists Gabo and Pevsner, done in Oslo, Norway; but this simultaneity is the only discernible connection. It is true that Tatlin, the founder of constructivism, had made relief constructions in Moscow as early as 1913–14, but Covert had no knowledge of these.

After six years at the Pittsburgh School of Design, Covert went in 1908 to Munich, where for four years he continued his academic studies on German government scholarships. Gabo was in Munich, too, as a student in another institution for a part of that time. Covert, however, says that he did not meet him—more, he met no modernists, had not the slightest interest in modernism. Going to Paris in 1912, Covert continued to paint his academic, realistic nudes and portraits,

[4] Marcel Duchamp in catalogue of the Société Anonyme Collection at Yale University, New Haven, 1941.

one of which was shown at the official *salon*, a tribute to his craftsmanship.

"I stayed," Covert says, "long after Big Bertha began plunking shells down on Paris—didn't leave until 1915. I didn't get to know a modern artist, or see a modern show, or even meet the Steins. It's incredible. I must have lived in armor."

Back in New York, Covert met Stieglitz, Duchamp, Picabia, and their group through his cousin Walter Arensberg. Arensberg was ashamed of him: he went right on with the academic work he had pursued for nearly twenty years. Covert was not a man to be hurried.

Then he went for the summer to Pomfret, Connecticut, with the Arensbergs. One morning, as usual, he went out to paint. "Suddenly," he recalls, "with the same trees and hills all around I couldn't find a subject. I tramped until noon, getting hotter and more disgusted by the minute, finally plopped down in the grass. The sun was blazing down from straight overhead so that each tree floated in its own shadow. Everything was trembling; it was like looking through molten glass; I was trembling, too. I was painting without knowing it: the trees were like gallows and the shadows, the hills, were triangles. I was sopping wet with perspiration when I carted it home. Tried to hide it—God knows I didn't know what I had. But nosey Walter saw it.

" 'Well,' Walter said, 'now we have a modern artist!' "

Covert immediately began making his extraordinary constructions. "I was on my feet eighteen hours a day," he says. "I was carpenter, upholsterer, painter—what have you. The stuff piled up in my studio but I never got tired. How can I explain it? It was play. It was work. It was happiness."

But it was happiness with a time limit on it. The years went by: one, then two, then five, then eight. The constructions piled higher and higher; no one bought them; even Stieglitz would not show them. The man who could not be hurried made up his mind again.

"In 1923," he says, "I woke up. There was nothing in the studio to eat and no money in my pocket. I reflected about the unquestionable fact that I hadn't been eating very regularly."

So the man who in one stroke had become an abstract artist now became no artist at all. He gave away a few pictures to the few who wanted them. Katherine Dreier bought one, and he gave her several more. Then he broke up all the rest—"the pile was halfway to the ceiling"—and went back to Pittsburgh. There he got employment with the Vesuvius Crucible Company, makers of steel-pouring equipment. John Covert could do well in any field. Soon a chauffeur was driving him from mill to mill to inspect the Vesuvius installations. "I was an open-hearth trouble-shooter," he says.

Now, in 1956, he lives alone, a wrinkled Billikin of a man three quarters of a century old, in a hotel just off Times Square in New York. He talks about steel readily enough, but it is hard to get him talking about art, that earlier thing. "They were happy days," he will finally say. "Too happy, I guess, to last."

And there was Gerald Murphy to expose the other side of the dilemma of the artist tied to the American situation. Poverty did not defeat him, but wealth did. Boston-bred Harvard graduate Gerald Murphy and his wife, Sara, were brilliant figures in the expatriate society of the 1920's, with their villa at Antibes on the Côte d'Azur and their yacht at St.-Tropez. Modernism involved everyone of intelligence; the Murphys were irresistibly drawn to the great figures of art and music, as well as literature; Picasso lived with them for a time; they were intimate with Erik Satie and with Milhaud and the others of *les six;* they entertained the whole modern coterie and the Americans, too—John Dos Passos, Archibald MacLeish, young Ernest Hemingway (as yet unpublished), and F. Scott Fitzgerald and Zelda.

Fitzgerald, who saw wealth as conferring on its possessors a kind of nobility without responsibility ("The snow wasn't real snow. If you didn't want it to be snow, you paid some money"), put the Gerald Murphy he knew, the poised, gay host, the rich playboy, into the character of Dick Diver in his novel *Tender Is the Night.*

Fitzgerald apparently did not know what only Murphy's closest friends knew: that he maintained studios, one in Paris and one on his Cap d'Antibes estate. Within these studios he led a different life. During the ten years from 1925 on, Murphy completed a series of semi-abstract canvases so complex in design, so meticulous in craft, and (some of them) so heroic in size (one is ten feet wide and over seventeen feet high) that their production could not have been without protracted and concentrated labor. The canvases, somewhat in the vein of the French purists Ozenfant and Jeanneret (the architect Le Corbusier) and the American immaculatists Demuth and Sheeler, strike an original note of their own, particularly in their complex design and in their wit.

Gerald Murphy showed his paintings in the Salon des Indépendants from 1926 to 1928. They were fine canvases. Artists noticed them. The less prominent ones who did not know him discussed the matter. "Who is this Murphy?" one would ask and be told: "Oh, a rich American who paints for fun." Then all would shrug their shoulders and turn away. Stronger even than in medicine is the cult of professionalism in painting. The "Sunday painter"—the humble postman, grocer, customs official—sometimes can be accepted as an artist. But you cannot patronize the rich man; the myth is too strong: he cannot be serious. Marcel Duchamp tells how the gifted Picabia was plagued in every café by the mocking salute "Hello, landlord!"

In 1935, nevertheless, more substantial recognition came to Gerald Murphy. The gallery of Bernheim-Jeune showed his work; Léger and Picasso wrote of it in praise. But the one exhibit was both *première* and retrospective. Murphy's career was over. He was forced to return to America at his father's death and assume the management of a large commercial concern. Burdened by onerous duties in the atmosphere at home, he never got started painting again.

So the work of Gerald Murphy remains unknown. Nevertheless, the paintings exist. And a painting is autobiography. As Abraham Walkowitz once observed in general, "A painting is your conscience hanging on the wall."

Murphy himself once summed it up in a letter:

> There is nothing to add except that I was never happy
> until I started painting, and I have never been thoroughly
> so since I was obliged to give it up. I wonder how many
> aspiring American artists have been claimed by the harm-
> ful belief that if a business is your "inheritance" that it
> is heresy not to give up all in favor of it? I hope not too
> many. We need real American artists. There *is* something
> to be painted by us that only we should do. And yet if

one *is* to be a painter of note nothing really prevents it, I guess. I cannot forget that Uccello suddenly gave up painting in favor of mathematics—but returned to painting after a long lapse.

Throughout nearly the whole decade of the 1920's, the abstract artist in America was a man almost without hope. He could not sell a painting; he could not even live by teaching. Throughout the land, scarcely one college or art school taught abstract art. There was no longer either honor or utility in starving in a garret; we ran on the success standard and measured success in terms of money. Thus, by a corrosion in the air, the confidence of our most advanced artists was slowly eaten away.

Besides Stieglitz there was only Gertrude Vanderbilt Whitney. Mrs. Whitney befriended artists out of a feeling of fellowship, without, in the last analysis, discriminating between the sheer, widespread need of help and those special talents which particularly needed to be saved. The millionaire collectors went on buying art from Paris as they do today, it being so much easier to spot greatness across an ocean.

As one talks with these pioneer moderns today—those who are still alive—one gets the overwhelming impression of bereavement and rejection. Theirs is sorrow, not bitterness. They had hoped for better from their country.

Yet such was the irresistible surge of the modern idea and its attractiveness to the more adventurous among the younger artists that the gaps in the ranks began almost immediately to be filled. Stuart Davis took up abstraction in 1921; one by one, others joined him: Arthur B. Carles, Jan Matulka, John Graham, Vaclav Vytlacil, Arshile Gorky. Unwittingly, struggling unnoticed and all but alone through a hard decade, these six performed the greatest of services as they kept abstraction alive and slowly and stubbornly gave it a more native cast. A new generation of Americans, then just beginning to enter the art schools, would build from it, creating a completely new modern style that would focus world attention on America. At last we would learn how to make friends and influence people.

But that was all in the future. Meanwhile, a completely new revolution had swept the world of art. The earlier revolution, which had begun in 1904, had successfully tried and convicted traditional art. This newer one sought to try man and all his works. It was a complex of the disillusion that came midway through a world war and a new and dual skepticism ushered in by physical science and the new psychology. Newton's old solid world was no more; matter was an illusion of the senses; without knowing it, we were on our way to the atom. Freud, examining that other eternal, comforting solid called Reason, had come upon Unreason, the nether world of the unconscious mind. Without knowing it, we were on our way to the psychoanalyst's couch.

The new revolution began in 1915 in New York and at about the same time in Zurich. One year later at Zurich it got its name. One of the new rebels, thumbing through a French dictionary, hit upon the name for hobbyhorse: *dada*. Dada spread like a mordant chemical, crystallizing into an act of reckless, gay, and bitter revulsion all the desperate questions of an intellectual generation. It immediately attracted artists, writers, poets, and philosophers. Dada centers sprang up. By 1919 there were Dada groups in New York, Zurich, and Paris and, with civil war already raging in

Germany, in Cologne, Berlin, and Hannover. Everywhere it found its natural leaders: in New York, Duchamp and Picabia, arch-priests already ordained by several prior years of iconoclastic activity, joined by the American Man Ray; in Zurich, Richard Huelsenbeck, Hugo Ball, Tristan Tzara, Hans Arp; in Cologne, Max Ernst, J. T. Baargeld, and Arp; in Paris, Tzara, André Breton, Louis Aragon, and Paul Éluard; in Hannover, Kurt Schwitters; and in Berlin, Huelsenbeck, George Grosz, Raoul Haussmann, and John Heartfield.

Even the ebullient futurists had not been so noisy; the Dadaists issued insulting manifestoes, staged demonstrations, disrupted public meetings and affairs, slaughtered "good taste" with vulgarity. They were violent, witty, and destructive. With it all, they made more than a little sense: it was an open question whether they or the times were out of step. The Dadaists needed no press agents; every eye was on them, and just by watching them, the whole world let off a little steam. Heaven knows, Dada was more destructive by far than cubism had been, but it unleashed far less acrimony. The world, while vastly amused, was also implicated, though not really understanding the matter.

For Dada, the Great Practical Joke, is actually a most complex thing. Some first-rate minds and talents were involved in it. Dada extended through many levels, from the custard pie in respectability's face to a cosmic questioning like that of the great clowns concealing anguish behind the laughing or cynical mask.

What the world saw in Dada was the mustache that Duchamp painted on a postcard of the *Mona Lisa*, or five people dressed in stovepipes performing a dance; what the world heard was a scandalous sonata played on typewriters and pot-covers, or three poets on a platform "seriously" declaiming simultaneously their several original poems. Poems like that by Tristan Tzara, which repeated the word "roar" one hundred and forty-seven times, then added the last line: "who still considers himself very charming," and Hugo Ball's "sound poem:"

> gadji beri bimba
> glandridi lauli lonni cadori
> gadjama bim beri glassala
> glandridi glassala tuffm i zimbrabim
> blassa galassasa tuffm i zimbrabim. . . .

The poetic literature of Dada surely culminated in Kurt Schwitters's majestic ode. Schwitters recited the letter W once only, and then barked like a dog.

There was the Dada "lecture" in 1917 at the first show of the American Independents—a gala evening audience of intellectuals and socialites and, staggering drunkenly to the stage, Arthur Cravan, a nephew of Oscar Wilde, a professed amateur burglar and even more amateur pugilist, whom Jack Johnson had once knocked out in a phony bout. Leaning over the table, Cravan began simultaneously to undress and to shout obscenities at the audience. He had not got far when the police seized him from behind and dragged him away while the meeting broke up in horrified indignation. Walter Arensberg went Cravan's bail. Society was badly put off, its leaders, Picabia's wife Gabrielle recalls, having been expressly invited for an initiation into the mysteries of modern art.

It was, however, a completely Dada gesture. Niceties had no part in the ruthless Dada program. " 'What a wonderful lecture,' said Marcel Duchamp, beaming, when we all met that evening at the home of Arensberg." [5]

Dada used the shock treatment in its public relations. To get at the core of serious ideas in Dada, it is more revealing to study the Paris work of Duchamp and Picabia beginning about 1911. In those years the two friends were facing in advance some of the fundamental problems that since have beset our industrialized age. They lived, Gabrielle Picabia has since written, in a "climate of invention, which has never since been retrieved," playing "games of exploration in an inaccessible dimension," the dimension actually being the future. [6]

Duchamp and Picabia, with a sort of clairvoyance, saw the machine clothed in its real meanings, animated with a non-human life, moving in ways that might as easily destroy as aid man. *Daughter Born without a Mother*, Picabia called one of his machinery paintings of this period—a newcomer, that is to say, issued from the mind of man without wife or midwife. The paintings of Duchamp, like those of Picabia, and even more meaningfully, became those of machinery— "strange personages of iron and steel," Gabrielle calls them. *The Bride* of 1912 is not a woman at all, even in outward appearance, but a machine built for voluptuous enjoyment and for a terrible, metallic insemination. She predicts the machine state of machine men, the strength of steel through the joy of steel.

Here are grim personages for a grim drama, no longer merely the war of men against men, but Frankenstein monsters against us all. These iron aliens burlesque human society in a satire as bitter as that of Jonathan Swift, but are deadlier

[5] Gabrielle Buffet-Picabia: "Some Memories of Pre-Dada: Picabia and Duchamp," *Transition*, April–May 1938.

[6] Ibid.

by far than his horse-people, the Houyhnhnms. Then, by 1913, we come to Duchamp's pencil drawing *Cimetière de uniformes et livrées* (*Cemetery of Uniforms and Liveries*). Duchamp was already thinking of "The Large Glass," which he would commence in America two years later. He was through with painting after what André Breton called a "meteoric flight," [7] and was the greatest Dadaist of them all even before the name was discovered and the movement begun. What could the success of his *Nude Descending a Staircase* and its scandalizing of a nation at the Armory Show have meant to such a man?

It is with the Goya of the *Disparates* and *The Disasters of War* that Marcel Duchamp really belongs. The pigeonhole of cubism is not for him, and he transcended Dada even while he foretold it. In the *Cimetière* he takes clothes—uniforms of service and liveries of servitude—as symbols of empty man and then depicts them, hard, sheathlike, and metallic, not even as machines but as machine-made gravestones for the machine-dug graves of the race. Goya himself was never more brutal or straight-seeing.

Marcel Duchamp's modestly pleasant and offhand social manner is deceiving. His real communication has always been through his pictures. It was there to be read all the time. All the strange things, all the grim things that he foretold have really come to pass in this cybernetic world in which thinking machines have "nervous breakdowns," in which people verge on becoming machines and machines on becoming people. Machines make machines; the human laborer begins to drop out. Now we can even dream of an "infallible" computing-machine to solve for us the final problems that we have posed.

Duchamp went through all this a long time ago to arrive

[7] André Breton: *Anthologie de l'humour noir* (Paris, 1940).

at an inevitable negativism before the existentialists were born. He made something positive of it in a very personal way; he arrived at complete detachment; he could participate in life without self-involvement.

Dada ended about 1922, having run its short, destructive course. Like the serpent-universe with its tail in its mouth, it swallowed itself. In the midst of its last orgy Duchamp had done a contradictory thing. He once remarked, in fact: "I have forced myself to contradict myself in order to avoid conforming to my own taste." [8] Duchamp's contradiction in this instance consisted of a highly constructive act: the great renouncer helped to found a museum.

In 1920, at Duchamp's urging, a new figure—painter and patron in one—entered the scene. This was Miss Katherine Dreier, who, in that year, incorporated in New York the Société Anonyme, subtitled *A Museum of Modern Art*. It was the first museum exclusively for modern art in America. It was, indeed, the first museum exclusively for modern art in the world.

[8] Quoted in Alfred H. Barr, Jr.: *Masters of Modern Art* (New York, 1954).

8. *Modern Art's First Museum*

Twenty years after the event, Katherine Dreier wrote
that her museum was founded with gaiety.[1] And yet with more
than gaiety, for she had recorded earlier that "the serious
works of serious men were shown and studied, and left to act
as the desired leaven in the art world of the community." [2]
Miss Dreier has left small doubt that Marcel Duchamp was
the central force. "Funds were only sufficient," she wrote, "to
make a demonstration, [yet] Marcel Duchamp, with the help
of Katherine S. Dreier, Andrew McLaren, Man Ray, and
Henry Hudson, had the courage to incorporate this Museum
of Modern Art as the Société Anonyme." [3] It is said, in fact,
that $6,000 comprised the total "funds" with which this
historic project was launched.

This modest amount even then might have bought only
one important modern picture by one of the recognized
contemporary masters. But, whatever her announced plans of
expansion and magnitude of operation, Miss Dreier actually
operated, not in terms of huge collections and important
buildings, but in terms of a continuing review of new developments. She was trying to provide the landing-field for new
ideas which modern art, as a living thing, so urgently required.

The Société Anonyme opened on April 30, 1920, at 19
East 47th Street, in quarters so small that the first show was
limited to sixteen paintings. It was almost like 291, which had
been closed for three years, come to life again. That there was
more than this one resemblance between the Dreier and the
Stieglitz ventures, time would show.

[1] Katherine Dreier in catalogue of the Société Anonyme Collection at
Yale University (New Haven, 1941).

[2] First Annual Report of the Société Anonyme, Inc. (New York, 1921).

[3] Katherine Dreier: *Société Anonyme . . . Its Why and Wherefore* (New
York, 1920).

Both of them, at least—Stieglitz's in 1907 and Dreier's in 1920—were ideas timely to the essence. The spawning development of modern art had made a permanent museum a crying need. Already in sixteen years it had explored more new directions, established more new schools than the entire preceding century. The work—from the conservationist's point of view—was piling up at an alarming rate and, paradoxically, becoming more expensive every day. Wealthy collectors were bidding in an international market, with dealers fully exploiting the situation. German industrialists, French capitalists, wealthy Czechoslovakians, American millionaires —even a fabulously rich Japanese baron—were grasping for the prizes. And there were the peaceful Swiss, who always have money.

In five years a new movement would already be historic, and its monuments would be disappearing from view into many a private mansion. How to preserve for the public the newly old and at the same time to collect the newly new while it was still underpriced had become a towering problem. One or two of our long-established museums were trying, finally, to get into the swim, but, already loaded down, they found the swimming difficult. The Brooklyn Museum had already become the first to show a French retrospective from Courbet and Manet through Cézanne, Van Gogh, and Gauguin to Picasso and Matisse. A commendable thing, but only a lone straw in a high wind.

Then, in 1921, the Metropolitan made a quick, exorcising pass at the situation. Plenty of people had been prodding the Old Lady of Fifth Avenue. Finally a committee that included Miss Lillie P. Bliss went to work, and the Met agreed— having no modern pictures of its own—to display pictures from important private collections. Walter Pach describes how Bryson Burroughs went to John Quinn's apartment on Central Park West to choose paintings and later "told with a gasp how, for several hours, workmen kept bringing in and removing paintings . . . passed in review for his choice." [4]

"Get thee behind me, Satan," said the Met, once the show was over, and for more years than one cares to count, never looked around again.

Already the big collections were starting to come onto the market to be broken up and dispersed. The custom of leaving these legacies to the public through its institutions was not yet general. The first big sale came when the collection of Oriental art dealer Dikran Kelekian was publicly sold in 1922. American collectors got some of the items, like the large Picasso *Green Still Life*, which Miss Bliss bought; but Paris dealers then began the practice of coming over to bid in many of the most important works to cart back to France. This same year the bulk of the important Jerome Eddy collection went on posthumous exhibit at the Art Institute of Chicago, an important exception to the rule of the time.

Chicago, it should be noted, was, to a degree, looking up. The socially prominent Arts Club of that city, incorporated in 1916, had entered the fray, and by 1921 had a room in the Art Institute. Here, as well as in its own quarters, it began showing advanced art from Europe: in 1923 Picasso, then Soutine, Toulouse-Lautrec, and others. Under the leadership of Mrs. John Alden Carpenter, the Arts Club put strong but discreet pressure on the Art Institute to liberalize its policy. To the remarkable Mrs. Carpenter's influence on her vastly wealthy uncle Joseph Winterbotham, the Institute owes his fund,

[4] Walter Pach: *Queer Thing, Painting* (New York, 1938).

which started their purchase of important modern painting from Paris. It certainly was none of the doing of the Institute itself, which in those days—long before the coming of Daniel Catton Rich as Director—quite evidently aspired to become the Metropolitan Museum of Michigan Boulevard, one of those anomalies which make the "wild" west not so wild, after all.

Even as late as 1926, when the Birch-Bartlett collection was bequeathed to the Institute, its trustees were divided about accepting it. The bequest included works of prime importance by Cézanne, Van Gogh, Gauguin, Rousseau, Picasso, Matisse, and Modigliani, and was crowned by the colossal Georges Seurat masterpiece, *Sunday on the Grande Jatte.* This high point of *pointillisme* and curtain-raiser for the discovery of abstract form had been bought originally for the collection for a reputed $45,000. Although the trustees knew this, they were not impressed, thinking no doubt that, as the old saying has it, a fool and his money are soon parted. They quite openly called certain Cézannes and Matisses—even the eye-filling Seurat—"obnoxious." The rumors of dissension spread. Finally, about six years after the Institute's uneasy acceptance of the bequest, a syndicate was formed in France to buy the Seurat. The offer was a cool $450,000. The trustees decided not to sell.

But it was Paris, Paris, Paris, in the minds of the great collectors and the great museums. Was there something sanctifying about the air of Paris? Apparently so. In any event, Marcel Duchamp, a French expatriate more durable than even the Marquis de Lafayette, commented with acid sarcasm on the belief. On a brief trip to Paris he had a pharmacist seal up fifty cubic centimeters of the atmosphere in a glass ampoule, which he brought back and solemnly handed to Walter

Arensberg. Arensberg as solemnly took it and added to his Duchamp collection.

All through that decade of polemics, individuals and organizations propagandized, argued, and persuaded in the cause of modern art—and through it all generally forgot to include the American modernist. One would have thought that he had resigned from the movement by coming home. And yet, perhaps, as native friend and advocate, he might have won the case himself and with greater benefit to all concerned.

Our contingent was fighting alone, like a detachment cut off from communications. Here we had our advanced abstractionists: Stuart Davis, Carles, Graham, and the others. And here, too, had sprung up independently the new movement called immaculatism or, less frequently, precisionism. Its beginnings had come as early as 1916, with the forthright machine pictures of Schamberg, an artist strongly influenced by Duchamp and Picabia. Then, about 1920–1, came Charles Demuth and his weaving of delicately precise machine forms into an over-all abstract design. Immaculatism soon included Preston Dickenson, Georgia O'Keeffe, and Charles Sheeler. With these varied artists, precisionism could include the extremes from O'Keeffe's female symbology to Sheeler's photography-like abstractions of factories and barns. The movement had its special local cult and no more; it was never given the opportunity of the comparison, which might have been more than favorable, with purism, the parallel French movement. Stuart Davis had to take his paintings with him to Paris in 1928 "to see how they stacked up over there."

On the whole, Katherine Dreier was not afflicted by this sort of shortsightedness. Herself an American artist, even though not one of profound accomplishment, and, too, under the liberal influence of Duchamp, she tried to give American art its part in the international picture. Her reach, however, exceeded her grasp. She thought in terms of accomplishment that she was not to attain, of a "chain of galleries" to "liberate the thoughts in the art world." [5] Nevertheless, she left a solid record of accomplishment as measured against her resources. In its first three years, the Société Anonyme originated nearly forty exhibitions, of which sixteen were in the Société gallery, others at various clubs and institutes in Greater New York, many still farther afield, on loan to Vassar, Smith College, the Arts Club of Chicago, and the museums at Worcester and Detroit. Miss Dreier actualized the idea of the traveling loan exhibition. In these shows, as listed in a Société report, thirteen countries (including the United States) were represented in the works of art, and fifty-seven artists, including all the great European names, as well as certain Americans: Marsden Hartley, Man Ray, Joseph Stella, and Abraham Walkowitz. And, of course, there was John Covert, though just a little late, for, as Katherine Dreier writes, "It was John Covert who started the collection of the Société Anonyme by giving six of his fine paintings to us when he entered the business world." [6]

The ice cap was slowly melting; the climate was changing. The rest of the country was beginning to call for a look at modern art as warm air spread out slowly but surely from the focal metropolitan centers. The art journals, so uniformly hostile at the Armory Show, had decided that the new art,

[5] Katherine Dreier: *Société Anonyme . . . Its Why and Wherefore*, op. cit.

[6] Katherine Dreier in reply to a letter from President Charles Seymour accepting the Société Anonyme Collection in behalf of Yale University, 1941. Marcel Duchamp tells that Miss Dreier bought one more Covert picture, thus accounting for the seven at present in the collection.

like the horseless carriage, had come to stay. Whether liking
and understanding it or not, they put up a good face, particularly as to whatever came from Paris. Of all the critics, only
the *Herald Tribune*'s Royal Cortissoz remained completely
intransigeant. Like the religious sects that from time to time
were mounting the rooftops, nightgown-clad, to hail the end
of the world, Cortissoz almost annually was oracularly an-
nouncing the end of modern art. It seems almost a pity that
such sublime faith—on the part of Cortissoz, that is—should
not have paid off.

Within six years the Société Anonyme had enough prestige and resources to assemble a large International Exhibition
for the Brooklyn Museum. It was on display from November
19, 1926, to January 1, 1927. Three weeks later the major part
moved to the Anderson Galleries in Manhattan, whence it
went on to the Albright Art Gallery in Buffalo. As a show of
current international developments, this exhibit, far out-
stripping the Metropolitan Museum exhibit of 1921, was the
most important public event of its kind since the Armory
Show. The paintings and sculpture were chosen by Marcel
Duchamp, who had the distinguished assistance of an international committee including Vassily Kandinsky, Piet Mondrian, Kurt Schwitters, and Fernand Léger.

Nearly fourteen years after the Armory Show, this new
International filled in an omission (futurism) that had kept the
earlier event short of being completely representative of the
scene in 1913, and added a résumé of the subsequent movements:

MONDRIAN and the Dutch *de Stijl* group;
PEVSNER, Gabo, and the Russian constructivists;

LÉGER and the *"extérieurs mécaniques"*;
CHIRICO and the *"intérieurs métaphysiques"*;
MALEVITCH and the Russian suprematists.

An admirable survey, but why was surrealism left out?
Duchamp, in a letter, explains. "In 1926," he writes, "although surrealism was in existence, it was not an established
movement because the self-called surrealists—Breton, Aragon,
etc.—had all been and were dadas fighting to separate themselves from the negative side of dada. There was still some
confusion."

Nonetheless, there had been a group surrealist show nine
months before the Brooklyn exhibit opened. It was at the
Galerie Pierre in Paris, and had even included Duchamp
under the Rrose Sélavy pseudonym. All of which, of course,
points up the extreme difficulty of staying *au courant* with such
a chameleon as modern art.

The International Exhibition was the high-water mark of
the Société Anonyme. It proved that the big shows could be
put on, but left unanswered the question of suitable quarters:
borrowing other people's museums for your exhibits was not a
good enough answer. It was too undependable, for one thing.
Not only was a large permanent gallery needed—it had been
needed for years. Already apparent was the paradox that has
haunted museums of modern art ever since: how to reconcile
this permanence, hallmark of the old-fogy museums, with the
brilliant, ceaseless transience of modern art?

But there was the need, the duty even, to preserve for
America the masterpieces that were already owned here but
were going on the auction block year by year. The fabulous
John Quinn collection had been broken up by public sale the

very year of the Société Anonyme's big International Exhibition. Establish the institution to welcome the bequests, and the bequests would come. Collectors did not relish the snubs of a Metropolitan.

As early as 1914, Arthur Jerome Eddy had discerned the responsibility of the large private collector. "I would like to own Raphaels and Titians," he had written, "and Rembrandts and Velasquezes. . . . I say I would like to *own* them; no, I would not, for . . . no man has the *right* to appropriate to himself the work of the great masters. Their paintings belong to the world and should be in public places for the enjoyment and instruction of *all*.

"It is the high privilege of the private buyer to buy the works of *new men*, and by encouraging them disclose a Rembrandt, a Hals, a Millet, a Corot, a Manet, but when the public begins to want the pictures the private buyer, instead of bidding against the public, should step to one side; his task is done, his opportunity has passed." [7]

A museum of modern art might have started out modestly enough in 1906 or 1910 and could have grown comfortably with modernism, buying examples of each new phase at moderate current prices. But by 1926 a lot of water had flowed under the bridge. Quantitatively and in price the task became more and more formidable—and more and more pressing— with each year that passed.

When John Quinn died in 1925, he left no provisions to bequeath any or all of his collection. Actually, an institution that could do justice to his fabulous assemblage of over two thousand works of art did not yet exist. It is a question, even, whether there was an institution that would have been willing

[7] Arthur Jerome Eddy: *Cubists and Post-Impressionism* (Chicago, 1914).

to accept them.[8] Promptly upon Quinn's death, Arthur B. Davies, an old man in whom the spark still burned, went to his friends Miss Lillie Bliss and Mrs. Cornelius J. Sullivan and talked to them earnestly about the immediate organization of a new museum to buy the best of the Quinn collection as its cornerstone. The ladies were not quite ready for such a venture, though Miss Bliss personally bought a number of the Quinn masterpieces. The great collection was dispersed; much of it went back to France.

Miss Dreier did not figure in Davies's plans. It had become evident that she would go so far, no further. People had been urging her for some time to expand her project by enlisting the help of some of the powerful friends of modern art in America, many of whom were her own friends, too. "Modern art," they were saying, "is too big for one person or even a small group. It has grown into a job for many." Still Miss Dreier held back. By 1928 she went so far as to start a building fund. But her heart did not seem in it. Soon the matter would be in other hands.

Like Stieglitz, although possibly not to the same extent, Katherine Dreier was a lone wolf. Unconsciously she had set her own limits at the very start when she had spoken of serving

[8] The Quinn collection included in part: examples of El Greco, Goya, Ingres, William Blake, Delacroix, Degas, Cézanne (the early *Portrait of Cézanne's Father*—1874, *Mme Cézanne*, *Mont-Victoire*, etc.), Gauguin (many, including a decorated ceiling from southern France), Van Gogh (*Self Portrait*, etc.), Toulouse-Lautrec, Seurat (very important group including *La Poudreuse* and *Cirque*—bequeathed to the Louvre), Rousseau (including the *Jungle, Sleeping Gypsy, Rousseau's Doctor*), Matisse (the monumental *Variation on a Still Life by de Heem*—Barr, p. 170 in color—*Bowl of Apples, Nude Reclining*), Picasso (earliest Paris period, Blue Period, cubist and analytical cubist, collage, neo-classic, etc.), Braque, Derain (a huge group), Duchamp (the early *Chess Players*, study for the *Nude Descending a Staircase, Peau Brune*), Duchamp-Villon (at least fourteen sculptures), Gris, Metzinger, Severini, Max Weber, Arthur B. Davies, and an important group of African Negro sculpture.

"the art world of the community." Why this acceptance of cultism? Why not the community? A museum is not a place for holding private picnics. At least, John Cotton Dana at the Newark Museum had not thought so. In his own modern imagery he had thought of the museums as "great engines for creating good individuals," and, as Holger Cahill wrote, "he realized too that the people as a whole are deeply involved in art whether they know it or not, through their daily activities as producers and consumers."

The same year that Katherine Dreier started her building fund, Arthur B. Davies died at the age of sixty-six. His death came as a deep shock to his old friend Miss Lillie Bliss. The old, patient, dynamic ally of modern art was gone. She was stirred into sudden action. Aroused at last to this matter of public concern, she moved with sureness and dispatch. In less than a year, mainly through the efforts of Lillie Bliss, modern art would find a worthy home in America.

The High Renaissance in Italy looms disproportionately large as the greatest age of art patronage. Such is the princely glitter, still, of the Medici. Then baronial wealth and churchly wealth vied—and often combined, in the single figures of the Medici Popes—in commissions for great artistic projects. It was much simpler then. There were no museums, no art dealers. If you had a lot of money and a strong taste for art, you went directly to the artist in his bottega and you bought it or ordered it. And then you had art's satisfactions, not the least of which, then as now, was prestige.

Actually, there has always been a lot of art patronage—a surprising amount, indeed, considering how little real general knowledge there has ever been as to what art is all about. There have been lulls when interest has turned to the past. There have been bad times when optical machines have been invented to do part of the artist's work: the camera for portraiture, the stereoscope for three-dimensional "scenery," the cinema to dramatize history. But the artist has always found something new, and probably better, to do; has found it, often, before the machine was even invented. Then there would be a new movement that would be ignored until it could be ignored no longer; taste would finally catch up and make amends. One of the great facts of art history is that the layman, proudly practical as he may be, is eternally fascinated by art and by the artist. This fascination runs deeper than a sideshow interest. A bearded lady and an eight-foot man are patent, even if engaging, facts, and are so looked at. But art is the kind of fact that language is, which is more than a mere collection of sounds: it challenges understanding.

It happens today that we have an art that, more than ever before, challenges understanding. We have, too, some pretty big and fancy art patronage. It is possible, even likely, that the two facts go together.

Modern art from Europe, as we have observed, attracted early and powerful support in America from the very moment that it first penetrated the walls of our isolation. Support for a new art comes usually from a certain chain of agencies. First comes the intellectual advance guard: artists, amateurs, critics, and laymen, a group seldom with much buying-power, but highly articulate. The advance guard argues, talks it up, and publishes little magazines—and it all adds up. Soon a brave dealer or two arises who on the one hand supports the new artist, often out of his own pocket, while on the other he waits as the market slowly grows. The dealer is the sub-patron. Next comes the private collector of means, who buys from the dealers. With him come the big private collections hung out of the general ken in mansions as they once were in castles. At last comes the general desire to see these pictures, these sculptures. Then we have the museum. It is all a little more complicated than it was in the days of the Medici, but ours is a more complicated age.

Here in America, however, the chain of agencies got jumbled about in order. We had the advance guard, all right, with whom Stieglitz must be grouped because, actually, he carried little weight as a dealer. Then, almost instantly, we had a huge public indoctrination through the Armory Show, and the great private collections were actually started before the dealers could enter the field. In fact, by March 15, 1913, as the Armory Show closed, America had had its first big look and was ready for a public museum of modern art, no matter how small. Had anyone realized it then, we would have today nearly every great masterpiece of modern art and most of the lesser ones—an accumulation of readily negotiable wealth which might easily reach ten figures of dollars (and that is a billion) in value. And it could have been bought in the early stages on a shoestring. For there was a time when the French openly laughed at the "rich American fools" who bought the work of Matisse and Picasso. For a long time, however, they have been coming here to buy it back, muttering about the coercive Yankee dollars that spirited such treasures from France.

Our patronage of modern art came first, mainly from the only aristocracy we recognize: the powerful *and* wealthy. In America that means wealth made at one time or another from trade or industry. Ours was the first great industrial aristocracy. In this light, the early acceptance by our industry of modern design principles—which came originally from the painters—is actually no more remarkable than our tycoons' buying of the art itself at that early day when cubism, like Henry Ford's Tin Lizzie, was a joke laughed at in the streets.

There was considerable talk here during the 1920's that modern art was being secretly subsidized by the French government, a gigantic fraud whose aim was to lure American dollars to war-torn and impoverished France. The rumor spread and took hold. "All that dough going for that stuff," the uninformed would say and then ask, "but does one cent come back to pay the war debts?" It was a neat theory without a shred of truth in it. The actual fact was that modern art was being subsidized in the main by American businessmen in their private capacity as collectors. The scions of a generation that had carted palaces over the sea and set them up here stone by stone were now buying the cubist "atrocities" at which

City Radiance, *1944, by Mark Tobey.*
Tempera, 18¾″ x 13½″.
Collection: the late Lyonel Feininger.

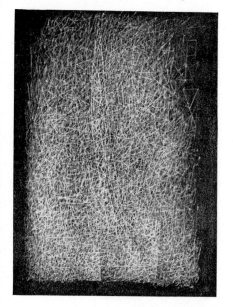

Umpferstedt I, *1914, by Lyonel Feininger.*
Oil on canvas, 51¼″ x 39½″.

Mark Tobey (left) and Lyonel Feininger, July 1955.
This is the last photograph of Feininger.

Standing Woman, *1930–3, by Gaston Lachaise. Bronze 8' high.*
Collection: The Museum of Modern Art.

their fathers had guffawed. One millionaire bid against another; the rivalry was intense, and from the early 1920's on, prices, obeying the ancient law of supply and demand, rose high, higher, and higher still. Modern art, far more than horse-racing, became the sport of kings. The kings made it so. Read a quick, partial roster of the names: Dr. Albert C. Barnes, Miss Lillie P. Bliss, Walter P. Chrysler, Jr., Stephen C. Clark, Chester Dale, Mrs. Simon Guggenheim, Solomon R. Guggenheim, Marie (Mrs. Averell) Harriman, Samuel A. Lewisohn, Samuel Marx, Duncan Phillips, Mrs. John D. Rockefeller, Jr., John D. Rockefeller III, Nelson Rockefeller, Cornelius J. Sullivan, Edward M. M. Warburg, Wright Ludington, Leigh Block, Ferdinand Howald, and John Hay Whitney.

In more recent years the big corporations themselves have become patrons and collectors. Among these, International Business Machines, Abbott Laboratories, Miller Lighting, and La Tausca Pearls have at various times formed large collections, while the Container Corporation of America utilizes the well-paid services of ranking artists to prepare its advertising formats. It is to be doubted that the French government under any circumstances could have done a comparable job.

Few stocks in the history of the Exchange over a comparable period can approach the phenomenal rise in value of the—shall we say?—gilt-edged modern painting. The advance in Van Goghs or Cézannes from the pittances paid for them sixty years ago—if one even sold—to the top amounts (around $125,000) that they command today is fairly well known. With Picasso, Matisse, and Braque, among others, we have seen similar advances in an even shorter period of time. But in order to illustrate that such appreciations in value (except in their rapidity) are not just part of a speculative present day, Arthur Jerome Eddy once recorded [1] all of the known fiscal history of a particular Rembrandt painting:

1734—sold in Antwerp (*after Rembrandt's death*)			$	109
1791—	"	" Paris		240
1814—	"	" London		525
1830—	"	" "		790
1831—	"	" "		792
1832—	"	" "		1,260
1841—	"	" Paris		1,576

and then we jump to:

1913—sold in Paris	220,000

It is all part of a pattern. Alfred Stieglitz, financially secure through his father's business efforts, made the first commercial modern art gallery in America, housing it as if by forethought in a commercial building. His 291 came about, as we have seen, largely through the urging of another financially secure American, Edward Steichen, who was able to commute at will between Paris and New York. Here the artists momentarily intruded, acting as their own advance guard of publicity by organizing the Armory Show. Immediately the financial hierarchy stepped in to establish the value of the new art in trade. After all of this, it should occasion no surprise that, two decades after 291 first opened, wealthy patrons would set up the present-day Museum of Modern Art in New York and, as if it were all in a script, house the new institution first of all on the twelfth floor of a Manhattan commercial skyscraper.

[1] Arthur Jerome Eddy: *Cubists and Post-Impressionism* (Chicago, 1914).

As we have seen, it was during the winter of 1928–9, closely following the death of Arthur B. Davies, that things began to happen. Touring Egypt, Lillie Bliss met Mrs. John D. Rockefeller, Jr. Miss Bliss was fired up. The Pyramids' "nineteen centuries" that had once "looked down upon" Napoleon, as he had said in Egypt, had grown to twenty centuries as the two women talked seriously about a museum for the newest art of the newest age.

The very next spring, 1929, back in New York, they began to form a committee on organization. The women involved were now three, Mrs. Cornelius J. Sullivan having joined them. Wanting a man to head the project, they invited A. Conger Goodyear to lunch on May 29.

The circumstances surrounding the invitation of Goodyear were rather extraordinary. Neither Miss Bliss, Mrs. Rockefeller, nor Mrs. Sullivan had ever met him, and Goodyear did not even know why he was being asked to lunch. He commented recently: "I found out later that a certain lady, a friend of mine, recommended me to Mrs. Rockefeller, I having fought, bled and died for old Albright." Goodyear had just been deposed as President of the Albright Art Gallery in Buffalo on the serious grounds of modernism.

Twenty years later, honorably resigning after continuous service as President of the Museum of Modern Art, Goodyear fell to reminiscing about that historic luncheon date. "Since as usual I had nothing to wear," he recalled, "I went out and bought a very dignified gray suit which my Buffalo friends thereafter always called the Rockefeller suit and appeared at 10 West 54th Street at the appointed time feeling rather like Aloysius in Wonderland."

At the luncheon table the ladies exploded their little

bombshell. Mrs. Rockefeller popped the question. Would Mr. Goodyear care to head a new museum for modern art? After due deliberation—one week—Mr. Goodyear said he would be pleased. He suggested additional committee members: Frank Crowninshield, Mrs. W. Murray Crane, Paul J. Sachs of the Harvard faculty. All were acceptable to the original three; all agreed to serve. Things thereupon began to move with astonishing rapidity.

Buffalo-born A. Conger Goodyear was a man of fifty-two in 1929, a seasoned art collector, a wealthy manufacturer, and a military man to boot—in fact, he was a general. He had gone to France in 1917 as captain in command of the 81st Field Artillery; by the 1918 Armistice he was a colonel; subsequently he became a major general in the New York National Guard.

In 1913 he had been an Albright director for two years. Then, like many another American, he was startled wide awake by the Armory Show. He was already a collector, too, but says now: "I don't think that I still own a single work of art bought before the Armory Show." His actual modern purchases began, not as has been often reported, at the Show, but in 1915, with some Matisse drawings from the Montross Gallery exhibition.

In his official capacity, Goodyear attempted gradually to lead the Albright Art Gallery into complete acceptance of modernism. He was among those responsible for bringing the Société Anonyme International Exhibition from the Brooklyn Museum to Buffalo in 1926. But with every move he met the most implacable opposition.

Finally in 1927 he overstepped: he was instrumental in buying Picasso's *La Toilette* for the Albright. He paid, he says, $5,000, congratulating himself, as well he might, for having got a real bargain for his home-town gallery. But, as he says, "All hell broke loose immediately. It was discovered I was a bad security risk."

The Albright elections were coming up; Goodyear's opponents seized the opportunity, and, as he says, "The generally automatic election of directors was non-automatic in my case." He was most unceremoniously out.

Only two years later, with the Museum of Modern Art under way, Cornelius J. Sullivan said to Goodyear, the latter recalls: "I'd like to own that Picasso."

Goodyear laughed a little ruefully and replied: "There's nothing standing in your way—least of all the Albright."

"What did you pay?" Sullivan asked.

Goodyear told him.

"What should I offer?"

"Five thousand," said Goodyear, who understood these things. "Or, better yet, forty-seven-fifty. Go easy and you'll own it."

But Sullivan was not so sure. To clinch the matter, as he thought, he made an offer that Goodyear remembers as near $15,000. Something like consternation ensued at the Albright. The directors changed quickly from bulls to bears. If it was that good, they decided, they would just hang on to it. They knew what they liked, but liking it, they saw, had nothing to do with it.

Goodyear commented recently on Sullivan's fiasco. "They thought up there in Buffalo that they had a lemon. They would have been tickled to death to sell for a slight loss. But *fifteen thousand dollars!* An art education in one easy lesson, *I* call it."

So in that year of 1929, the year when Robert Henri, first

of the twentieth-century American art rebels died and the stock market very shortly did likewise, the Museum of Modern Art was born. Katherine Dreier always felt that a name she had thought of, and at that time was still using, had been preempted. Goodyear, however, explicitly states that when the organization committee took the name they did not know it had been used by Miss Dreier, having always heard her organization referred to only as the Société Anonyme.

About July 1 a manifesto was issued. It promised complete representations of modern art—American and European—from Cézanne onward and the establishment of a permanent public museum to acquire collections of "the best modern works of art." Beyond that, so great seemed the possibilities, it was considered unwise "to lay down too definite a program."

Next, a three-year plan was laid out in terms of organization: a salaried staff of director, superintendent, stenographer, four guards, and an agent in Europe. There would be nine exhibitions each year. It was immediately shown how long overdue was the project as the subscription drive got under way: by July 12, $39,000 annually had been pledged for three years; by July 31 the ante had risen to $50,000 per year; and then within mere weeks the desired $75,000 per annum had been secured. Best of all, not a few, but many, were assuming the responsibility: by wise agreement, no single individual was asked for more than $10,000.

Paul J. Sachs, with his teaching background, proved useful when it came to finding a Director. He suggested a "very young man," a teacher of art at Wellesley by the name of Alfred H. Barr, Jr. Barr was invited. He accepted, and then submitted a carefully thought-out long-range plan (since known simply as The Plan) that extended beyond the fine arts to the "practical, commercial, and popular (visual) arts." The Barr plan was accepted, though it would not begin to go into effect as a whole until some years later. The staff was soon complete. It included, besides Director Barr, Jere Abbott, Assistant Director; Mary Sands, Secretary; and Genevieve Carpenter, Assistant.

On August 29, Conger Goodyear sailed for Europe to borrow pictures for the opening exhibition. There had been disagreement about the first show. The men—Goodyear, Sachs, Crowinshield, and Barr—had wanted to open the new museum with a show of the outstanding earlier American painters: Winslow Homer, Thomas Eakins, and Albert P. Ryder. The women—Miss Bliss, Mrs. Rockefeller, Mrs. Sullivan, and Mrs. Crane—held out for a show of the French proto-moderns, the so-called Four Titans. The men gave in.

In Europe, Goodyear was amazed at the interest in the Modern Museum project. By word of mouth, news of it had already reached every nook and cranny of the foreign art world. There was no difficulty in securing the most important and precious works: dealers and collectors vied in loaning them.

At home, meanwhile, Frank Crowninshield turned an experienced hand to the getting of publicity. By early September, following a luncheon he gave for the press, the first notices began to appear. The *New York Times* observed that "nothing has recently stirred more interest in art circles—and outside them for that matter—than the project to establish in this city a modern art museum. The artistic direction and financial backing are already assured. . . . It will not compete with any existing museum.

"It must occasion a little surprise, not to say regret, that the first exhibition is to be French. . . . Yet there can be no doubt that the sponsors of the new Museum intend to be hospitable and even generous to American artists. . . . It is so gratifying . . . to make a beginning . . . that few will dispute . . . which foot we ought to start off [on]. . . ."

The *New York Evening World* spoke of the apathy toward current painting in America: "The average woman never buys any of it . . . the average man has never heard of it." Despite this opinion, the Armory Show was far from forgotten by Manhattanites. Taxi-drivers still talked to all who would listen about the *Nude Descending a Staircase*. The *World* was on more solid ground in pointing to the shortcomings of then-existing museums exclusively "devoted to old pictures." This gave the impression, said the daily, that modern art "is to be thought of only with contempt. . . . A museum given over to modern pictures ought to wake us up to our folly."

The anticipation was eager. Only the *Herald Tribune*, fortress of Royal Cortissoz, struck a sour note. Modern art, said Cortissoz, was to be on trial. He scarcely bothered to conceal his expectation of the imminent public verdict: incompetent, irrelevant, and immaterial.

By September's end Goodyear was back, and on October 3 the new trustees met to elect officers. Goodyear became the first President; Miss Bliss, Vice-President; Mrs. Rockefeller, Treasurer; and Crowninshield, Secretary. These four, plus Mrs. Sullivan, Mrs. Crane, and Paul Sachs, formed the Directorate. Very shortly after this, the Board was increased to fourteen by the election of William T. Aldrich, Stephen C. Clark, Chester Dale, Samuel A. Lewisohn, Duncan Phillips, and Mrs. Grace Rainey Rogers.

A skyscraper eyrie had been found: galleries made over from twelfth-floor offices in the Heckscher Building, on Fifth Avenue at 57th Street. There, early in November, only a little over five months after Conger Goodyear had lunched with three determined ladies, the Museum of Modern Art opened with its first show. Viewed from any angle, it was a most impressive achievement.

No less impressive was the show itself: 101 canvases by the great forerunners of twentieth-century art, Cézanne, Van Gogh, Seurat, and Gauguin, a historical backdrop for all modern shows that might follow. Included were impressive and almost priceless examples like Cézanne's *Still Life with Apples*,[2] Van Gogh's *L'Arlésienne*, and Gauguin's *Spirit of the Dead Watching*.

Impressive, too, was the attendance, even if it did not match that of the Armory Show nearly seventeen years before. The initial, wall-leveling explosion of that first unpreconditioned American view of modern art—that first "pure primordial amazement"—could never be repeated. Nevertheless, "47,000 people," as Goodyear writes, "crowded our six small rooms in a month. On the closing day of the exhibition, December 7, fifty-three hundred visitors tried to get a last look." [3]

The critical reception was rapturous. *Art News* spoke for all when it said: "Tremendous, breath-taking, and if the exhibition has a flaw, it is that of too great power."

The Arts decided that "in one move our youngest museum has stamped itself upon the public's imagination by the superb

[2] This picture came to the Museum of Modern Art in 1934 as a part of the Lillie P. Bliss Bequest.

[3] A. Conger Goodyear: *The Museum of Modern Art: The First Ten Years* (New York, 1943).

quality of the pictures . . . by good taste, elegance, dignity, seriousness of purpose."

The *New York Times* called the show "so superb . . . that those of us . . . prepared . . . to deplore the decision to start off with a French show face palpable embarrassment. Quality disarms."

Yet, most impressive of all in the long retrospect may well be merely the appearance of such a museum at such a time and in such a place as America. Modern artists never studied with Dale Carnegie. Their art is monumentally and historically uncompromising, disdainful of making friends. It is violent, thorny, and certainly, much of it, supremely ugly as judged by the standards of several preceding centuries. It is a curmudgeon that conceals only too well its courage and honesty. It called for these qualities in those who supported it then and built for it a public place.

Only six days after the opening show closed, the second exhibition, "19 Living Americans," went on view. Now the *Times* and other proponents of American modernism were to have their chance to crow. Enthusiastic at the prospect, they were loudly and unanimously disappointed at the event. "Drab" was the consensus, which was not far from the mark.

If not actually drab, the show, it must be admitted, was far from brilliant. The new museum played it politic; what was to have been, one would have supposed, a modern show lost itself in saluting every currently notable name in American art. Pioneering was far from evident. Here were John Sloan and Ernest Lawson, survivors of The Eight; realists unbesmirched by modernism, like Kenneth Hayes Miller and Eugene Speicher; and realists of the exotic on the order of Maurice Sterne and Rockwell Kent. Here, too, were

Charles E. Burchfield and Edward Hopper, heirs of the Ash Can School. Everyone was talking of the "psychological over-tones" of their otherwise literal scenes. They were fashionable.

Even by generous standards, only seven of the "19" art-ists qualified as modern: Charles Demuth, Preston Dickinson, Lyonel Feininger, John Marin, Georgia O'Keeffe, Jules Pascin, and Max Weber. Nowhere to be found were Stuart Davis, Arshile Gorky, Macdonald-Wright, Alfred Maurer, Joseph Stella, Man Ray, Arthur G. Dove, Karl Knaths, Charles Sheeler, or Patrick Henry Bruce. Living, too, was John Covert. Some of these men were young and struggling, some were old and had given up the struggle—no matter, all were a part of modernism's American history in a sense in which the Sloans, the Kents, the Hoppers, the Millers never were.

The Museum's opener, the Four Titans, had been a backdrop for modernism. This show might have been a back-drop for the whole struggle of modernism in America. Right then and there, instead, the impression was fostered that our modern art was, on the whole, second-rate and a far less vital part of American art than it really was.

Then, in January 1930, came the exhibition "Painting in Paris," with special emphasis on Picasso, Matisse, Derain, Bonnard, Braque, Roualt, and Segonzac among the twenty-six artists represented. Popular response carried this show an extra two weeks and dictated—as earlier at the Armory Show —raising the entrance fee at certain hours to keep the attend-ance down. No public apathy to modern art was shown by the fifty-eight thousand people who jammed the small rooms in the Heckscher Building; other tenants complained of monop-olization of the elevators by the gallery-goers and even threatened eviction proceedings: they wanted to put the baby museum out on the Fifth Avenue doorstep.

The press was ecstatic. Henry McBride in the *New York Sun* went completely overboard, writing that this third show was "even more important than the Armory Show. That was a promise; this is fulfillment."

Actually, there was no comparison. The present show, again, saluted everyone of current note. Only Matisse was strongly represented; Picasso was shown mainly by his Blue and Classic periods, with only one cubist canvas; all the Derains were late and unimportant. A fine Delaunay was overbalanced by poor Chagalls, a good Chirico by three bad later ones. The Bonnards and Légers were fine; the good Braques included no cubist pictures. As for Vlaminck, there were two potboilers and only one Fauve still-life. As for the rest, a host of names: Kisling's calendar art, Marie Laurencin's French pastry art, Lurçat, Gromaire, Fautrier, Dufrèsne, Survage, Segonzac—and some inexplicable earlier inclusions: Forain and Vuillard.

Nonetheless, everyone cheered. It was from Paris. Our attitudes were solidifying.

The Museum of Modern Art was like a young pitcher warming up. The next pitch was right over the plate: a large retrospective of the work of Max Weber, unchallenged dean of American modern art. It was altogether fitting that he should have the first one-man show at the new museum. Shown simultaneously with Weber were twenty-seven sculptures by Lehmbruck and Maillol and a small roomful of the delightful fantasies of Paul Klee.

The next show bore the cryptic title "35/46" to indicate the showing of the work of forty-six painters and sculptors under thirty-five years of age. It was more than a gimmick: thus was continued a personal penchant of Director Alfred Barr. His philosophical and almost mathematically logical mind has a strong liking for numbers. It had appeared earlier in the second show, "19 Living Americans"; it would appear again and again over the years.

Homer, Eakins, and Ryder, who had been the choice of the men for the opening show, now finally came on the scene. The strongly original and strongly American work of these three pioneers drew serious critical attention and crowds of viewers. At the show's conclusion on June 5, total attendance for the first seven months had reached an approximate hundred thousand. The first season was brought to a close by a general retrospective that put on view (to apply the Barresque numerology) 4 sculptors, 50 painters: 8 sculptures, 102 paintings. Despite early and perhaps inescapable mistakes, the season had been a great achievement. The deeds in a short season, the struggle to meet genuine needs, the impact of the venture—not in America only, but throughout the world—not even an Alfred Barr could reduce to mere numerals.

These accomplishments, too, and the confidence that they inspired were reflected in some real and solid numbers. By December 6, 1929, only one month after its official opening, the Museum of Modern Art reported $115,000 subscribed annually for the next two years. These were the big, already deflated dollars of the very real depression that had already begun. More numbers and facts: the Board of Trustees grew from fourteen to twenty-one, and a building committee was appointed. The Museum was to move from rented skyscraper rooms to a home of its own.

The fall of 1930, opening with a copious show—one

hundred and fifty items in all—of neglected proto-modern phases of the work of Corot, together with the early social commentary of Daumier, proved the international status already achieved. For the first time in history, the Louvre in Paris and the National Gallery in Berlin lent works of art to an American museum. Even the Metropolitan had never had this honor. The mountains were coming to Mahomet.

But, despite the affluence of the Museum of Modern Art, the big fact in America was the lowering clouds of the Great Depression. America, suddenly impoverished, was becoming social-conscious. Even the Museum, in hanging the work of Daumier, showed that it was not unaware of the new facts of life.

10. *The Artist Is the Man Next Door*

The Great Depression of the 1930's, when suicides plummeted from skyscrapers, war veterans marched on Washington, and the suddenly poor peddled apples on the street corners, was the time, remarkably enough, when America recognized the artist as a citizen and the artist recognized himself as an artist. All at once the casteless one was one of us. It was the unlikely, unpredictable, almost fantastic result of a time of sorrow. In the midst of all that vast insecurity the artist found security.

Although the Depression's WPA was a thing of controversy which has been cantankerously chewed over ever since, it may stand as the most important single emergency measure of a desperate time. It was the finger in the dike when despair threatened to engulf the Republic. Certainly, anyway, one branch of the many branches of the Works Progress Administration—the art subsidiary—will stand as the most salutary thing that ever happened to the American artist and American art.

America's idea, as expressed then, was that it is the right of the individual to work for his living rather than to stand in a bread line. And the right of the individual is the duty of a democratic government. That pair of simple propositions did the trick for the artist.

For some eighty years, at least, he had latterly lived as an alien among us practical people, his work considered a kind of non-essential play, while his pride was reduced to a defensive vanity or turned into an impotent anger. Then, suddenly, he was hungry, too. His right to eat was obvious; his right to work was granted; the second right restored dignity and meaning to his work; and then we found out that all along he had been the man next door.

The Depression was well under way before the Works Project began. The problem was acute; local agencies were staggering under the burden. Even then a few people remembered the artist along with all the others. One who remembered was Manhattan's beloved "Little Flower," Mayor Fiorello H. La Guardia. He sponsored two gigantic exhibition sales of American art in Rockefeller Center. The first was in 1933, with over five thousand items selected by a committee of museum directors. The second, the year following, was assembled by a short-lived group of artists under the name Salons of America. But already in January the Federal government had begun to take hold.

La Guardia's attitude toward art, uncomprehending but friendly, forecast the position that official Washington would take, the position that the great majority of Americans would take. It deserves a better name than tolerance. It is a kind of friendly waiting to see, the atmosphere of the first social call on the new neighbors. A photograph has survived of La Guardia standing with Arshile Gorky in front of a Gorky drawing. Serious Gorky, dark-mustached, beetle-browed, brooding, and inches over six feet, towers above the five-foot, rotund, witty dynamo that was La Guardia. The occasion was the opening in December 1935 of a gallery sponsored by the WPA. Gorky's design was for a mural, *Aviation*, intended for Floyd Bennett Field.

It was Gorky who later reported what the Mayor said. La Guardia shook hands with the artist, looked in bewilderment at his picture, and shrugged his eloquent shoulders. Then he smiled and said: "Happy to meet you, Mr. Gorky. Introduce me to your painting."

The only thing to mar this meeting of everyday America

with art was reported by the *New York Herald Tribune:* "An aggressive salesman for 'Art Front,' publication of the Communist John Reed Club, jumped into one picture so that the negative recorded . . . the cover of the magazine. The Mayor laughed . . . and the photographer took another picture."

The first Federal aid for art came in 1934. This was PWAP—Public Works of Art Project—which lasted six months and then was killed by Congress. Harry Hopkins allocated funds from the Civil Works Administration and placed Edward Bruce, a businessman who had become a painter, in charge. PWAP, as its name implies, laid stress on murals executed for public buildings. For a brief successive period the FERA (Federal Emergency Relief Administration) concerned itself with art. It was administered through state projects without national direction or control.

Then in 1935 came the WPA Art Project, which operated until 1943. Some of the community art centers established by the Art Project are still functioning. The new project grew out of the desire of Hopkins and his assistant, Jacob Baker, to expand the activity on a national basis.

Holger Cahill, who three years earlier had been temporary director of the Museum of Modern Art in Barr's absence, was suddenly summoned to Washington. Cahill went reluctantly, feeling sure that he would be asked to head the project. He had just retired from administrative work and wanted to write, but he was prodded into going and urged to accept the job by the abstract artists in New York.

"If you don't take the job," said Stuart Davis, "Jonas Lie will, and every modern artist will get the brush-off." Lie, a dyed-in-the-wool National Academician, was also up for the place, and his appointment was being strongly urged. Cahill, however, was offered the post, accepted, and took the reins immediately.

It was a time of action, not debate. "Have your organizational plans and your policy ready by tomorrow morning," he was told. Cahill was ready on the dot. His policy, formulated in two sentences, put into operation a liberal and enlightened Project whose effects were to be basic and constructive: "We shall not tell painters what to paint or how to paint it," said Cahill. "Whatever an American artist paints will be American art so far as we are concerned." It was no more a time, he saw, for modern art exclusively than it was a time for the exclusion of modern art. As the Project went on, artists were given directives. They worked them out, however, in their own way.

The organization, Cahill decided, would be run by local directors acting under state directors, who in turn would act under regional directors. Cahill was a realist. If a tyro, perhaps, in national politics, he knew well the machinations of art politics. Moving to prevent them as far as possible, he reserved the right to appoint every director, large or small, assuming responsibility for them all.

All over the country the WPA Art Project swung into action. Copyists of nature, from "calendar artists" up to portraitists whose smart clientele was no longer sitting for likenesses, commercial artists of a commerce that no longer existed, modernists of every ilk and persuasion from semi-representationalists to geometricists—all set to work together. The old, stubborn wounds left by the Armory Show almost healed. Painters of autumn foliage met cubists. They even liked one another. Even the gripes at "foreign art" were stilled as alien artists—Yasuo Kuniyoshi, Gorky, Willem de Kooning, and many others—were allowed on the rolls until, somewhat later, Congress banned them. Most of them later became citizens.

Murals began appearing in post offices and other government buildings everywhere. To the general public these represented the full extent of the WPA art activity. There was considerable talk about "boondoggling." This new word, which means loafing on a job that you cannot be fired from, was promptly welcomed into the American language by H. L. Mencken. Actually, a vast amount of work was being done, and it was as diverse as the men doing it. Even, perhaps, more diverse because Holger Cahill was at the helm.

To Cahill's interest in our native folk art we owe the twenty thousand or more magically lifelike colored renderings of Americana that are now in the National Gallery of Art. The method of executing these replicas, which are as much paintings as they are drawings, is typical of the altogether amazing way in which the Art Project was able to unify the work of many highly individual artists on a given program. The technique was developed by the painters working on the common problem. It combines a number of hitherto separate mediums; once it had been elaborated, scores of painters used it in a uniform manner. It is lovingly faithful to the loved object, to the last blister in the paint of a ship's figurehead, to the smallest flake of red rust on a hand-wrought iron weather vane. The color camera could not have done so well; it would have caught the rust, but not the magic of the rust, settled like a minute fragment of history, of a long and glorious time on a new continent. Cahill somehow infected the artists with his own sense of the abiding enchantment of these things of ancient use, so that, most of all, it is the magic that comes through.

From the huge files of this visual catalogue of our ancestors' daily life came a now famous book, the *Index of American Design* (1950), which overnight revealed to America at large the almost forgotten heritage hidden away in many an attic and barn. This WPA sub-project supported and in some cases initiated the great private and public collections and restorations that now preserve this heritage for us, among them, Du Pont's Winterthur Museum in Delaware, the Rockefeller restoration of Colonial Williamsburg, Henry Ford's Dearborn Museum and Wayside Inn (recently destroyed by fire) at Sudbury, Massachusetts, the prime collection at Cooperstown, New York, and Shelburne Village, reassembled by Mrs. J. Watson Webb in Vermont. Possibly even more important in the long run is the host of small collectors of moderate means whose newly educated eagle eyes now save these humble objects, the junk of yesterday, from careless destruction.

The brick walls, the sidewalks, and all the minor jobs done by WPA artisans are now forgotten. The great dams and the new lakes that they shoulder back, however, changed the face of America and our life as well. The creative projects of the WPA as a whole brought a deep change, too. We learned to look not only at the artist, but at our own country too with new eyes. The Writers' Project that gave us guidebooks of a new kind for our states and great cities; the interviews of old settlers and frontiersmen and wrinkled survivors of Negro slavery, all of them nearing the grave; the many-faced portrait of the implements and the simple adornments of our daily life—these add up to a wise husbanding of our finest national resources. When America, that "last and greatest hope," seemed lost and foundering, all together they affirmed: "Here is your country."

So we grew up to our artists. They grew up, too. Even the most embattled of them had concealed at least a trace of uncertainty. It was a simple but great thing to be accepted as workmen living by their work. Willem de Kooning, then an unknown, now one of our most celebrated modern painters, has told how it felt: "I had been doing odd jobs to live and to have a little time to paint," De Kooning says. "The WPA made me think of myself as an artist. There were a lot of odd jobs still, but they came second in my mind."

The artist found out how vital a thing art could be, how practical and how necessary. Midway in the WPA, war drew closer and closer to an unarmed America still fighting to cure the anemia of depression. The feverish preparations began as on one hand we bolstered a hard-pressed Britain with absolete destroyers and on the other tried to milk armaments from our nearly prostrate industry. Men were called to arms—and we had no arms to give them. But they were trained, nevertheless, with "mock-ups" of the new weapons—working models prepared by the WPA sculptors—and by enormous explanatory prints engraved and printed by the artists. One of these was of the revolutionary new Garrand rifle, which then existed only in factory blueprints.

A lithograph of immense size was prepared which was in itself a work of art, if a somewhat grim one. It was rendered and shaded in certain sections with the realistic technique of the Americana drawings, while other sections were intricate and accurate cross-sections of vital working parts of the new gun. Hundreds of prints were made from the lithographic stones. In front of these the lecturers stood, explaining to the

green inductees how to handle this twentieth-century descendant of that first weapon of our freedom, the Revolutionary
Long Rifle.

The thirty-foot lithograph of the Garrand was almost a
miracle. Any single artist would have said that it would take a
year to do, if it could be done at all. The group did it in weeks.
It was a composite of hundreds of individual prints, each the
size of an ordinary lithograph stone. The technique—the
method of shading and highlighting, the range from lightest to
darkest tone, the direction from which the light would fall—all
of this was worked out on a single pilot print. Then each artist
was handed a section of a blueprint and a stone to draw and
etch, and all set to work simultaneously with no waste of
precious time. When the first prints were pulled and the
gigantic, unproved jigsaw puzzle was thumbtacked together
on a wall, every part fitted and the joining lines were lost in the
unity.

America has never known how much she owed in those
months to her artists. Soon came the black Sunday of Pearl
Harbor. Many a War Bond was sold, many a volunteer en-
listed, through the persuasions of the thousands of posters designed by the WPA artists. We need remember only one
famous one: *A Slip of the Lip May Sink a Ship*. A measure of the
deep change in society's attitude toward artists is to be seen in
their altered role in war. In 1917–18 they were handed rifles
and sent into the trenches. In World War II those in service
were, on the whole, employed in their special capacities. At
home, in addition to the WPA work, they worked with
psychologists in the hospitals on art therapy that eased the
tedious recovery of some of the casualties, drew others back
from mental darkness.

With all its unity of effort upon occasion, however, the
Art Project was not one long feast of amity. It was torn by two
dissensions. One of these came from the wave of nationalism
which was gripping America as it was gripping countries
everywhere. In its most virulent racist forms in Germany,
Italy, and Japan, it led, of course, to the war. With us it was
more mild. A direct result of it was the school of regional painting called the American Scene, led by Thomas Benton of
Missouri, Grant Wood of Iowa, and John Steuart Curry of
Kansas. It may be seen as a remote descendant of the Hudson
River landscape school of the nineteenth century grafted on to
the genre pictures of Winslow Homer and J. G. Brown and the
homy sculpture of John Roger—and as a nearer descendant
of the Ash Can School.

But the American School was something more than these.
When its touters and campfollowers got to work, it became a
pressure group crusading for conformity. The Hudson River
work is simply and naturally American. "Americanism in Art"
was the self-conscious program of the new men. They pulled
every stop of nationalist appeal. When their espoused critic,
Thomas Craven, beat the drums, one could almost imagine
Tom Benton repeating the words of "I Am an American"
over and over like an incantation while he painted in a flag-
draped studio. The Ash Canners at least were fighting for
freedom of subject matter. With Wood, Curry, and Benton,
the subjects *must* be American. Even Curry's Kansas pigs,
which looked so much as pigs do in any land, must have had
an American smell.

The regionalists—and, in particular, Craven—were
determined to force their views on all artists. Nothing less than
an American renaissance, with "foreign abstraction" given the

heave-ho, was their avowed aim. It is hard to believe the pressure that was brought to bear. But any number of today's generation of painters will testify to it. There is Jackson Pollock, for instance, one of the most talked-of younger abstractionists in the world today. He once studied under Benton at the Art Students League in New York. "They put the screws on with a vengeance," Pollock says. "You were only trying to find how you needed to paint and you were un-American. I noticed that some damned fine American painters, men like John Marin, for example, wouldn't touch the movement with a ten-foot pole."

The flurry is long since over; artists, as always, were violently opposed to the goose-step. The paintings of the three leading regionalists, like all other paintings, must await the verdict of time shorn of the benefits of special advocacy.

More sinister and even more violent was the pressure of the social-significance school led by left-wingers and their fellow travelers. Art that was not socially conscious, that was not propaganda for the great proletariat, was not art at all, they claimed. In the midst of the collapse of business and property values, and with the memory of the wave of bank closings still fresh, the Communist pressure was more insidious and effective by far than that of the American Scene group. Their claim, "Capitalism is dying," seemed for the moment as though it just possibly might be true.

But that was not the only string to the Comintern bow. "Prepare for the new state tomorrow," was only for those who scared easily. Those who did not received the full mental massage: brotherly love, that evil war-mongering capitalism, Big Brother Bear—our good Russian friend—over there fight-

ing the Nazi horde for us. Every other phrase began: "It is the
artist's duty . . ." and the alternate ones commenced: "With
your great talents you have no right. . . ."

One artist who suffered through it remembers the bar-
rage: "One day you didn't even know these guys; the next day
they were sitting in your lap; and the day after that you were
asking yourself, 'Am I a lone Judas betraying the whole
human race?' "

This was the great day of the Mexican radical artists,
Orozco, Rivera, and Siqueiros. Rivera had done his murals
in the San Francisco Stock Exchange, and was preparing an
even greater controversy on the walls of the RCA Building of
Rockefeller Center, while Orozco's new frescoes at Dartmouth
College were mercilessly flaying an educational system liberal
enough to commission his work. The Mexicans painted hammers and sickles all over the place and then left for home with
their pockets lined with far more than a WPA salary. They
were big-leaguers: they bit the tycoons' hands. They had it
good while it lasted. The art world hailed Mexican art.
Everyone listened to these new Isaiahs: they were the Givers
of the Law.

With it all, a number of American artists, on the WPA
and off the WPA, gave in. A few joined willingly; many, many
more felt vaguely guilty while continuing to paint in their
own way. Between the American Scene on the one hand and
the social-signifiers on the other, a number of New York galleries had a field day. The ACA Gallery, in particular, then
on 8th Street in Greenwich Village, was the center for the
new "social school."

The left-wingers stirred up no end of trouble on the

WPA Art Project. Their grievance committees made life miserable for the state and regional directors, and even harried Cahill himself. They would secretly insert Communist symbols or insulting portraits of wealthy citizens in murals here and there, then draw their weekly pay of thirty-five dollars. Next day, thinking perhaps of their more fortunate Mexican comrades, they would be back complaining of "this miserable pittance." Cahill finally got a bellyful of the whole thing. He summoned the ringleaders, wound up, and began pitching.

"What is this prattle of 'social significance'?" he all but roared. "Take a good look at this project of your government's if you want to see something of social significance.

"You talk of pittances, but you draw them and spend them. And then bite the paymaster's hand. These 'pittances' add up to billions of dollars. They add up to more than money —to the greatest act of responsibility ever made by any government."

Twenty years have passed since the group that so suddenly discovered a conscience were the Alger boys of the New Day. For all the hue and cry, most of their names are all but forgotten. It is hard to believe that history will ever place them with that sparse, noble roll: Goya, Hogarth, Daumier, Forain, the non-political Picasso of the Blue Period, the George Grosz of 1918 meeting Imperial Prussian brutality with the cold brutality of truth.

Out of all the list, it is chiefly the name of Ben Shahn which endures. It is likely that, with or without the pressure, with or without the Depression, he would have painted the same way. It is a way, a style, a point of view which he found for himself. The true humanist is a humanist every day of the week; his humanism is not a "line." His paintings are less footnotes to a period than perpetual re-enactments of the human drama.

The Museum of Modern Art's opening exhibition in 1936 was a salute to the Art Project of the WPA. "New Horizons in American Art" was made up of a wide variety of work done by artists on the Project rolls. It was directed by Dorothy Miller of the Museum staff. There was no censorship of the work that was shown. The social-signifiers were shown along with the rest. One canvas in particular, *The Feast of Pure Reason*, created a storm in the Museum inner circles. This painting by Jack Levine portrayed J. Pierpont Morgan in a murky underworld setting with unsavory political and police characters. Levine made clear his belief that all were pals in skullduggery. Behind the scenes the millionaire Board of the Museum was embroiled in controversy. Reasonableness won out, and *The Feast of Pure Reason* remained on the wall. It has been shown a number of times since. With each successive showing its topical melodrama approaches nearer and nearer to the level of the adventure comic strip.

The exhibit title, "New Horizons," showed an awareness of the far-reaching social and artistic effects of the Art Project. The art critics sensed these wider implications. One pointed out that the United States government had finally recognized the artist as a member of society; another observed that, perhaps unknowingly, it had become the greatest art patron in the world. The *New York Times* felt that the Art Project was revolutionizing "the whole attitude toward art in this country" and saw "quickened appreciation on the part of millions of people whose lives art had not before touched."

When the WPA folded, a vast quantity of art was left.

A small proportion of it, at least, was very fine work. The government could not sell it without incurring the charge of exploitation of labor. Anyway, to go into the art business had not been the purpose of the Project. So political foes leveled instead the charge of "criminal waste"—this in a country where waste is a trained reflex, where each year millions of scarcely old automobiles are added to the piles already rusting in the junkyards. The WPA art, at least, was not destroyed as was gasoline and unused war equipment on many a South Pacific beach. It was gradually allocated on indefinite loan to museums, hospitals, schools, and other public institutions.

Many felt that with the end of the Project the time had come for setting up a cabinet post of fine art. It did not happen. Perhaps it is just as well. It bears thinking about, the prospect of making art a political football. One has only to imagine art administered by an Oveta Culp Hobby or to try to answer the general question: "Are Democrats more artistic than Republicans?"

The vast majority of the WPA artists actually had already answered the whole question. By rejecting political ties and dictation, they were showing the keen instinct for self-preservation which is typical of their species. The independence of the artist, like that of the scientist, is a safeguard of society. Both serve best when not servitors. And they know it.

11. *Passage to Permanence*

The year 1931 started normally enough for the Museum of Modern Art with Royal Cortissoz's annual prediction of the imminent demise of all modern art. Then, about six weeks after this pronouncement, which the dean of the no-men gave out on February 1, there actually was a death keenly felt by all modern art-lovers. Miss Lillie P. Bliss succumbed. "During the period of less than two years preceding her death," Conger Goodyear wrote later, "the Museum had become her chief interest. . . . Her questioning, understanding and friendly eyes, her criticism, sympathy and support were of the greatest inspiration in the early days." [1]

Over the years the Bliss collection had grown to one of importance, notable especially for the Cézannes—eleven oils, as many watercolors, and numerous drawings and lithographs. It was well rounded out with work by Daumier, Degas, Seurat, Picasso, Gauguin, Derain, Matisse, Redon (including *Silence*, the first sale at the Armory Show), Pissarro, Modigliani, Renoir, Rousseau, and Toulouse-Lautrec.

The Bliss collection went by bequest to the Museum she had helped to found. To the best of her ability, Miss Bliss had made up to America the loss that it had suffered when so many of John Quinn's treasures had left the auction block to go back to France. For there is small doubt that Lillie Bliss had never ceased to regret her failure to respond in 1926 to Arthur B. Davies's urgings to help save the Quinn collection. She did nobly, nevertheless. *The Arts* noted quite accurately "the transition of the Museum from a temporary place of exhibitions to a permanent place of lasting activities and acquisitions."

[1] A. Conger Goodyear: *The Museum of Modern Art: The First Ten Years* (New York, 1943).

Permanence was not yet a pedestal, however. The Museum could scarcely allow itself to become a reclining figure at that stage. Modern art was still far from general acceptance, and all was not yet sweetness and light. The bitter controversy first unloosed in 1913 still boiled away, perhaps particularly among the artists. Many older ones, especially, remained disoriented by any departure from the actual appearance of things: the more extreme forms of abstraction, even cubism, seemed to make their blood boil. An example of this at that time was the veteran painter Henry Rankin Poore, who wrote an open letter to the Museum. Cortissoz gave him great space in the *Herald Tribune*. Poore fairly spat out his words: "At your gallery you have touched bottom. . . . Nothing . . . could go deeper into the mire. . . ." Now, too, with a real depression on hand, native artists resented more than ever the American money being poured out for art from Paris.

Faced by such accustomed assaults—however they may have disconcerted some of the Museum of Modern Art's Trustees—the protagonists of the modern relaxed in their native climate of defiance and vituperation. Modern art, they could tell from such goings-on, was still modern and very much alive. Jerome Eddy had once pointed out that it "thrives on controversy—like every human endeavor. The fiercer the controversy, the *surer*, the *sounder*, the *saner*, the outcome." [2] Abraham Walkowitz once footnoted Eddy's comment with his "famous three words": FEAR (any change)—SNEER (when it comes)—CHEER (when it's here to stay).

Anyway, it will be time to worry, modernists think, when no one howls, no one shouts, no one is angry, baffled, or amused, when cubism, futurism, expressionism, and all the

[2] Arthur Jerome Eddy: *Cubists and Post-Impressionism* (Chicago, 1914).

other wonderful "isms" that have made our century so lively come finally to share the same walls with the Rembrandts and all the old masters, stared at Sundays by the mute, shuffling crowds. Time to worry when the truths that set a generation fighting are no longer even put to question. Time to worry, or time, rather, to look for new fighting truths, to strike out for the unknown once more.

However, this sad state of affairs was not even on the far horizon when, two months after Miss Bliss's death, the Museum of Modern Art opened a memorial exhibition of the complete bequest, a show that, as Conger Goodyear observed, showed the "quality of the woman" quite as fully as the "value of the collection." [3] Certainly—although the paintings were removed from the climate of her home to museum walls —the highly diverse showing evoked a clear impression of a single remarkable personality. Collecting, it is clear, can be far more than mere acquisitiveness: it can in itself be a creative act. Marcel Duchamp once made a sharp distinction between the "Wall Street collector" and the real collector who "paints himself a collection." [4]

The Bliss Bequest carried the condition that the Museum must be put on a sound permanent basis through capital endowments before the collection would change title. As Conger Goodyear points out, this presented a problem as "through the following years the United States languished in a vale of depression. It was not thought advisable to undertake a long term drive for the endowment fund. . . . Instead it was decided to wait for the more favorable conditions

[3] Goodyear, op. cit.
[4] Quoted from *Abstract of Proceedings*, Western Round Table on Modern Art, San Francisco Museum of Art, April 8, 9, and 10, 1949.

that it was hoped the New Deal might produce."

The New Deal did all right—far better, in fact, than had been hoped. By early in 1934 the conditions were met. Goodyear notes that by appealing "solely to the known supporters of the Museum's policy, over $600,000 was raised in a few weeks. There were only 125 subscribers to this fund, 93% of them already members." In five years the Museum of Modern Art had progressed from a luncheon-table topic to an endowed institution owning an important permanent collection housed in separate quarters. For in April 1932 the Museum had moved to a leased building at 11 West 53rd Street remodeled for its occupancy.

The last show in the Heckscher Building suite had been one that was long overdue and that would have lasting effects on the physical appearance of this country. This was the architectural show directed by Philip Johnson, which presented no less than fifty architects from all over the world working in what Alfred Barr was the first to term the International Style. The catalogue included short papers on Frank Lloyd Wright, Gropius, Le Corbusier, Oud, Miës van der Rohe, Hood, Howe and Lescaze, and Neutra. The architectural show was the first Museum of Modern Art exhibition to circulate. It went to ten other American museums and one department store, thus inaugurating an activity that has developed great importance in our present cultural scheme and has spread the name of the Museum far and wide.

In 1932 Alfred Barr, exhausted from overwork, went on a year's vacation; his place, as we have noted, was temporarily filled by Holger Cahill. For the ensuing two years the exhibitions, following Cahill's bent, leaned heavily to the American —both Early and Late. In 1930 and 1931 Cahill had put on

Man-eater with Pennants, *1945, mobile by Alexander Calder.*
Steel rods, sheet iron, 14' high and about 30' in diameter.
Collection: The Museum of Modern Art.

Gizmo, *by Jimmy Ernst—*
"electronically disintegrated and reassembled every fourth Monday night."

*Opening of the first exhibition at the Museum of Modern Art,
730 Fifth Avenue, New York, November 7, 1929.
Left: Van Gogh Fruit, 1886–8. Center: Seurat Side Show, 1889.
Right: Cézanne Still Life, c. 1885.*

*Summer exhibition at The Museum of Modern Art, June 7 to October 30, 1932,
in the original brownstone house on West 53rd Street, New York.
Installation to show historic evolution of ideas: Cézanne, African mask,
Picasso Negroid, Braque cubist, Léger mechanistic, Mondrian complete abstraction.*

three important shows of this sort at the Newark Museum: "American Folk Art," "American Primitive Paintings," and "American Folk Sculpture." Each of these, it is believed, was the first museum exhibition of its kind anywhere. Cahill tells that New Yorkers came over to Newark "in droves," and the metropolitan papers carried glowing accounts. Newark momentarily took the play away from the big city across the Hudson.

In the larger arena afforded by the Museum of Modern Art, Cahill immediately staged a sweeping show of American folk art. Its honesty and beauty struck home. No propaganda, no labored exegesis, was necessary. These modest archaic objects of use—trade signs, weather vanes, ships' figureheads, cigar-store Indians, and all the rest—spoke to us like soft, friendly, forgotten voices from the past. "They touch the heart," wrote Henry McBride in the *New York Sun*. "It is impossible to regard them, even casually . . . without a nostalgic yearning for the beautiful simple life that is no more."

It was indeed the period, those years, of the "New Vision," when American art of many kinds from times past was being looked at afresh. Dramatic events happened. In New York, for example, a one-hundred-year-old artist standing at the brink of the grave was suddenly discovered, suddenly acclaimed. Almost at the same time an old, old woman paid a sensational visit to her native America, to receive the homage due to royalty—which she was not—to be admired, even adulated, by millions, to create a flurry still well remembered.

The year was 1932.

The man in question was modernist Alfred Maurer's

father, Louis M. Maurer, a man who so hated modernism that he had said long before, when he first saw his son's modern work from Paris at Stieglitz's 291: "I have buried my son." [5] And yet here he was, old Louis, a sudden hero solely because modern art had brought us a new view that could include the utilitarian, the popular, and the fine arts—barberpole, parlor "chromo," and serious painting. For Maurer, Sr., had been a popular artist in almost the humblest sense of the term.

It was a New York print dealer, Harry Shaw Newman, who discovered that Alfred Maurer's father was the last survivor of the group of artists who once had drawn for the nineteenth-century Currier and Ives prints. So with one burst of glory the crabbed centenarian had his blinding moment in the sun. Then, having achieved his twin ambitions of the one-man exhibit ("just to show Alfred") and the century mark in living, he quietly expired.

The woman in question is not dead yet. She is, at this writing, about one hundred and fifty years old, and there is a distinct possibility that she will never die. She is a figure in a picture, one of the half-dozen most famous pictures in the world, painted in 1869 under the title of *Arrangement in Black and Grey* but universally known as *Whistler's Mother*.

She was part of a Museum of Modern Art exhibition, "American Painting and Sculpture," that covered a period of seventy years. There could be some argument as to just how old Mother was in 1932. As a canvas she was sixty-three; however, allowing that she was older than that when "Jimmy" Whistler painted her, she could logically have been figured as nearer to a century and a third.

[5] Jerome Mellquist: *Emergence of an American Art* (New York, 1942).

She once had been obscure and not even acceptable socially. While her paint was still fresh, she had been turned outdoors by the British Royal Academy, and for the next twenty years she had moped around her son's studio. By that time Jimmy, who had reached fifty-five himself, was getting cranky. Then the French government, quite unaware that it just possibly was subsidizing American and/or British art thereby, took pity on the old lady and housed her in a rather noted museum. Mother was sold into this distinguished bondage for a mere bagatelle: $400.[6] She aged well and profitably. Forty-three years after she had moved to Paris, when her benefactor the Louvre (rather unexpectedly to all concerned) consented to let Mother visit her homeland, the officials insisted that she be insured for a tidy half-million dollars. This figure represented a considerable concession on her landlords' part. They had first asked one million.

Whistler's Mother stayed around New York about a month, and when she left, the town was misty-eyed and had a catch in its throat. She then rode on to hold homy court in other museums throughout the country. She was guarded like a potentate on her travels—in one city by roaring squadrons of motorcycle police, in another by armored cars and rumbling army half-tracks, in still another by a troop of cavalry. It was clear that they were guarding a lot more than the mere money involved. We send a half-million around the streets any old day in one poor little armored car with just a couple of men.

The United States government made a postage stamp of

[6] This figure is from Goodyear, op. cit. Eleanor Dunne, in "Let's Put Whistler's Mother in Her Place" (*American Mercury*, October 1954), gives the purchase price as $800, but cites no authority.

her, our Bureau of Engraving, which has labored long and successfully to make our stamps among the drabbest and ugliest in the world, outdoing itself by cheerfully altering Whistler's much-admired composition as it saw fit. The traditional proportions of a bit of gummed paper, the Bureau felt, were more important than a painting. Alfred Barr, restless on vacation, happily took up the cudgels, and considerable publicity attended his strenuous but beautifully worded efforts to convince the unconvinceable engraving bureaucracy that it had no business tampering with great paintings.

Before it was all through, Mother had America on its knees. The triumph of what Philip Wylie calls Momism was seemingly assured by her visit; Mother's Day was finally and inexorably saddled on this country by the florists and the gift-card manufacturers; and a reputed million copies were sold of a record of Bing Crosby's called "The Whistler's Mother-in-Law."

It is not too difficult to imagine what Mother's son, acid-tongued Jimmy Whistler, would have thought of this great, big, beautiful, tearful jag. It is best that he was not around to witness it. He, who once sued Ruskin, would have had a good libel case against the whole country. He might even have gone on to ask: "What does all this have to do with *modern* art?" A lot of people, in fact, were wondering about that.

Mother stayed on for the 1933 Chicago Century of Progress Exposition, where she had the company of another female, also famous in a high degree, but with the far different aura of a far different century: *Nude Descending a Staircase.* So far as is known, no ballot was taken to determine the relative popularity of the two women. It is just as well. Americans could hardly have brought free and unbiased minds to bear on such an onerous choice.

In 1934 the Museum of Modern Art had just completed its fifth year while the press, filled with Joseph Stalin's pronouncements, was much concerned with Five Year Plans. Conger Goodyear had observed that in "five years the value of a museum should be proved or disproved." The proof was in the pudding. Modern art was becoming more and more palatable; the public gobbled it up more and more avidly portion by portion as it was served. Not only a museum, but the new art—even as Cortissoz had said—had been on trial. Both had come through that testing half-decade triumphantly. There seemed no limit on the future.

The overlapping five years from 1932 to 1937 were lively years during which, step by step, the Barr Plan would go into operation, the Museum would consolidate its world leadership, and actual construction would start on a magnificent new building of the Museum's own. If one were writing the biography of a man, one would say that these were the fruitful, vigorous, adventurous years of his prime. Many, indeed, believe that the comparison is not amiss, that those years— despite all the accomplishments since—were the Museum's years of venture when the whole field lay ahead still to be explored, years before the weight of accumulating prestige ruled out the taking of chances, years when eye and judgment were still quick and when the staff, still relatively small, was as flexible as muscles in their prime.

In 1932 we find the art library being established and space being found for it in an attic room of the remodeled brownstone house in 53rd Street to which the Museum had just moved. This important department was placed under the direction of Miss Iris Barry as Librarian, and the first chairman of the library committee was Philip Johnson, succeeded somewhat later by Walter P. Chrysler, Jr. Conger Goodyear gave the first nucleus of books, which was shortly to be enriched by Chrysler's donation of an important collection of surrealist literature.

Museum publications are fittingly considered in connection with the library. The Museum of Modern Art has greatly enriched art literature by a long series of handsome, scholarly exhibition catalogues that are models of their kind, as well as by several important books written by Alfred Barr. In its first ten years the Museum published some fifty volumes. By 1955 an impressive total of 204 was reached, out of which at that time and despite mounting printing-costs, 65 items had been kept in print. Many are indispensable reference works, and at least two are virtually monuments: Barr's giant volumes, *Matisse: His Art and His Public* (1951) and *Masters of Modern Art* (1954).

Early in this fruitful period the huge Matisse retrospective exhibition proved that America was growing up to the controversial onetime King of the Wild Beasts. "The press was a chorus of praise, with the usual Royal exception," Museum President Goodyear wrote, referring of course to Royal Cortissoz, who damned Matisse as "the veriest dabster." [7]

At this time, too, as evidence of wide-ranging interest, the Museum in 1933 assembled an exhibit of Mayan, Toltec, and Aztec art under the rather remarkable title "American

[7] Goodyear, op. cit.

Sources of Modern Art." This is noted because, unlike African and Oceanic art, it has never been shown that the ancient art of Central America was an influence on Matisse and Picasso or later masters. Its influence at that time on American artists was still negligible, although, of course, contemporary Mexican art was largely based on it, and, much earlier, Frank Lloyd Wright, in his individual, solitary way, had absorbed elements of the Mayan architecture. The title, anyway, was prophetic inasmuch as this remarkable art so remarkably shown forthwith did become an influence on American modernists.

In 1934 the Barr Plan quickened its tempo. Motion pictures and industrial art came on the scene. The film library was established under Iris Barry's direction, and Philip Johnson arranged the "Machine Art" show.

Miss Barry, with the notable co-operation of the Hollywood film industry, began to assemble a priceless and unique collection of motion pictures of all countries, types, and vintages. After two years of public projection at the Museum, their circulation began throughout the country by way of museums and educational institutions. In five years, by 1939, the film library had acquired the mildly astonishing total of one million feet of film. By 1955 the library, presently under the curatorship of Richard Griffith, held the nearly astronomical total of thirteen million feet of film history.

The year in which the film library began saw three notable Museum exhibitions: the controversial but ultimately influential "Machine Art"; the show "Art of the Theatre," arranged by Lee Simonson; and another that rhetorically asked the question "America Can't Have Housing?"

Within five more years the Museum of Modern Art itself would question the optimistic answer to the housing question at this 1934 exhibition, which opened with a broadcast during which Mayor La Guardia was one of seven speakers. In the catalogue of the 1939 show, "Architecture in the U.S.," is to be found this statement: "The critical problem . . . today is not . . . construction, function, esthetics . . . [but] the humanitarian and social problem of trying to provide decent homes in decent communities for those millions of our people who do not have them." In simple language, this means decent houses at a decent price.

It had been pointed out that in 1910 the same modest price paid either for an automobile or for a good, well-built one-family house. Already the house cost far more than the car, and at the same time the car had grown and the house had shrunk. The process, like Alice alternately nibbling at the two mushrooms, has continued disastrously ever since. Soon migrant war workers were living in trailers. By the war's end a large percentage of the citizenry of the richest country in the world was living in houses the size of huts. Many began to move out of them and back into the trailers for the sake of more room. Finally, today the trailers are being mounted on concrete foundations and are being called "mobile homes." There are, of course, the "electric servants"—washing machines, dish-washers, mixers, choppers, and ironers as well as the "entertainers": radio, television, home-recording sets, and the electric phonograph. Progress-hounds point with pride to all this as Margaret Mead soberly proves that, in spite of all the time-saving gadgets, our housewives have less free time than the families that still, in backward communities, do most of their work by hand. Perhaps, as Marcel Duchamp once observed, "Progress is merely an enormous pretension on our part." [8]

The "Machine Art" show directed attention to the vast change that the "New Vision" had already wrought in industrial products, and in architecture and interior decoration. By 1940 the change would be visible to anyone. The automobile would have lost its last link with the "antique" car—the running-board—while fenders were sinking out of sight into "faired" contours inspired by Brancusi and the airplane. Cars began, in fact, to look more and more like bathtubs, not unfittingly, perhaps, in a nation that boasted of more of the latter than could be found in the rest of the world. Chairs were earnestly streamlined as if for a trip to Mars; stationary household objects of every sort gave the illusion of being in the air and on their way; and electric refrigerators were sleek white sculptures with that rounded top—which many of them still retain—so well calculated to start loaded plates and glasses sneakily sliding to crash on the floor. Our modern designers had obviously learned the alphabet; perhaps someday they would get around to the language.

The year after the unveiling of "Machine Art," 1935, was one so lively at the Museum of Modern Art, and so significant, that it represents an early climax. "African Negro Art," six hundred items of it, finally received a full-dress show. The exhibition, arranged by James Johnson Sweeney, elicited the comment: "Probably for the first time the layman art lover will understand why so much importance was attached to Negro sculpture by the artists of the cubistic era." The judgment, certainly, slighted the pioneer work of the Brooklyn Museum nearly fifteen years before—which was surprising

[8] *The Museum of Modern Art Bulletin*, Vol. XIII, Nos. 4–5 (March 1946).

because the comment appeared in the *Brooklyn Eagle.*

With important new collectors arising all over the country, the Museum of Modern Art for the second time in its history showed an American collection in its entirety. The first occasion, of course, had been the posthumous showing of the Bliss Bequest; the second was in the nature of a salute to an advance-guard collection started in the 1920's and still in the process of building. The collection of Mr. and Mrs. Sidney Janis [9] was built along historical lines; its keystone was the gigantic Rousseau canvas *The Dream*, completed in 1910, year of the artist's death. In 1954 *The Dream* would become part of the Museum's permanent collection as the gift of Nelson Rockefeller. It is a famous, important, and quietly sensational picture. In the middle of a nocturnal forest, Yadwigha lies nude on a sofa, staring with wide, somnambulist eyes prophetic of the surrealist Freudian imagery and the "dream sequences" of the movies that were still to come when Rousseau painted it.

But one single event of 1935–6 overshadowed all others. This was the Museum of Modern Art's monumental retrospective of the work of Vincent van Gogh, which traveled across the country. America had grown up to Van Gogh forty-five years after his tragic death. The New York attendance at this one show was 123,309, in contrast to 85,974 at the six preceding shows of that year.

Publicity reached such fantastic levels that when the exhibition reached the San Francisco Museum of Art the attendance there totaled 227,540. It was extraordinary. From as far as nine hundred miles away, trains marked "Van Gogh

[9] Janis served for twelve years on the Advisory Committee of the Museum of Modern Art.

Special" rolled into San Francisco loaded with pilgrims. Van Gogh was shown in ten cities, while forty more applied in vain. Then came two final added weeks in New York, during which 19,002 more people came. The final nation-wide attendance count was 886,631.

The public had been prepared for the Van Gogh show by Irving Stone's best-seller *Lust for Life,* which had been published two years earlier. This highly fictionalized and rather lurid biography had aroused great interest in the Dutch artist's life and work. The book helped to bring people to the show, but, once they were there, fiction was left behind as they looked at an art of tragic immediacy. Everyone felt its elegiac and momentous force. The *New York Times*'s "most vivid . . . projection of a personality that art has witnessed in our time" ranks as almost an understatement. It was no mere art show, even a very great one—it was a his-toric event with the most solemn overtones, something not altogether unlike a visual requiem mass for the memory of a great and tortured man.

There is not a Van Gogh to show every year. Neverthe-less, the Museum continued to make life interesting in 1936. There was Alfred Barr's "Cubism and Abstract Art," as well as "Prehistoric Rock Pictures in Europe and Africa," which Barr also arranged.

"Cubism and Abstract Art" was a masterpiece-studded survey that extended from painting and sculpture to construc-tions and remoter fields that had been touched by the two art movements: photography, architecture, industrial art, theater, films, posters, and typography. It did not, however, extend from Europe to America. This, Barr explained in a modest preface to the catalogue, was because in the preceding year "a large exhibition of Abstract Art in America was held at the Whitney Museum of American Art." In fact, there was a plan—already under way for four years—to correlate the activities of the three big Manhattan museums: the Whitney, the Modern, and the Metropolitan.

Barr put together the "Prehistoric Rock Pictures" exhibition from painted reproductions or facsimiles that he had recently seen in Germany. These had been made by artists who went along on the many cave expeditions of Professor Leo Frobenius, which had ranged all the way from Scandinavia down to the Cape of Good Hope. Barr's apologia for the show was in part as follows: "That an institution devoted to the most recent in art should concern itself with the most ancient may seem something of a paradox, but the art of the 20th Century has already come under the influence of the great tradition of prehistoric mural art which began around the 200th Century B.C."

No apology, actually, was needed. Robert J. Goldwater wrote in the *Magazine of Art*: "A Museum of Modern Art needs no pretext for the exhibiting of the works of art produced by the prehistoric peoples. The very discovery of these paintings and drawings and their study in the last sixty years is an outstanding example of that historical spirit by which modern art was at first so much affected."

The horizons of modern art, its sources, its influences, and its interests were by now becoming very wide indeed. By 1949 a book could be published in London called *40,000 Years of Modern Art*, a title that would not only sound logical but almost, in fact, like a retrospective view of the modern movement.

The show of cave paintings was not in the brownstone

house, but in the great modern cliff-dwellings called Rockefeller Center. The Museum of Modern Art had moved to
temporary quarters there for a very good reason: a modern
building was being built for it where the brownstone had
stood.

The pedestal was being readied.

12. *Termite, Time Capsule, and Pedestal*

In 1939 the Time Capsule lay fifty feet down in the mud of Flushing Meadows, launched on its sedentary "5000-Year Journey" into the future; a large and costly building was opened for the Museum of Modern Art; Hitler marched into Poland and then almost immediately sat down in front of the French Maginot Line; a host of famous modern artists was fleeing from Europe to the United States. These events are not listed in the order of their occurrence or necessarily in that of their importance. They are merely happenings in another chapter of the drama: Change against Permanence, or, Time against Man.

Poland was ancient in a sort of off-and-on way: once more it had been; now, once again, it was no more. The Maginot Line was "permanent, impregnable"—we would be finding out about that soon enough.

As for the Time Capsule, people crowded around the narrow open well to gawk down at the slim seven-and-one-half-foot copper alloy cartridge awaiting the day when the well would be sealed as the bugle blew "Taps." The contents were common knowledge: a woman's hat, a razor, cigarettes, a toothbrush and cosmetics, hybrid seeds, dictionaries, a microfilm packed with current lore. The magazine *Time* called it "a miniature museum." No one knew, however, whether Westinghouse Electric's "memento to the future" would ever be dug up. For time the termite worked in the mud around it; change was sealed in the capsule together with all those perishable souvenirs of a harried yet hopeful day.

The new Museum building, designed in the International Style by architects Philip L. Goodwin and Edward D. Stone, was publicly opened on May 10. That part of the tremendously valuable real estate fronting on 54th Street behind the building was set aside as a garden for eventual use as an open-air sculpture gallery and as a possible site for building expansion. Here, a mere decade after the founding of the Museum of Modern Art, was permanence behind a glass façade that spelled Today just as impressively as the Metropolitan's great stone pilasters spelled Yesterday.

And yet, if the Time Capsule was "a miniature museum," it was equally true that this Museum was a Time Capsule full of costly souvenirs. It was dedicated to change, for it was dedicated to "modern" art—and yet change, that darting chameleon, could not be caged. How permanent, even, might this great box of glass and stone prove to be on that strange isle of Manhattan, where buildings are grown and cut down like crops?

As always, anyway, there were some mightily impressive numbers. The Museum's total attendance for its first five years had been 851,219; for the succeeding five, 1,611,040. To look into the future, this figure in turn would mount during a succeeding decade (1944–54) to over 5,000,000. And yet figures can mean many things, as we all learned in school when we tried to multiply ten apples by fifteen cows. For at the New York World's Fair, dedicated to transience, the first five days' attendance would soar far above that of the Museum of Modern Art's first five years. Well, for that matter, America that year produced 25,000,000,000 pins.

The drive for permanence grew stronger every day. The permanent collections were growing in size, value, and importance. Within five more years Alfred Barr would be able to state quite truthfully: "The Museum's collection of modern sculpture is already the best in existence," [1] and its collection of modern painting would be only a step or two behind. As valuable as currency—yet what about the currency of events, the new movements and the new artists in America, the creative ferment that was sizzling all around? For all of the first plans or the unformulated hopes, the Museum of Modern Art had been patterned substantially along the lines of existing museums. At one end of the scale lay the old-time museum, at the other the newsreel. Did the true role of a new museum for new art lie, perhaps, somewhere between the two?

Even then a few people wondered about this, a little fearful that the big new building would actually become a pedestal of permanence. They feared that this new museum, so active, so promising, might climb up there for a nap and become one of those reclining figures which are so classic in art, partly because posing models become tired, partly, too, because artists become tired.

There was already a famous reclining figure on Fifth Avenue, with Cleopatra's Needle at her back like an alarm clock that would never go off again. Fame, wealth, prestige, authority—chisel marks in the marble—were we to have a new Metropolitan Museum on 53rd Street?

Meanwhile, art did not stand still. The vanguard of the army of change had made a beachhead; the main force was on its way. For the decade of the Depression, American artists had virtually ceased ambling off to Paris. Now Mecca itself was coming here.

It was an impressive list. Salvador Dali, erstwhile leading

[1] Alfred H. Barr, Jr.: *The Museum Collections: A Brief Report* (1944, unpublished).

surrealist, had arrived with his suitcase of dreams. Amédée Ozenfant, French purist, had come in 1938, and would soon set up an art school in New York. Sculptor Jacques Lipchitz and surrealist Kurt Seligmann landed a year later. By 1941, Max Ernst, André Masson, Yves Tanguy, Marc Chagall, and the poet André Breton having arrived, the surrealist hierarchy would be in session here.

In 1940 came great, grizzled Fernand Léger, one of the original masters from the time of cubism. Englishman Stanley Hayter landed, to set up here his Atelier 17, which for thirteen years had worked in Paris with artists like Picasso, Miro, and Ernst in developing new methods of print-making. From Paris came Matta (Roberto Matta Echaurren), Chilean surrealist, and from Germany, Ladislas Moholy-Nagy, symbolically bearing with him the famous Bauhaus—outlawed by Hitler— to set it up again near the shore of Lake Michigan in Chicago. Soon, too, we were permanently joined by three of the leaders of the International Style of architecture: Walter Gropius, Miës van der Rohe, and Marcel Breuer. Gropius, Bauhaus head ousted by Hitler, his similarly fated successor Van der Rohe, and Breuer found still other old colleagues already here: Lyonel Feininger, great American abstractionist who had lived in Germany fifty years, returning to his native land in 1937 in time to do two murals for the New York World's Fair; and abstractionist Josef Albers, who had been here since 1933 and was head of the Art Department of Black Mountain College. These six, plus others—notably typographer Herbert Bayer and photographer-designer Herbert Matter—began spreading the Bauhaus idea of *Gebrauchs-Kunst*, "Art for Use," thus reinforcing and enriching our native ideas of industrial art.

Another German modernist, Hans Hofmann, had settled here in 1932, setting up an influential painting school in Greenwich Village in 1934. All of the Central Europeans have stayed on: Gropius became head of Harvard University's Architecture Department; Breuer ended up in private practice; Moholy-Nagy died in 1946. Earlier still, of course, had come two artists to grow up with American painting and to become two of its leaders: Armenian Arshile Gorky and Dutch Willem de Kooning. Save for one more important name, the list is completed by that distinguished transatlantic traveler Marcel Duchamp, who came in 1942 to settle here for good and, in 1955, became an American citizen.

The one important name is important indeed: Piet Mondrian, Dutch *de Stijl* leader and greatest pioneer of geometrical abstract painting. It was in 1940 that Mondrian arrived in New York, where he painted a number of historic canvases. The vertical and horizontal elements of his primary-colored linear painting became broken and more complex as befitted multitudinous and bustling New York and the jazz and boogie-woogie that he came to love for their rhythmic vitality, tensions, and balances. Mondrian called his art neo-plasticism; through the "horizontal vertical division of the rectangle" he found, he said, "tranquillity, the balance of duality: individual and universal." Only four years later, at the age of seventy-two, Mondrian died in the plain 59th Street studio that, with its furniture built of orange crates, was as spare and as austere as the artist and his paintings.

But Mondrian left his mark here. The influence of this one painter of modest presence, but of passionate yet ordered intellect, is easy to trace. His presence lent strong support to younger American painters working in completely non-objective abstraction—that is to say, painting with no reference to natural appearances. Led by Harry Holtzman, these painters in 1935 had formed their own group, American Abstract Artists, and it was Holtzman who brought Mondrian to New York.

Holtzman had originally called together a small group of artists which included Gorky, Carl Holty, and Vaclav Vytlacil, all of whom were dissatisfied by the inadequate representation of the more abstract American work in the museums. The American Abstract Artists in the beginning were, like abstract painting itself, divided between partly representational and completely non-representational work, but almost immediately the group tended strongly toward the latter. Within a few years they were holding biennial shows at the Riverside Museum at 103rd Street and Riverside Drive. By this time they included so-called post-Mondrian painters like Burgoyne Diller, Fritz Glarner, and Holtzman himself, as well as cubist abstractionists like A. E. Gallatin, George L. K. Morris, and his wife, Suzie Frelinghuysen. Then Mondrian came and contributed his new work. The exhibits continue to the present day.

The surrealists' impact is popularly likely to be measured by the antics of Dali, who moved with reporters and photographers frothing in his wake. For a dozen years his bizarre and sensational actions were flooded by the light of publicity. His first one-man show in Paris in 1929 had set the tone of sensationalism. Here in America he planned a "Dream of Venus" sideshow for the amusement area of the New York World's Fair, but even before the Fair opened he had been briefly jailed for riding a bathtub out of a Fifth Avenue display window, through the plate glass, and on to the pedestrian-crowded sidewalk. To give Dali his due, he was somewhat justified in this weird adventure, which was an accident and not a prank.

All the newspapers agreed on the following facts: Bonwit Teller engaged Dali to design and install two window settings; they formed a pair and were called "Night" and "Day," or, alternately, "Sleep" and "Narcissus." The *New York Journal American* reported Dali's fee as $700. All agreed that the window called "Narcissus" was altered by Bonwit Teller soon after Dali completed it, and without so much as a by-your-leave. The *Daily Mirror* described "Narcissus" as Dali left it:

> There is an old-fashioned claw-footed bathtub, draped with a cover of black Persian lamb, and containing water. Emerging from the water are three wax hands, each hand holding a mirror.
>
> On the edge of the tub, Señor Dali placed an old-style figure of a red-haired woman, somewhat buxom, clad in a coque feather coat, gazing into the mirrors.

That was all. It sounds tame enough, but Dali, as everyone knows, can pack a world of macabre and—shall we say?—Freudian suggestiveness into a few rather ordinary objects and as many otherwise unobjectionable anatomical details. There was *something* about that window—just what, no one knew, but a certain number of window-shoppers took violent exception to whatever it was. As the *New York World Telegram* observed, "Bonwit Teller's maintains a staff of public demand interpreters. This staff, lurking by the windows, had clocked the opinion of the populace." So the management took out the 1900 wax figure with her Folies-Bergère build and substituted a streamlined model in a tailored suit. Just then Dali strolled by, saw the change, turned purple to the collar, and rushed inside, shouting incoherently in French and Spanish.

This account has Dali saying: "Michelangelo is traduced. Raphael is bespattered with grime. An act of contumely is perpetrated against the great Vermeer, against Pieter Breughel the Elder, against me."

His protests being spurned, Dali dashed into the show window and took action, "a young man in a fawn suit pulling with great agitation at the bathtub, splattering the water on the floor, dousing mirrors and walls. Suddenly he yanked at the tub. It tipped, toppled, and surged up. The young man teetered with the sudden motion and came crashing through the window.

"Two detectives, passing on a Fifth Avenue bus, saw it with horror. The young man was on the pavement, prone, and just above his head, like a guillotine blade, wavered a huge sheet of plate glass. It seemed to fan slowly out and then it crashed. The young man's neck was six inches from the blade-like edge."

The detectives asked no questions but hauled Dali off to the East 51st Street station. He was arraigned at night court on charges of malicious mischief preferred by Bonwit Teller. The dispute fizzled out with Dali's expressions of polite regret and the department store's reduction of the charges to disorderly conduct.

Disorderly conduct, the *Telegram* observed, "was a mere trifle for a Catalonian painter who remembers his father as a grasshopper, puts sides of beef in grand pianos, and decorates the pellucid brow of a beautiful woman with a maggot."

Americans paid considerable attention to Dali. There was

something about his painting, just as there had been about that ill-fated Bonwit Teller window. Even while laughing at the limp watches in the macabre flatlands of his famous painting *The Persistence of Memory*, we felt the slight, cold shudder of recognition. Already well under way was our great national trek to that recumbent throne of the guilty dream, the psychoanalyst's couch, and Freudian jargon was the fashionable thing.

As far as surrealism is concerned, Salvador Dali is rather a case to himself. For a little over ten years he was a surrealist painter of stature who combined an almost miraculous technique—worthy, indeed, of a Vermeer—with genuine surrealist vision. A Dali painting of this early period is a truthful simulacrum of the unseen, a glimpse into the drama of the unconscious and the landscape of dream. No one excelled his immaculately factual painting of the enigmatic symbols of this submerged world.

America decided that it would buy Dali. Almost overnight he was rich and famous. The inner torment that had made him great subsided. The change was not immediately apparent, however, because the technique became more brilliant and persuasive as the vision faded. The madness became wholly methodical; Dali became a fashionable portrait painter. In 1947 he made his last fling, participated in a sensational International Exposition of Surrealism in Paris, and then, renouncing "Freudian nightmares," confessed his sins and re-entered the Catholic Church. Now his large religious canvases are being hung in the Metropolitan.

Although surrealism is based on Freud, its best pictures are as haunted as a medium's trance, and mystic painters, like spiritualist mediums, sometimes lose their "powers." Through their leader, poet André Breton, the surrealists at one early stage employed hypnosis to release their creative powers through the channel of "automatism." Sustaining these powers is often another matter, as is evidenced by the case of Giorgio di Chirico. The pictures Chirico painted from 1913 to 1919 made him the precursor and patron saint of surrealism. Then suddenly he lapsed into the bored mediocrity of technical competence. At the same time, as he saw his early pictures becoming more and more valuable, he tried the role of imitator of his own mastery. But the old magic touch was gone. With all his competence, he could no longer match the twilight colors into which he had once mixed his own lonely sadness. There are, sometimes, unknown colors not born of chemistry on an artist's palette.

Despite Dali's defection, the coming of the surrealists was important to American painting. Although no strong native surrealist school came out of it, and although social intercourse was limited, the effect of this distinguished visitation was profound. The mere presence here of the whole hierarchy of a new "ism" was impressive; many of these men, so arrogantly assured and so acclaimed, exerted a strong personal influence on our younger men. They were assuredly the most rugged of rugged individualists, triumphantly disdainful of custom and social cliché, and theirs was the strong odor of revolt. The American artist, reborn with the WPA, had a lesson in the uses of freedom. Now a member of society, he learned how to stay free of the meshes of mediocrity and the coils of conformity.

The men of the new generation were eager students. When the surrealists came, Jackson Pollock and William Baziotes were twenty-seven years old; Robert Motherwell was twenty-four. And in the same generation, though older, one must include Willem de Kooning and Arshile Gorky, both thirty-five, as well as Mark Rothko and Adolph Gottlieb, one year older. These were the men most strongly influenced by the surrealist spirit that seems in retrospect so much a part of that unsettled time. Motherwell, in particular, has stated how strongly they all felt it.

Remarkable in retrospect, too, is the scant attention paid to it all by the Museum of Modern Art. It is true, as Peggy Guggenheim (later married to Max Ernst) writes, that the Museum assisted Ernst in getting through Ellis Island.[2] As a German—even though a survivor of the Hitlerian concentration camps—Ernst was in serious difficulties with the immigration officials. Even so, according to her, it was the presence of Max's son Jimmy, then a Museum employee "of a menial order," which saved the day for his father.

The attention of the Museum of Modern Art was elsewhere. It was busy picking up the marbles. Through purchase and through gifts, the rarities poured in. From Stephen Clark came Lehmbruck's *Standing Woman* and the historic Brancusi *Bird in Space*. Mrs. Rockefeller's gifts were many. They had begun in 1930 and they continued at frequent intervals up to her death in 1948, a series following, as *Vogue* observes, "her amiable custom of keeping pictures for a few years and then giving them to the Museum."[3]

Among other important donors was Mrs. Simon Guggenheim, from whom the Picasso *Girl before the Mirror* came in 1938 and the Henri Rousseau *Sleeping Gypsy* a year later.

[2] Peggy Guggenheim: *Out of This Century* (New York, 1946).
[3] "The Big Gamble," *Vogue*, November 1, 1954.

The beautiful Rousseau canvas had disappeared right after the 1897 Salon des Indépendants in Paris. Rediscovered in 1917, it was bought by John Quinn and, as *Vogue* relates, "when he died in 1925, he had the painting in front of him."

Without doubt, however, the most important single acquisition in this period was Picasso's *Les Demoiselles d'Avignon*, eight feet high, which Alfred Barr accurately calls the first cubist canvas ever painted.[4] A remarkable history, that of the *Demoiselles*: executed in 1907, the big picture was never publicly shown until the 1937 Paris Exposition, though for several years, from 1907 on, painters had seen its faceted planes and masked faces derived from West African Negro sculpture while it leaned against a wall in Picasso's studio. Barr calls its women—who "loom like giantesses"—"forbidding, formidable, even frightening." *Vogue*, concerned with its little starved clotheshorses, describes these cubist apparitions as "five of the least seductive females in history," but they seduced a generation of painters. Picasso never gave this masterpiece a title. Years ago an appalled but worldly-wise observer grimly remarked that they looked for all the world like the girls in a certain brothel on Avignon Street in Barcelona. Picasso was well satisfied. He had been born near Barcelona.

Lillie Bliss posthumously gave the *Demoiselles* to the museum she had helped to found. To meet the price, a Degas canvas from her bequest was traded in as part payment. A. Conger Goodyear tells of Barr's excited urgency as he broke the news to the Trustees that the great painting could

---

[4] ". . . the *Demoiselles* has justly been called the first cubist picture . . ."— Alfred H. Barr, Jr.: *Matisse: His Art and His Public* (New York, 1951).

be had. It had just been unpacked at the New York branch of Seligman et Cie. Cornelius J. Sullivan wanted to see it forthwith.

It happened that the great Seligman had a more obscure neighbor, Arnold Seligman, Rey, antiquarians by trade. In his excitement, it was into the shop of the latter that Sullivan dashed, to be met ceremoniously by a frock-coated attendant.

Cheeks red and eyes glowing, Sullivan came right to the point: "Show me the *Demoiselles!*"

The frock coat recoiled a pace, and, shocked but still deferential, said: "Surely the gentleman has come to the wrong place."

As collecting and cataloguing took more and more time, the Museum of Modern Art increasingly concentrated on "survey" shows emphasizing past history. As early as 1933 there had been "American Sources of Modern Art"; in 1935, "20 Centuries of Mexican Art" (in which the Mexican government collaborated); and, a year later, "Indian Art of the United States," in which for possibly the first time in history the Navajos created their fantastic ceremonial sand paintings in public view.[5] The survey shows have continued ever since. For example, "Arts of the South Seas" went on view in 1946. The dramatic installations were frequently designed by René d'Harnoncourt, at present Director of the Museum. D'Harnoncourt climaxed his achievements along this line in 1954 with the exhibit "Ancient Arts of the Andes." The Andean show was rich with Inca sculptures, slotted tapestries, and feather work, and glittered with objects of the virgin gold

---

[5] This show was arranged with the co-operation of the U.S. Department of the Interior.

that had tempted Pizarro and cost the Incas their empire.

The survey show is like a gigantic steam shovel. Sooner or later—generally later—everything that happened in art gets scooped up. At its best, the survey temptingly combines scholarship with eye-filling displays of treasure. Management, on the one hand, takes no chances; the audience, on the other, has only to skim the pages of authority and come away feeling learned and artistic. It is a glorified Chautauqua. The Museum of Modern Art has shown skill in managing the survey show, which can so easily degenerate into a circus or a bazaar. At least once, however, the ground floor of the Museum has looked for all the world like a department store. This was in 1955 in the show "Art of India"—not arranged by D'Harnoncourt—with its core of valid art that had been touched off by the Alexandrian invasion all but concealed amid silken textiles hung and draped with the window-trimmer's dexterous and decorative eye.

And there was one crackerjack of a show which the Museum's critics in one breath denounced as a circus. This was the last show of 1936, in which the Museum of Modern Art finally got around to ten-year-old surrealism. It scooped up the already venerable "ism" in a grand shovelful: "Fantastic Art, Dada and Surrealism." It was a fine show, a real shocker.

But it was late. Five years earlier the little Wadsworth Atheneum in Hartford, under the direction of A. Everett Austin, Jr., had become the first museum in the world to show surrealism. This was the sort of pioneering for which the Museum of Modern Art presumably had been founded, and yet in 1931, after two years of operation, and with funds and foreign connections the Wadsworth never dreamed of, the Museum of Modern Art gave this important new art movement not even a nod.

Three years later Austin again presented surrealism, this time as an opera: *Four Saints in Three Acts*, a collaboration of librettist Gertrude Stein, composer Virgil Thomson, scenic and costume designer Florine Stettheimer, and an all-Negro cast who looked like Spanish Colonial saints in their brocaded vestments while they sang Gertrude's delightfully sibylline syllables. Gertrude was a genuine proto-surrealist, as she was the first to write whole pieces in what is now called stream-of-consciousness style. To everyone's surprise, *Four Saints* was an instant success and had a Broadway run.

Meanwhile Julien Levy's little midtown gallery carried on the pioneering for surrealism. Levy had helped Austin with the Wadsworth Atheneum exhibit of 1931, the first year of his own gallery. Levy introduced Max Ernst to New Yorkers and discovered Joseph Cornell, perhaps the most authentic American surrealist, one by grace of instinct—for when Levy first met him, Cornell knew nothing of the movement. He is not a painter, but a builder of objects: magic windowed boxes filled with strange, memoried things—old photographs, theater tickets, sea shells, fragments of jewelry and colored sand, and other things less explicit, more muted.

Julien Levy introduced Dali, Tanguy, and the sculptor Giacometti; showed films like *The Andalusian Dog* (*Le Chien Andalou*), by Luis Buñuel and Salvador Dali; and found time to write the first book on surrealism to be published in this country.[6] *Le Chien Andalou* opened with the shocking sequence of a human eyeball being slit by a knife, an optical deflowering

[6] Julien Levy: *Surrealism*, published in 1936 by the Black Sun Press.

at which even Freud might have shuddered.

Then the Museum of Modern Art caught up with events and put on its shocker. Barr scheduled "Fantastic Art, Dada and Surrealism" over the protests of some of the Trustees. The seven-year-old Museum, having got around to it, really kicked up its heels. The newspapers burst into a rash of head-lines: FAREWELL TO ART'S GREATNESS and MUSEUM OF MODERN ART RESEMBLES PENNY ARCADE.

The controversial exhibition was a historical résumé of the strange, the outré, and the ridiculous in art from Leonardo da Vinci and Archimboldo to Salvador Dali and Walt Disney, the latter represented by the *Wolf-Pacifier Machine* from the cartoon film *The Three Little Pigs*. It was an unknown and modest entry, however, that knocked everyone for a loop almost as Marcel Duchamp's *Nude Descending a Staircase* had done at the Armory Show. This was a bewildering little object of the highest integrity of workmanship, it being exactly what it was represented to be: a real cup, a real saucer, and a real spoon, all completely covered with real fur. Swiss surrealist Meret Oppenheim's *Fur-lined Teacup*,[7] as it came to be called, unhinged people who just looked at it. They walked away talking audibly to themselves. Overnight the fur-lined teacup was an American legend and a part of our slang. We spoke of fur-lined eggbeaters, fur-lined false teeth, fur-lined Cadillacs; fur-lined medals were being awarded right and left.

Goodyear quoted a critic's description of the reaction of a "solid, substantial" banker to another of the objects, an enormous mask "ornamented with a strange miscellany of household utensils, including a mousetrap, bits of wire, hair

---

[7] Correct title of this object, now owned by the Museum of Modern Art, is *Le déjeuner en fourrure.*

brushes, etc." The banker's first reaction was one of "awe-struck astonishment." Then, turning to his wife, he said un-smilingly: "Never throw anything away." [8]

Many of the 694 items in "Fantastic Art, Dada and Sur-realism" came from abroad, and yet not one, as Goodyear notes in astonishment, caused trouble with the customs officials from the fur-lined teacup to Max Ernst's touched-up botanical chart crisply entitled: *The gramineous bicycle garnished with bells the pilfered greybeards and the echinoderms bending the spine to look for caresses.*

Perhaps the authorities had given up. Only a few months earlier they had acidly compared a futurist bronze by Boc-cioni to a "wrecked Buick fender." In a historic case ten years before, the customs men had taken one look at Bran-cusi's polished, propeller-like *Bird in Space* and had yelped: "It ain't art." Into the courts came Picabia and Jacob Epstein to say firmly: "It is, too, art." The court decided for the *Bird*, even though it had no feet nor feathers nor yet "any re-semblance to a bird without the exercise of a rather vivid imagination." So the *Bird*, which *Vogue* once called a "whoosh of metal," ended up in the Museum of Modern Art.

In such cases, the intellectual shrugs and says: "American officials!" But not so Stuart Davis. They are all brothers, he says, under their various uniforms. When Davis sailed in 1928 for his first visit to Paris, he took along two of his own ab-stractions. At the *douane* a big hassle began, Davis speaking no French but intercepting dark glances and words like "Ruhr" and "Maginot."

"It dawned on me," Davis said later, "that these palookas

[8] A. Conger Goodyear: *The Museum of Modern Art: The First Ten Years* (New York, 1943).

did not even know that these were paintings—thought that they were maps of strategic areas and fortifications."

Finally the chief inspector was summoned. He was polite, spoke English: "What are these things?"

"Paintings, for Chrissake. Cubist paintings."

"Ah, *cubisme!*" said the inspector with relief. "But of course," and immediately released them.

The delayed timing that had been evident in the Museum of Modern Art's belated showing of surrealism in 1936 became glaring ten years later with its show "11 Europeans in America." An exhibition intended, no doubt, to be current had all the aspects of a retrospective, for by that time most of the visiting artists were already home or else preparing to leave. It was a backward look at what might have been: all the exciting shows of an art temporarily transplanted to the New World, the invaluable personal contacts, the round tables of discussion.

The Museum may very well answer that its concern is with art and not with artists. That it is property-minded is obvious. It seems much more at ease with paintings than with painters. It is understandable that painters can bring most difficult pressures to bear. Perhaps the Museum seeks to avoid these. Yet the dealers who for many years have done most of the pioneering work meet these pressures every day.

The Museum of Modern Art, after its first brilliant years, began to show a slight uncertainty, if not uneasiness, as to its real role. By 1936, only seven years after its founding, it was already apparent that it was winning its first big, dynamic battle, that of gaining public acceptance of modern art. The tact and force with which it accomplished this cannot be overestimated. But after this victory, what then? To win the public, the Museum had had to invest itself with authority. Should it now be risked on new bets, or should the Museum take its winnings and quit the table? To go on meant becoming a kind of museum which had never before existed. Who even knew what that was? You could find out only by risking your stake. Or you could become a museum in the old sense, investing your funds of prestige in the proved stocks and bonds of the already acceptable. One thing was certain: art would not stand still for the Museum of Modern Art or any other museum. It would go right on spawning isms. As the older kids moved into the museums, there would be new brats about. They would brawl in the streets until you could hardly sit quiet to study.

The Museum of Modern Art got worried. It hired an art professor, Artemas Packard of Dartmouth College, to answer the question: where do we go from here? The professor ground away for several years and then, as the Museum prepared to move into its new permanent building, he rendered a report of 138 typewritten pages. The report has never been made public, and even within the Museum its contents are labeled "confidential." When questioned about the Packard Report, Museum officials answer in effect: "Ask the man who owns one."

Professor Packard pointed out that the Museum of Modern Art, though "patterned in most respects on . . . the older museums," needed "to carry the concept of the public museum beyond that which now generally obtains," adding that "the only guarantee of life and health for an institution such as this lies in its perpetual hospitality to new interests as they arise."

Packard attacked the fallacy of the "static" museum:

Braque-Picasso show at Stieglitz's "291" in 1915.

*Surrealist gallery of Peggy Guggenheim's "Art of This Century,"
New York, 1942. Frederick J. Kiesler, architect.*

International Surrealist Exhibition in the ballroom of the Whitelaw Reid mansion, Madison Avenue, New York, October 14 to November 7, 1942, seen through Marcel Duchamp's mile of string.

The Dada Exhibition at the Sidney Janis Gallery, New York, 1953. Show installed by Marcel Duchamp.

"the . . . conviction that art can be made to survive in a commercial civilization only by isolating it from all other interests." He observed that "the arts have flourished most conspicuously in prosperous commercial societies, such as those at Athens, the communes of the thirteenth and fourteenth centuries, Florence, Venice, the trading cities of Germany, the England of Elizabeth, the Dutch Republic."

Packard then outlined some of the activities proper to a "dynamic" museum. "The museum," he wrote, "becomes less important as a safety deposit vault for the preservation and classification of art objects and more important as an agency for stimulating new creative effort." The dynamic museum should stimulate "confidence in American creative capacity" and spread "throughout the country . . . respect for our own creative capacities."

The Museum of Modern Art, said Packard in effect, must stay in the game. He then defined "timeliness," not as "mere accidents of chronology which provide convenient excuses for anniversary or memorial exhibitions . . . however great their academic appeal" (remarkable words for a professor), but as "current interests and needs."

He advised the Museum to set about placing some new bets. Of art films, he said: "The opportunity for pioneering in this field is very great indeed" and pointed to the Museum's own claim that "as a direct result of the Museum's Film Library cinema projectors have been installed in classrooms in a great many schools and colleges." You are the ones to make art films, he said. Of radio, Packard observed that "it would seem reasonable to expect a Museum of Modern Art to go somewhat further than other museums in helping to develop this important medium of education."

Packard's conclusion was that, "since the radio and the cinema are the vehicles which, more than any others, secure the attention of the masses, it is extremely important that educational programs devised for these vehicles should be deliberately cued to the largest possible popular appeal. The Museum of Modern Art is in a very favorable position to take the lead in this sort of enterprise." Then he added: "The world will naturally look to the Museum of Modern Art for developments in this direction."

Packard's language was the professorial equivalent of the football coach's between-the-halves remarks to players who read their clippings. "Get out there now and hold that lead," he was saying. And none of this standoffishness. He called attention to the Museum of Modern Art's "responsibility for wise guidance and encouragement to the living artists" as "one of the greatest opportunities for usefulness that any museum has ever had." And against the need for authority he placed equally "the need for substantial recognition of contemporary talent."

Well, the Museum of Modern Art never made an art film. It never put on a series of radio programs. It worked itself into an ideal position so that, when television came along, it would have to do just as little as possible. But from time to time it betrays an uneasy consciousness of sins of omission. Midway in the lively and historic decade (1943–53) when American abstract expressionism was fighting its way with scarcely a peep of encouragement from 53rd Street, James Thrall Soby as spokesman made a statement of purpose: "The Museum," he wrote, "is an educational institution: it is one by charter and in conscious purpose. Consequently, in whatever it does . . . it feels itself responsible to the public and only indirectly to artists." [9] Then, as if answering an unspoken criticism, Soby added that the Museum had helped the artists indirectly far more than it could ever have helped them by direct subsidy. Ever since the WPA, "direct subsidy" have been fighting words to the artists.

And yet in 1940 the Museum had had the Mexican painter José Clemente Orozco busy on the premises painting a mural to order while the public watched. Orozco, indeed! If it *had* to be imported, Léger was here. But why not American? Max Weber, for example: instead of Orozco's murderous steel tank and dive bomber draped with a corpse, why not Weber's living figures, monumental yet warm? And three of our men had just proved at the New York World's Fair that they were muralists of real stature. Gorky had decorated the Aviation Building. Lyonel Feininger, whose international fame was surely beyond question, had flung one phenomenal painting clear across the 120 feet of a Marine Transportation Building wall. Not to be outdone by Gorky and Feininger, Stuart Davis had created a panel 45 feet high by 132 feet long for the Hall of Communications. The World's Fair murals have disappeared with most of the exposition art. Orozco's mural, however, is safe somewhere in the Museum basement.

Anyway, the Museum of Modern Art, through Soby, had had its say: the painting is more important than the painter. Start the Bible of art with Exodus.

The Soby statement was made in 1947. By that time most of the foreign artists who had sought haven here during the war were back in Paris. They had found the melting-pot a little cold for comfort, life in Manhattan too formal and too difficult.

[9] *Museum of Modern Art Bulletin*, Vol. XIV, No. 2 (February 1947).

"It was hard to see one another in New York," said Max Ernst. "Café life was lacking. . . . Here you would have to 'phone and make an appointment in advance. . . . There is more loneliness—more isolation among artists than in France.

"However," Ernst concluded, "this situation cannot be changed."

Ernst was wrong. Even as he spoke, the situation had already been changed, and by the Americans themselves, a new generation of young modern artists. On that tiny distracted island of Manhattan, staggering under its fantastic payload of people, they had found the will to make a new Bohemia and a little space to crowd it into.

A string of firecrackers: these were the isms exploding for the first fifteen years of modern art. Fauvism—before the red paper fragments could settle to the ground, it was over and done with. Then two bangs almost together—cubism and futurism—and the whole string began to go. Orphism and synchromism, vorticism, expressionism, rayonism, constructivism, and suprematism. Ism, ism, ism—the very suffix became a separate word, a symbol and a standard joke of the time.

Was it new? Was it nutty? Then put it down as just another ism by those wild young artists. Do you call that a picture? My four-year-old could paint better than that!

While we watched the artists, some giant crackers—the foot-long, dollar kind—were letting go: anarchism and nihilism. Then the bugles blew. It was our First World War, and we touched off our own firecrackers: patriotism and nationalism. Fought the war through and found our own little string going off: communism, fascism, national socialism —and isolationism.

Then there was Dadaism, and the artists were laughing at us. And we're off again: neo-classicism and neo-plasticism, non-objectivism, purism and immaculatism, surrealism and magic realism. Our private joke of common sense had long since worn thin. We grew uneasy; there was just too much noise. The kids' firecrackers began to seem more like sticks of dynamite in the foundations. Anyway, the house was undoubtedly falling apart, beginning with the cornerstones: Love, Marriage, Home, and Peace. The props that were offered to take their places seemed pretty flimsy: for Love a two-by-four called Biological Urge, and for Marriage a dry stick called Divorce. The corner called Home kept collapsing, and each successive prop grew thinner: the Bungalow, the Duplex, the Motor Court, and, finally, the Trailer. Peace had been a marble block inscribed "1918." We shored up that corner with the Kellogg Declaration, then with Universal Disarmament, then forgot about it. So it caved in completely. Then we boarded it up with a shaky fence called the Cold War.

Inside the house, things were even worse. What had gone wrong with Matter—you know, iron, wood, solid stuff like that? The antique table that had been Dr. Samuel Johnson's was falling apart. Or worse: the cabinetmakers looked at it and said: "It isn't even there. It is merely a void filled with electrical charges," and sent in their bill. In the living-room, which we used to call Mind—so comfortably decorated once by Kant & Descartes—the floor was nearly gone. People kept falling through into a wet, dark cellar called the Unconscious Mind.

What a nightmare until we woke up and rubbed our eyes! We—the human race—had had a moving-day, had moved from one Period House to another. In the old days you could take one hundred thousand years to move from Stone Age to Bronze Age. But now it gets faster and faster. That's the Atomic Age. Reach the speed of sound and you begin critically eying the speed of light. Miss tomorrow morning's paper and you may be living an age behind the rest of the people.

So we awake from the nightmare and begin looking around us, using that New Vision which was formerly the exclusive faculty of the artists and the scientists. We admire the new machines and begin buying them on the installment plan. We talk about fission and space satellites.

Finally we got around to looking at art—all those awful isms. So we looked at the Fauves. That insanity of paint now seemed gay—in fact, actually lyrical. And cubism, that ultimate pre-war madness, was now a sober brown refuge of contemplative thought. How they have changed! But wait a minute: "Paintings do not change, people change."

"When does an ism become a wasm?" The old vaudeville gag line is still a neat question.[1] Let us take Fauvism. It exploded at the *salon d'automne* in 1905. By 1907 it had disappeared from the scene; Matisse, Derain, and the others had gone on to newer things. But let us look on both sides: before Fauvism and after Fauvism.

Looking earlier, we find Fauvism's writhing lines in Toulouse-Lautrec and the Art Nouveau, its strangely shaped masses in Gauguin, its violent brushwork in Van Gogh, its prismatic color in impressionism, and, through all its violence, strangely conveyed, the quietude of Cézanne. Or, we can go back to 1892 and a little Vuilliard canvas called *Au divan japonais*, take it out of its context, and say: "A Fauve!"

After Fauvism in Paris? It went to Germany about 1908; Germanicized, it became the early expressionism of Kandinsky, Marc, and Jawlensky. Then it went permanently into the vocabulary of a new language, appearing here in one man's

---

[1] Sample dialogue, vintage 1914: Two straw-hatted song-and-dance men enter. One is limping and has a black eye.

BOB: Where did you get that shiner?

DICK: I decided to be an artist. I took up futurism.

BOB: Oh, you took up futurism, eh?

DICK: Yes, I painted a futuristic portrait of my wife.

BOB: How did she like it?

DICK: Well, let me tell you there's no future in that stuff. (Points to his black eye.) Futur*ism* is a futur*wasm*.

(Orchestra seguays into "That Futuristic Rag" and the team goes into an eccentric tap dance.)

color, there in another man's line or another's form. It grew
less explicit, more abstract. Forty years after that historic
salon d'automne, and nearing mid-century, Fauvism, in the
expressionist guise that it had assumed in Germany, would
explode all over again as one of the many detonant elements
in a completely new international style, American abstract
expressionism.

That is the history and pre-history of the first and presumably one of the most short-lived of the modern isms. It is
like a laboratory demonstration of the law of the conservation
of energy: *no energy is ever lost*. Or, put another way: *nothing
ever comes out of nothing*.

"Ism," the word, is almost a synonym for "search." Each
of the important ones has been a search for reality by the
adoption of a new point of view. This may sound strange
when we consider the purple trees of the Fauves, the exploded
planes of the cubists, the bare horizontal and vertical lines
of the neo-plasticists. A chorus of voices will ask: "And just
what does all this have to do with reality?"

Well, the artists say, seeing is not necessarily believing,
and believing is not necessarily seeing. There is that table
which Sam Johnson pounded on to refute (so he thought)
Bishop Berkeley's denial that matter, as such, existed. Everyone knows what a table looks like—a drawing of any table
will do as well as a drawing of Dr. Johnson's original one.
But any table looks like a table only because a bunch of
atoms have decided to stay together. So what about *that*
reality? How do you draw a realistic picture of an atom, a
thing that the eye has never seen? You don't. You *express* it
with that ominous little hieroglyph of three slim interlaced
ovals which every schoolboy recognizes today; he recognizes

it and doesn't even care that the atom symbol is abstract art.

Artists are frank about it: they are more than a little bored with all the hue and cry about "abstract" art. The most realistic painting, they point out, is abstract in one sense: it is certainly not the thing depicted, but only a set of painted symbols for elements abstracted (drawn) from the original. Then they turn it around: even Mondrian's most non-objective canvas is not abstract, for each of its elements is completely real in and of itself, and it was with these elements and these only that Mondrian was working. Patient Mondrian himself once referred to the "new realism" of his paintings. Artists like to quote Guillaume Apollinaire on the subject. Many years ago Apollinaire rebuked a critic of the "abstractness" of Picabia's paintings. "This is not a case of abstraction," he said. "Would one say that the flavor of a peach was an abstraction?"

Artists are more than bored, they are openly impatient with all the talk that they do not "communicate." Recently even a Director of the Metropolitan Museum described modern art as a "form of private communication . . . divorced from the area of common human experience," adding that it was humiliating and patronizing.

Artists all but frothed at the mouth when they heard this dictum. "We are not loudspeakers," they said, "and our pictures are not singing commercials. We have something to say. Let people take the trouble to learn our language. The ones who will study a foreign language, or a special one like mathematics, are the very ones who expect a painting to sing them to sleep."

Nevertheless, there are two sides to the matter. Abstraction *is* confusing, and, worse still, there are two kinds of abstraction. One starts with nature and consists of making the subject more and more unrecognizable. The other, properly called non-objectivism, does not start with real objects at all. Non-objective pictures are simply creations of line, form, and color. It makes a difference to know this in advance.

Fauvism, really, was simple enough, though shocking. Its landscapes were quite recognizable, though color used purely as color led to such things as shocking-pink skies and blue trees. The trouble began with cubism: all natural color was bleached out into browns, grays, and luminous brown-blacks, and the thing being portrayed exploded into a thousand pieces. If the idea of the jigsaw puzzle did not come from cubism, it might well have done so. It was like looking at something through a crystal so that all the surfaces became flat planes displaced in space. Then Picasso introduced the "circulating viewpoint." He simply wanted to see an object from all sides simultaneously and thus better express its real nature. No more unreasonable, actually, than the mechanical draftsman's superimposing of plan, elevation, and cross-section in one working drawing, but vastly confusing to picture-lovers. It was somewhat as if a camera, fitted with a crystal-shaped lens, and with its shutter open, had moved around a subject, recording what it saw in overlapping multiple exposures on one negative—and then the result had been printed in sepia. Unrecognizable as the picture might be, Picasso knew where it had all started, and labeled the end result *Violin* or *Guitar*. With that signpost you *could* decipher it and have a lot of fun doing it, provided you were not too angry. And after the fun, inevitably, would come the profound thrill of genuine esthetic experience, because Pablo Picasso, first and last, is an artist.

But things happened a little too fast. Right then Kandinsky came along to paint some completely abstract paintings, the series of *Improvisations* which began in 1911. After several years of expressionist landscapes, he suddenly began painting pictures about nothing at all except the way he felt. Like improvised music, these paintings grew spontaneously in free, swirling lines and rhythmic, emotional masses of color. Kandinsky, too, was an artist. These paintings can thrill us today by their own intrinsic poetry. But in 1911 people had nervous breakdowns trying to find cows and trees in them.

Then, about 1915, Kandinsky began to plan these abstract, non-representational canvases in advance, incorporating geometrical elements with the free forms and lines from which the *Improvisations* had spontaneously evolved. This phase went on for a few years and then Kandinsky's painting became complete geometric non-objectivism.

Thus, German expressionism—at least in the work of its leader—is perhaps unique in having successively embraced the polarities of modern art: initial reference to natural appearances and complete rejection of them in the two different accepted ways—the intuitional or poetic and the geometric or scientific.

The parallels between science and art, though often pointed out, are still remarkable in view of the fact that the methods of artist and scientist are so diametrically opposite. Although art seems at times to presage science, and perhaps does so, the artist generally follows the scientist or (sometimes) works simultaneously on the same problem, converting factual data into esthetic experience and formulas into poetry. The parallels, indeed, go back to the beginnings of modern science. Some of the Renaissance artists were scientists, too. And by the 1820's the English landscapist Turner very nearly reached complete abstraction when caught up by Goethe's theories of light, first propounded in the 1790's. The French impressionists went on from Turner, strongly influenced by the discoveries of the German physicist Helmholtz and the theories of complementary colors advanced by Chevreul.

The cubists, following Cézanne, avowedly broke up the forms of material things along the principles of solid geometry. However, following the practices of descriptive geometry, they discarded the deep space that solid geometry implies, overlapping their different views on the flat two-dimensional picture plane of the canvas.

The cubists made no point of the question of light. Perhaps, in their choice of monochromatic color, they felt that they had discarded light as they had discarded deep space. Yet the cubist pictures are strangely alive with light, diffused and seemingly sourceless. It came from the electric light, still a novelty in France when cubism began. In the cafés where the cubists met, bare bulbs were just being hung. From their multiple positions came the uncertain source and the diffusion and, as can readily be demonstrated, complex, overlapping shadows that look like passages from a cubist painting. Artists are as sensitive to appearances as musicians are to sounds. Then came the act, no doubt unconscious, of poetic transposition. In a cubist picture by Picasso or Braque, solid volumes become airy shadows, crossing and interpenetrating penumbra in a mysterious void of light.

Here, too, was a physical beginning as actual as the still life of guitar and wine bottle. Such a beginning cannot be traced in the *Improvisations* of Kandinsky. There one must look inside the man for the beginnings. For a while Kandinsky simply let his subconscious mind do the work. He did so with no knowledge of the fact that Sigmund Freud was busy charting that unknown organ. In any event, the light that Freud was about to shed on man himself would soon be obsessing artists.

By 1922 Dada had reached its own dead end. It had attacked the vanities of reason and logic, undermined permanence, derailed progress, and dynamited dignity. It had embraced the irrational as the true. It was the Critique of Pure Un-reason. It had nothing left to do.

Freud, with Adler and Jung at either hand, was the evangelist of the unconscious, the explorer of man's submerged half. Like the madmen in *The Cabinet of Dr. Caligari* who take over and run the asylum, the Dadaists hailed the new psychology with cries of joy. Everyone was irrational—had they not been saying that for years? They conferred, wrote a manifesto—and, in 1924, surrealism was born.

The movement swarmed with poets: leader André Breton, Paul Éluard and Tristan Tzara, Louis Aragon and René Crevel. The great German Dada painter, Max Ernst, was in at the beginning; soon others joined: Joan Miro, Salvador Dali, André Masson, Man Ray, Yves Tanguy.

Surrealism, the surrealists decided, had always existed. So they voted honorary memberships to Hieronymus Bosch, Archimboldo, Uccello, and Henri Rousseau. They claimed Picasso, Duchamp, Picabia, and Chirico as their own. Posthumous literary memberships went down a long list from Coleridge to Edgar Allan Poe, through Rimbaud and Baudelaire to the Comte de Lautréamont (Isidore Ducasse). Modern psychology not having invented the phenomena it describes, the surrealists staked their claims at will among the past denizens of that ancient "misty mid-region of Weir," as Poe had called the land of Psyche, where wisdom and madness meet.

When surrealism came onstage the after-war letdown was past. Even Picasso had evidenced the general disillusion or uncertainty by a return to non-cubist representational work called neo-classicism, which began in 1918 and lasted for several years. Art reactionaries in both France and America hailed his backsliding and triumphantly announced that abstract art was through. But in 1921 the mercurial Spaniard had foiled them again by launching into a period of incredibly heaped-up and distorted still-lifes that are rather vaguely called synthetic cubism.

Meanwhile, two parallel movements had sprung up in France and America, called, respectively, purism and precisionism. In France the leading purists were Amédée Ozenfant and Jeanneret, the latter the architect internationally known as Le Corbusier. Both movements stressed pure or "clean" painting—the Americans were also called The Immaculates—and the incorporation of machine and architectural forms into abstract design.

Precisionism was our big native art movement of the 1920's, and purism made something of a splash in Paris. Both movements, however, were a little obvious and mundane, and over them towered the giant figure of Fernand Léger, who used machine forms with poetry and authority. The scene was obviously ready for a new idea and new personalities.

The surrealists had an idea. There was no question that they were personalities. Their idea was to use as subject matter the symbolism and the imagery of dreams and daydreams, the stuff of the unconscious. True, a mystic or two had done this in every generation. But the surrealists were in partnership with the mighty Freud; they would collect the material and systematize its use. Their strategy for releasing the hidden springs of creative inspiration somewhat paralleled the functioning of deep analysis. But each surrealist, so to speak, was his own analyst. Each morning he jotted down all that he could remember of his dreams, not to cart them to the couch in exchange for normality—heaven forbid!—but to use them in still-lifes and landscapes that are unquestionably among the weirdest that the world has ever seen. He practiced going into semi-trances, working arduously to perfect the technique known as automatism.

The surrealists worked at it with passion and devotion; they practiced even when they played at games. For them, surrealism was a way of life. In a little while it got so that you could recognize surrealist women or surrealist men partly by the way they dressed, partly by their actions, but mostly by the faint swamp atmosphere that clung to them.

Someone would start a story on a long roll of paper, then fold out of sight all that he had written except the last line. The next player went on from there, adding any strange events or wild imaginings that occurred to him. Then he, too, would fold out of sight all except the last line and hand the manuscript to the next in turn. Around the room it would go until the last player had written the last line. Then it would be unfolded, and Breton would read it aloud with dramatic inflection. The writers were diverse and genuinely gifted; the results generally were extraordinarily evocative of the quick, shifting scenes and moods of a dream.

The painters had a similar game that they rather daintily called "Exquisite Corpse" (*Cadavre exquis*). At its conclusion the folded paper was smoothed out and everyone had a good shudder—or, perhaps, a good laugh, because a lot of Dada was left in surrealism. Some of these composite "corpses" have been shown in museums.

Surrealism, with its tolerance of individual styles, its residue of Dada's gay, destructive, reckless wit, and its promise of the release of creative power, was extremely attractive to artists. That it was the complete opposite of cubism was not the least of its attractions. In the mid-1920's young painters were beginning to rebel against the already long reign of Picasso and of cubism in its various guises. Many began joining the new movement—Victor Brauner, René Magritte, Richard Oelze, Kurt Seligmann, Paul Delvaux, and others. It was slow in reaching America, however. Not until 1931 was surrealism publicly exhibited here.

Representation, narrative, and literature—so resolutely barred for years—came flooding back into art via surrealism. The old outer world had been painted and photographed, the old stories retold to the point of boredom. Here, real though inward, was a brand-new world to picture, and the utmost fidelity of brushwork, color, light, and shade was permissible. In fact, as Dali demonstrated, you could go the whole way to a photographic still in Technicolor (painted, of course) and make the horror more intense. Here were stories to tell, even though they were tales of night and of fright fleeing naked through nightmares.

Delvaux used a similar naturalism more lyrically; Magritte used it with Dada wit; Ernst seldom needed it to convey the wit and the macabre horror that combine in his work. The naturalistic element attracted certain artists, for the instinct toward representation is strong. Later on in

America surrealism was used as a faint flavor for a school called magic realism which is only a variation of the old American Scene school.

The naturalism of some of the surrealists greatly facilitated public acceptance. People could look at an early Dali and feel: "Well, no matter what it *means*, we can tell what it *is!*" That, of course, was the first glance across those endless plains with no barricades of inhuman geometry or cruel distortion. It was when they kept on looking that things started to happen. They were shocked beyond measure, but somehow they always came back to Dali for another look.

Surrealism was as shocking as cubism had been, perhaps in a way even more so, because it was interior to all of us, working directly with the hidden materials of personality. It did not transmute or transform a dream; it gave us the dream itself. We could not stand off from a strong piece of surrealist work. If we looked at it, we were involved in it in those days of its first impact. The Raven flew down from the bust of Pallas to sink his claws into our shoulders while Loplop, Max Ernst's mythical King of the Birds, screamed at us from the darkest corner of a haunted bedroom.

If surrealism has lost its shock, it is less from familiarity than from the fact that the surrealists overdid it. They swamped us with surrealism, and when surrealist styles for women and surrealist advertisements and surrealist window-displays became the order of the day, the real thing had lost its punch. But the surrealists did some never-to-be-forgotten things. Their exhibitions were like nothing before on heaven or earth. To the medicine men and voodoo horrors of the past they added the terrifying modern lore of abnormal psychology. Each room was a chamber of horrors in an amusement zone built for Frankenstein monsters.

Such were the rooms in the International Exposition of Surrealism of 1938 at the Galerie Beaux-Arts in Paris when the movement was nearing its climax. *Life*[2] pictured the Nightmare Room: ". . . floor of dead leaves, chair covered with ivy, pictures of strange dreamlands. Beside the bed . . . a phonograph (old horn-disk type, table model) called 'Never' with a woman's legs entering the trumpet and a hand" coming out the other end instead of a pickup and needle.

Eric Sevareid reported firsthand in the Paris edition of the *Herald Tribune*[3] that "by the time top-hatted dignitaries of the art world had moved down the gallery as far as the third wax lady with light bulbs growing out of her ears," the show was temporarily closed by the gendarmes for fear of violence. "In the courtyard," Sevareid continued, "visitors were confronted with a closed car in which a dry skeleton sat at the driving wheel, while in the back seat, deep among flourishing weeds, a semi-nude lady relaxed with a sewing machine at her side and a heavy rain pouring down upon her head."[4]

Visitors entered the Exposition through a gallery that was a travesty on museums, walking between endless rows of nude standing wax figures garlanded with mushrooms, stuffed bats, and other incongruities. One waxen sylph suffered all through the show with eggs broken and splattered over her breasts and with bits of sea shell congealed and clinging. Each figure was the chef d'œuvre of a different surrealist of note.

After the gallery, as Sevareid noted, visitors came to

[2] February 7, 1938.
[3] January 18, 1938.
[4] The *Taxi Pluvieux*, or "Rainy Taxi," was Dali's work. He did this on his own without the sponsorship of Bonwit Teller or even General Motors.

"the first of two rooms, which has a ceiling consisting of empty gunny sacks." Here they "stumbled through thick and dank autumn leaves, peering at surrealist pictures with the aid of flashlights cheerfully furnished by the management. In each corner a modern double bed with luxurious silk coverlets and the purest of white pillows stands in swamp water and thick mosses." Amid these surroundings "an art lover could stand at his peace, shoes snugly covered with foliage, and let his fancy wander free."

The second room was shockingly well lighted, and "here the utilitarian and practical side of the surrealists' nature was expressed in umbrellas made of sponge, vases of goose feathers, wheelbarrows satin-lined." [5]

The 1938 Surrealist Exposition was organized by Breton, Éluard, and Duchamp with the counsel of Dali and Ernst; the lighting (and lack of it) was executed by Man Ray. It closed amid the warning sounds of approaching war. The surrealists dismantled the exhibition and began packing their personal effects for an exodus to America. Four years later they would be ready to stage a New York show that would be the high-water mark of the movement. This was on view from October 14 to November 7, 1942. Of all the unlikely places that might have been selected, the surrealists chose the old Whitelaw Reid mansion on Madison Avenue, a block-long brownstone that is shared nowadays by a publishing firm and the Catholic Archdiocese of New York.

[5] Among these "practical" objects was a stool with three stocking-clad feminine legs in high-heeled slippers. Kurt Seligmann designed the stool and called it: *Ultrameuble* or "super furniture." A historical note is in order here. In 1900 in Berlin there occurred *Der Erste Grosser Berliner Ulk-Kunst Ausstellung*, or, "The First Great Berlin Joke-Art Exposition." Here was shown a stool, draped with lingerie, with three feminine legs terminating in boudoir slippers. Its designer, one B. Möhring, listed it as *Überstuhl*, or "Super Stool."

The New York show was sponsored by a distinguished list of men and women of the world of art, including Peggy Guggenheim, the Walter Arensbergs, Sidney Janis, Marian Willard, Katherine Dreier, James Johnson Sweeney, and Elsa Schiaparelli. The French War Relief benefited from the gate receipts and the proceeds from an opening-night auction of surrealist art works. The catalogue credits read: "Hung by Breton. His twine: M. Duchamp." The twine, one full mile of it, was stretched through the huge ballroom, back and forth below the ceiling, at every conceivable angle, crossing and crisscrossing. With diabolic cleverness Duchamp saw to it that every picture and object had to be viewed through this incredible maze of taut string.

During installation, the string caught fire as if, not Marcel Duchamp's fatalism, but Buster Keaton's, was inevitably inviting disaster. After the quick flare-up was extinguished, another mile of string went up as replacement. There were no more fires. The cause was never determined, but Duchamp placidly ascribes it to spontaneous combustion. "I was just standing there," he says, "when the black spots appeared and in another second glowed and burst into flame." Marcel had purchased sixteen miles of string. "It would have been fatal to run short," he says. That left fourteen miles unused. "I gave it away," he recalls. "It made someone very happy—a kind of insurance, string enough to last him the rest of his life."

The preview evening was invitational, distingué, and dressy. First the arriving guests were confronted by the string jungle. Then their ears were assailed by the happy shouts of children at play. The whole ballroom, in fact, looked like a public playground. A day before, and unknown to anyone, Duchamp had said to Sidney Janis's eleven-year-old son Carroll: "Get some friends together and I'll send taxis for you." Then he outlined his plans, concluding: "And pay no attention to anyone. Just play all evening."

The guests had no choice but to pick their perilous way through this juvenile Olympiad. A half-dozen boys were vigorously and lightheartedly playing a sort of combination game with various types of balls. They wore football helmets, baseball pants, basketball sneakers, and gym shirts. A like number of girls were in little groups, skipping rope, playing jacks and hopscotch.

Some foolhardy guests tried admonishing the children: "Why don't you little dears go out in the street and play, where you belong?"

"Mr. Duchamp told us we could play here," was the invariable answer.

Mr. Duchamp, of course, could not be found. Having arranged the show, his final Dada gesture was not to attend.

It was the guests who finally broke down. By the time the auction began, most of them were playing with the children. Bejeweled society women, holding their trains with one hand, were skipping rope, and tailcoated gentlemen were punting and forward-passing.

Duchamp's installation proved that Dada's spirit was still very much alive and indicated by inference that surrealism's gruesomeness, like an over-diet of horror movies, was beginning to pall. In place of wax dummies crawling with live snails, there was an automaton that played checkers; guests dodged string and baseballs instead of stumbling through moldering leaves; and the pictures were plentifully leavened by Steig cartoons and the likenesses of Superman and Father Divine.

There was a little storm of publicity even though the Museum of Modern Art's show of "Fantastic Art, Dada and Surrealism" had occurred six years earlier. The surrealists, most of them, would soon be returning to Paris. They had left a deeper mark in America, however, than the dent made by the shindy in the Whitelaw Reid brownstone. By their example they helped, before they left, to shape a new American art movement.

The surrealists' reckless creative spirit profoundly impressed a whole new generation of our painters and sculptors. Even though Breton, refusing to learn English, sulked and fretted, there was considerable meeting between the distinguished foreigners and our younger men. Peggy Guggenheim was the catalyst. Her gallery and her home were always open to the two groups. She was hostess, interpreter, and artistic *agent provocateur*.

Most important of all, perhaps, the young Americans felt themselves part of the international scene. Here in America, Breton, a tyrannical leader, surprised everyone by relaxing the surrealist bylaws and admitting certain non-objective abstractionists into the sacred ranks. Here, once more, the roads lead to Marcel Duchamp, for it was Duchamp who persuaded Breton to let down the bars. Thus Gorky, Robert Motherwell, William Baziotes, and others received the cachet.

It was a bit of practical psychology, this gesture by a master of the abnormal kind, the extra little boost of encouragement that a rugged new generation needed.

In 1920, as museums went, the Société Anonyme was a lonely little outpost without neighbors. If—to translate it into familiar American terms—the Société had been the initial model house of a new real-estate tract, the salesmen might well have given up. The new subdivision, in fact—if we may call it that—had been surveyed years before by Stieglitz and then had been thrown open to buyers—if there had been any—by that grand public barbecue, the Armory Show.

Katherine Dreier—and one must recognize that it probably was Marcel Duchamp who first conceived it—was the first to implement the idea of a wholly *contemporary* museum. The belief that a museum must be a repository of the past was very deeply rooted. Even John Cotton Dana, then still active at the Newark Museum, did not quite grasp the necessities of the time.

Art had pulled itself up by the bootstraps and had changed its direction in a completely unprecedented way—at least within the memory of a century or more. And that century was the time in which museums had begun. Despite the proverb, here was the new thing under the sun. Or so it seemed. Older museums approached it with a long stick as one handles a rattlesnake. There were heavy investments, financial and emotional, to be considered. It appeared a matter of loyalties: to embrace the new, one must divorce the old. In that raw first close-up, certainly, to hang a Picasso next to a Rembrandt or even a Goya or an Ingres seemed to set the scene for Mayhem on the Wall.

Since Adam, however, no human has been born without parents. Nor does any human work—even art—spring out of nothing. But this *new* art! It was a prejudiced time, and this was the black child. Better to be discreet than to pry. Only in time could we open our eyes, legitimacy be established, and the family be made whole again. Now, of course, the great survey shows proclaim the oneness of art as if we had wisely known it all along.

Once Miss Dreier had made the jump, however, others braved it. Within a couple of years or so she began to have neighbors. A. E. Gallatin turned his private collection into a museum that he called the Museum of Living Art. And in Russia the modern wave that carried constructivism and suprematism with it had not yet brought up full force against the immovable wall of Communist reaction. The Communists themselves confiscated the great Russian private collections of Matisses, Picassos, and the rest, and made a vast modern museum in Moscow. But soon the commissars—long before Hitler—would scent subversion in a free art that they really did not like anyway, and would abate and padlock the nuisance—cannily holding on to the valuable paintings, however. And cannily reopening the museum for brief periods from time to time for propaganda reasons.

The really surprising thing was the lack of action in France. It would be many years before the Musée de l'Art Moderne would open in Paris. Which only points up the fact that Paris is not France, or the other way around, either. The beautiful city by the Seine is an international, even more than a national, capital. It is the locus and the focus of a state of mind. It exists apart from French officialdom.

Then, in 1929, just as Wall Street, to quote *Variety*'s famous quip, laid an egg, there came that remarkable gesture of confidence, the Museum of Modern Art. Its founders went farther, even, than Herbert Hoover. He promised us prosperity around the corner—they gave us modern art.

Almost immediately after this, Gertrude Vanderbilt Whitney put together her American collections and her hopes and a very genuine love for her fellow artists and, from some unlikely old brownstone houses in Greenwich Village, brought forth, in 1931, the Whitney Museum of American Art. There was by now indeed a new neighborhood of congenial friends. It no longer seemed to make much difference what the Metropolitan Museum was doing or not doing.

Best of all, the new happenings were not confined to New York City. By 1935, for example, San Francisco, building its two great stone twins, the Opera House and the War Memorial, reserved the top floor of the Memorial for a modern museum, allocated maintenance funds, and had the acumen to place progressive Grace McCann Morley in charge. One year later the Museum of Modern Art established a branch, the Boston Museum of Modern Art. It had distinguished sponsorship, glittering with such *Mayflower* names as Saltonstall. Soon the parent museum relinquished control to the sponsors, who have since had a lot of fun renaming their museum. Successively it has been the Institute of Modern Art and the Institute of Contemporary Art. Granted that none of the terms we have concocted for the maverick art we have on our hands is wholly satisfactory, Boston, even so, has an unusual interest in semantics. No small amount of the Institute's energies seems to have gone into these rechristenings.

Soon museums began springing up and old ones began converting all over the country. As the pioneer collectors, getting older, began making valuable bequests, museums like the Baltimore and the Philadelphia started to look at things differently. The topnotch Duncan Phillips collection became the Phillips Memorial Gallery in Washington, D.C.

Smaller galleries adapted themselves or sprang up. Many of them, adopting Dana's advanced ideas, set out to serve their communities rather than to be great display cases with prominent signs reading "Don't Touch." The Walker Art Center of Minneapolis is one such; the Munson-Williams-Proctor Institute of Utica is another. Director Harris K. Prior worked something of a miracle at Utica. Three mansarded Victorian family mansions—the Munsons', the Williamses' and the Proctors'—sitting in a row behind big trees in the center of the busy town became the Institute. It houses a growing collection of art, modern and old, primitive and sophisticated, American and European. But, most of all, community things happen there: children finger-paint and dance and put on original plays of their own; ceramists fling pottery and weavers weave cloth; young and middle-aged and old paint and make sculpture; and the auditorium—an old drawing-room wisely left as it was—is busy with lectures, longhair music, and jazz. Munson-Williams-Proctor can show how John Cotton Dana's legacy—as endless as the loaves and fishes—has been divided up all over America.

However, the biggest splashes after the Museum of Modern Art came with the fabulous Guggenheims. When Mrs. Simon R. threw in her lot with the Rockefellers and the Museum of Modern Art, the Guggenheims were far from through. After all, there were seven brothers who, singly and not collectively, could have made Crœsus look like a man with a merely modest competence.

In 1939, Solomon Guggenheim established the Guggenheim Museum of Non-Objective Art in New York, stocked it well as a starter, and placed a real countess in charge.

Then, finally, came a stormy little bird with ruffled

feathers, Peggy Guggenheim, granddaughter of banker James Seligman and Meyer Guggenheim, daughter of Benjamin Guggenheim, and niece of Benjamin's six famous "copper king" brothers: Isaac, Daniel, Murray, Solomon, Simon, and William. Peggy had been fledged in a warm copper-lined nest on New York's East 69th Street, where the nearest neighbors had been the Stillmans, the Rockefellers, and General Grant's widow.

Peggy Guggenheim could be expected to be both willful and original. From one side of her family—the Seligmans— she inherited a trace of what had been notable eccentricity. One aunt, so Peggy tells in her autobiography, was an "incurable soprano" who would burst into *solfège* and trills while waiting for a Fifth Avenue bus. One uncle "lived on charcoal [and] in a zinc-lined pocket . . . carried pieces of ice which he sucked all the time." This uncle kept a mistress concealed in his room and finally shot himself. Another uncle, rather miserly, always arrived at mealtime disclaiming hunger and then ate everything in sight. After dinner he entertained by wriggling on his stomach across a row of chairs in a game he called The Snake. "The other two uncles," Peggy confides, "were nearly normal. One . . . spent all his time washing himself and the other wrote plays that were never produced." [1]

Peggy assures us that the Guggenheims were merely rich and not eccentric, as if this made them less interesting. But from them she inherited her share of a fortune reaching an amount that itself was little short of eccentric. The *Encyclopedia Americana* states that at times "the family income exceeded $500,000,000 per annum." Simple arithmetic reveals that this

---

[1] This and immediately succeeding quotations are from Peggy Guggenheim's autobiography, *Out of This Century* (New York, 1946).

is more than one and one-third million dollars every day, and this at a time when the income tax was not even a glint in a Washington politician's eye. What, one wonders, does a little family do on $1,369,863.01 every twenty-four hours?

When Peggy Guggenheim flew out of the nest with its marble staircase and its tapestried, four-story, domed hall, it was into a lively whirl of several marriages and many more chance meetings on the wing. She has had a gay life and yet a serious one. During the 1930's in France she made her most lasting marriage: she fell in love with modern art.

Peggy entered the modern museum scene in 1942 with a weird and wonderful gallery that she called Art of This Century. She stayed with this New York venture only a few years and then flew on to buy an old palazzo on the Grand Canal in Venice, but no one has ever forgotten that marvelous place where sculptures hung in mid-air and paintings leaped out at you on invisible arms from the walls, where miniature pictures revolved in peepshow cabinets, where Marcel Duchamp displayed his life's work in a suitcase, tables became chairs, and chairs became pedestals.

There on 57th Street the hidden child in Peggy Guggenheim built an enchanted museum out of the enchanted dollhouse "containing bearskin rugs and beautiful crystal chandeliers" which had been the one nostalgic, bright memory of a "childhood excessively lonely and sad [and] filled with torments."

Peggy's Art of This Century was a place where things happened and where things that were happening on the outside found a door wide open with welcome. With all the museums and all the doings, hers were almost beyond a doubt the most important of all in that brief historic half-decade from 1942 to 1947 when events reached a crisis and a new American modern art was struggling to get born.

With museums mushrooming and collectors both large and small springing up all over the place, a new day dawned for the dealers in modern art. There was Marie Harriman (wife of the present Governor of New York) and there were Julien Levy and Pierre Matisse, all of them set up in business by the early 1930's. Marian Willard first established the East River Gallery and by 1940 had opened the gallery that bears her name. Buchholz (later Curt Valentin) set up trade, and so did Carl Nierendorf from Berlin. Along came the ACA Gallery, and from Paris the renowned Paul Rosenberg.

Many of the early pioneers continued to hold their own: Valentine Dudensing, J. B. Neumann—whose advice was so important in the early years of the Museum of Modern Art— Edith Halpert and her Downtown Gallery, and the famous Parisian, Seligman (not a relative of Peggy Guggenheim).

57th Street became the foreshortened Miracle Mile of Modern Art.

The Whitney Museum of American Art, even as it stands today in its imposing new building on 54th Street, is a museum that did not intend to be a museum. The Metropolitan Museum of Art, although it may not like to think so, had a great —in fact, a vital—part in its founding.

Gertrude Vanderbilt Whitney was a famous heiress at a time when American heiresses, like British princesses, were supposed to grow up in well-defined and well-regulated ways. They could exude glamour, make their debuts, marry the one right man, and, perhaps, raise a new heiress or two. They had rights, but not at all those "Women's Rights" which noisy persons like Carrie Chapman Catt and Sylvia Pankhurst were parading around and loudly demanding. The American heiress, in short, stayed in her own world.

Gertrude Whitney, however, had ideas of her own. She liked art, but not the arts of china-painting or embroidery or watercolor as taught in the finishing schools. She put on a smock, seized mallet and chisel, and became a sculptor. Worst of all—this was in 1908—she fled the Whitney mansion and took a studio at 19 Macdougal Alley in Greenwich Village. There, a lone girl—and a blooded one, too—she carved away amid the riffraff of that early Bohemia.

She liked this new world, liked the people in it. Soon she was wrapped up in art and artists, fighting with them in those first almost pathetic rebellions against the Academy. Practically and completely without condescension, she bought their work. She helped them to go to Paris, helped them stay there. Never by gifts, but always by that real boon of buying their work. In a thoroughly nice way, Gertrude Vanderbilt Whitney threw her weight around. Perhaps she was not so selective as she might have been—an artist was an artist to her—but some now-famous names were among the many that she aided.

In 1913, Mrs. Whitney was ready with checkbook to help the Armory Show. One year later she took another step by founding the Whitney Studio. She remodeled part of an old house at 8 West 8th Street into rent-free studios where needy artists could work, and into galleries where their things could be exhibited and sold. Her policy ran parallel with that of the new American Independents. In 1917 she, too, announced a policy of no prizes and no jury of awards in her annuals. This policy still obtains in the museum that bears her name.

Gertrude Whitney had quite an institution going. As can be well imagined, her collection was growing by leaps and bounds. It began, actually, to become a problem to her. Finally, in 1929, the year in which the Museum of Modern Art was established, she decided to give it all to the Metropolitan Museum—her collection of "over six hundred works by American artists, probably the largest collection of contemporary American art." [2] Her secretary, Mrs. Juliana Force, accordingly conveyed to the Metropolitan's Director the first part of Mrs. Whitney's offer—namely, title to the collection itself. The second half of the offer was to be "to build and endow a wing to house it. The latter subject was never broached, because the collection was flatly refused."

Literally within hours after this unmerited rebuff, Mrs. Whitney completed the plans for her own museum. She proceeded to remodel into one building the houses at 8, 10, 12, and 14 West 8th Street. There, barely two years later, the Whitney Museum of American Art opened its doors to the public. Mrs. Whitney thought of her institution as one never to be complete, an "organism that would grow as we grow."

It grew. By 1954 it removed from Greenwich Village to occupy the new building on 54th Street, behind and connecting with the Museum of Modern Art and opening into the same garden. The next year the art branch of the New York Public Library opened in new quarters on 53rd Street across from the Museum of Modern Art. Directly north of Rockefeller Center, something like its art counterpart has lately begun to take shape.

1929 appears to have been the year when the Metropolitan Museum of Art outdid itself. The Armory Show pioneer Walter Pach might just as well have included the Whitney,

[2] This and immediately succeeding quotations are from the catalogue of the Whitney exhibit "Juliana Force and American Art" (1949).

too, when he made his oft-quoted remark: "It is not too much to say that the Modern Museum is the greatest mistake the Metropolitan ever made, bringing about, as it did, the creation of the newer institution through intolerance of the latter-day masters." [3]

Long after Mrs. Whitney's death, her inclusive point of view toward art is stamped on her museum. Its annuals remain catch-alls like the big Independent Shows of 1917–18, with no great degree of qualitative selectiveness. It was not until the 1940's, really, that the Whitney annuals began to include more than a token or so of abstract painting. And there still is an evident effort to "balance" the abstract with the representational, whether or not this arbitrary balance exists on the current art scene.

Immediately upon the Whitney's founding in 1931 it became apparent that a museum dedicated by its bylaws solely to American art could be a valuable thing. The Museum of Modern Art, only two years old, was facing the almost insuperable task of representing an international art that included America, too. So speculations began, spurred on by necessities. Could the Whitney shoulder the native part of that burden? Could the Metropolitan (extravagant thought!) become repository for modern works as they aged into New-Old Masters? And so the idea of the Inter-Museum Agreement was born.

It began with a pragmatic, informal agreement between the Modern and the Whitney to synchronize and separate their respective fields of exhibiting and collecting. The hope of including the Metropolitan persisted. It happened that at the moment the younger museums could claim a powerful friend

[3] Walter Pach: *The Art Museum in America* (New York, 1948).

Arshile Gorky dancing at a wedding, New York, c. 1940.

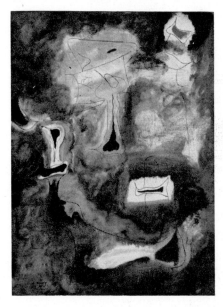

Charred Beloved No. 2, *1946,*
by Arshile Gorky.
Oil on canvas, 60″ x 54″.
Collection: Martha Jackson.

Arshile Gorky and Willem de Kooning, New York, c. 1937.

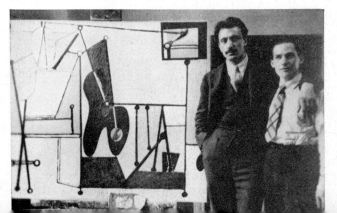

Woman I, *1950–2, by Willem de Kooning. Oil, 75⅞" x 58".*
Collection: The Museum of Modern Art, New York.

Willem de Kooning, 1955.

at court, the Metropolitan President, William Sloane Coffin. Coffin, although by no means the whole of the Metropolitan, was personally sympathetic to modernism. In 1932, in fact, the Metropolitan head saluted the Museum of Modern Art in this vein: "If this museum will always remain modern, retaining faithfully the pioneer spirit of faith and adventure, you will have found what the ages have sought—the fountain of perpetual youth, whence shall well forever the spontaneous creative art of the future."

As Coffin spoke, a plan was already formulated and under way: the Metropolitan would buy and keep on view the historic older moderns; the junior museums, with freed space and funds, would move on ahead; the public would gain a perpetual panorama of art from the Old to the New.

It was a beautiful plan. Then in 1933 Coffin died. Men with other ideas took over. But the idea, so practical, so simple, and so logical, did not die. In 1947 it became a thing on parchment, complete with three sets of signatures and ribboned seals: the Inter-Museum Agreement. The Museum of Modern Art made a public statement that was a justifiable sigh of relief. There was peace; the senseless Cold War of the Museums was over.

The Museum of Modern Art immediately handed over Daumier's *Laundress*, and the Metropolitan in turn lent Maillol's monumental sculpture the *Torso* and Picasso's historic *Portrait of Gertrude Stein*. Pledged to the Metropolitan in addition were fourteen nineteenth-century American folk paintings and sculptures and twenty-six European works of art. Under an option clause, the junior museums could be paid immediately for pledged works, but could retain them for ten years longer. This clause recognized the Metropolitan's vast funds, and was intended to help the Modern and the Whitney in making timely and important purchases. With its endowments that have multiplied and accrued for seventy-five years, the Metropolitan is a Crœsus compared with its new neighbors. An official at one of the younger institutions puts it this way: "We are like millionaires in Texas. We run errands for the billionaires."

Now Alfred Barr's Torpedo Plan, conceived in 1933, was ready to function, with its nose "the ever advancing present, its tail the ever receding past." The Museum of Modern Art collections, as Barr had hoped, might now "always be kept within [a] period of the previous five or six decades," the Metropolitan would be enriched with no risk of prestige by "works which have stood a severe preliminary test of time," and the Museum of Modern Art would "remain a museum of modern art." [4]

But again something happened. Just what no one would say, but the Torpedo Plan exploded, all bets were off, a gentlemen's agreement became a gentlemen's disagreement. In 1948 the Whitney canceled its share of the Inter-Museum Agreement, and for several years things went along with no direct evidence of whether or not the remaining two thirds of the pact were functioning.

Finally, early in 1953, John Hay Whitney, Chairman of the Board of Trustees of the Museum of Modern Art, announced a "change of policy." The Museum, he stated, "now believes it essential . . . to have permanently on public view masterpieces of the modern movement, beginning with the latter half of the 19th Century." Specific galleries would be

[4] A. Conger Goodyear: *The Museum of Modern Art: The First Ten Years* (New York, 1943).

set aside for this in the same building—except for a relatively small added wing (The Grace Rainey Rogers Memorial Building)—of which Barr had complained nine years earlier: "Three or four times as much space is needed." [5]

Whitney emphasized that his Museum's collection could not remain static, must "attempt to include all significant and promising aspects of today's artistic production." The serious aspects of vast accumulation were resolutely faced: there would be "periodic reconsideration of the major part of the collection and the creation of a permanent core." As for the rest? Obviously, like the Quinn collection, it must go on public sale and—in this case, reversing historical process—pass from the public domain into the private.

The words of the Museum of Modern Art's Chairman were mild words even while they publicly announced the cancelation of an agreement upon which such hopes had been pinned. Painfully polite and evasive, they tried hard to put a good face on a matter very bad indeed. And there, still, the matter stands.

With all this going on, the Museum of Modern Art could pay scant attention to current artistic events. Exciting things happening in American art and in art abroad were demanding coverage. Again the art dealers filled the bill as Stieglitz had from 1908 to 1915, then Daniel, and then, during the 1920's, a devoted few like J. B. Neumann and Valentine Dudensing. Now in the 1930's it was Julien Levy introducing Max Ernst, Dali, Magritte, Delvaux, and the American Joseph Cornell; Marian Willard sponsoring the so-called Northwest Painters, Mark Tobey and Morris Graves; Pierre

[5] Alfred H. Barr, Jr.: *The Museum Collections: A Brief Report* (1944, unpublished).

Matisse showing American Loren MacIver, Chilean Matta, Cuban Wilfredo Lam, the new French sensation Jean Dubuffet, and the newest works by his famous father.

Meanwhile, in 1939, Solomon R. Guggenheim, then seventy-eight years old, made his incredibly youthful gesture. He opened and gave his name to the Museum of Non-Objective Art at 24 East 54th Street, only two blocks from the Museum of Modern Art. This followed a two-year tour by his collection to a series of eastern cities. It was an unexpected move by a noted lover of more representational painting, who, as his niece Peggy tells, lived in his Plaza Hotel apartment "surrounded by the most beautiful Picassos, Seurats, Braques, Klees . . . Gleizes, Delaunays, Chagalls . . ." [6]

The American Abstract Artists, a group that had long deplored the general neglect by the museums of the extreme forms of non-representational abstraction, immediately took heart. But they were soon disappointed. Hilla Rebay von Ehrenwiesen, Guggenheim's Director, paid them scant heed, concentrating instead on the German non-objectivists. The Blue Four, Feininger, Jawlensky, Kandinsky, and Klee, were wonderfully represented, with special emphasis on the last two.

It was in extending its collections beyond this admirable core that, in those years, the Guggenheim erred. In using the enviable Guggenheim funds, the Countess Rebay followed her own personal predilection: a German abstractionist named Rudolf Bauer, who, like a lazy echo, copied each Kandinsky period ten years after it was over. Bauer was all over the place. But those who fondly believed that artists are made by bally-hoo and promotion could only be sadly disappointed in the

[6] This and the succeeding quotation are from Peggy Guggenheim, *op. cit.*

result. All the Guggenheim money, so unwisely used, could not make an artist out of Bauer.

Peggy Guggenheim writes of first visiting her uncle's museum: "It really was a joke. There were about a hundred paintings by Bauer in enormous silver frames which over-shadowed the twenty Kandinskys. . . ." [7] Peggy then quotes Max Ernst, her distinguished husband of the moment. Max, in sly punning reference to the nondescript painter Bauer as well as to the German Bauhaus that had inspired the Guggenheim Museum, called the Guggenheim "the Bauer House." An inveterate quipster, Ernst then went on to de-scribe the Museum of Modern Art as "the Barr House" and the A. E. Gallatin Museum of Living Art as "the Bore House." Gallatin's collection was then at New York University on Washington Square. "It really was boring," Peggy comments, "because, although he had some nice abstract paintings, the surroundings were so dull that one had no pleasure in looking at them." She might have added that the students never so much as glanced at them in the library where they were hung. Gallatin, having a fancy idea that "living art" should be dis-played in a place where life went on, had chosen a university library as the liveliest place he could think of.

In 1939, modern art, as a whole, was still so esoteric that the Guggenheim policy of non-objective art was distinctly caviare to the general, a specializing within a specialty. Early in 1948, a year before Solomon Guggenheim's death at the age of eighty-eight, the Guggenheim moved into a palatial remodeled mansion on upper Fifth Avenue. In 1952, James

[7] As listed in its catalogue at its opening, June 1, 1939, the Guggenheim Museum owned 231 Bauers and 108 Kandinskys. Peggy's observation is probably accurate: the Bauers and Kandinskys were usually displayed in about that proportion.

Johnson Sweeney became its Director. By degrees Sweeney has shifted the Guggenheim policy from the exclusively non-objective to more generalized exhibitions and collections.

In 1956—eight years after his death—the long hand of Solomon R. Guggenheim was still being felt. The Solomon R. Guggenheim Foundation (which supports the Guggenheim Museum) announced a lavish set of cash prizes—national and international, ranging from one thousand to ten thousand dollars—to be awarded biennially for contemporary paintings. Art's new universality was recognized by the assignment of prizes to each of sixteen different countries. Art's new importance here was acknowledged in the announcement that President Eisenhower would personally present the first International Grand Award.

During World War II, art activity, far from diminishing, spurted strongly in all its phases, particularly in creative work by a whole new group of American modernists. Peggy Guggenheim's Art of This Century on West 57th Street, both museum and sales rooms, became their arena. Peggy had made her own collection abroad, and it was kept safe in southern France during the early part of the Occupation. Peggy bought art in a passionate fury ("My motto was 'buy a picture a day' and I lived up to it"), but with an instinctively good eye of her own plus Marcel Duchamp's counsel. Her collection had both personality and quality.

Peggy finally succeeded in spiriting both her paintings and sculpture and an assorted group of artists—including Max Ernst—out of France under the very noses of the Nazis. The art work came out as household goods surrounded with linens and blankets. Peggy and the artists came via neutral Portugal on Pan American Clippers, many of the escapees in space reserved for them in New York by the Museum of Modern Art.

Peggy, who had been trying to set up a personal modern museum in England with Herbert Read, had decided to have one in New York. So, finally, her collection—which ranged diversely from cubism to surrealism—was unveiled in galleries so novel that even New Yorkers were startled.

Architect Frederick Kiesler was given a free hand by Peggy. Kiesler in 1922 had startled his native Vienna with stage settings for Kapek's drama of the robots, *R.U.R.* Then, for Eugene O'Neill's *Emperor Jones*, he had built an abstract mobile setting with a background that, as Harriet Janis describes it, followed the O'Neill text, slowly changing "the visage of the jungle to keep pace with Jones' frantic and lost wanderings." [8]

Kiesler ran the gamut for Peggy. The surrealist gallery, a *grand guignol* shocker, became famous overnight. Long, narrow, and sealed with outcurved walls, it was as remote from the world as a surviving fragment of Atlantis. It was uterine architecture as involute as the subconscious mind from which were born the paintings themselves. This strange salon of the surrealist stirred the imagination of each visitor according to his capacity: to one it was a Quonset hut, to another a subway station plastered with posters, to one a bomb shelter, and to still another a tunnel to the future.

To walk from it out into the main gallery was to awake out of quiet nightmare into a harmlessly mechanized world. Here floated and jutted and tilted the rest of Peggy's personal collection: paintings and sculptures hanging in mid-air on guys of taut cord or cantilevered into space (and into your

[8] Harriet Janis: "Mobiles," *Arts and Architecture*, February 1948.

face) while still others rested on amorphous wooden forms that in one position or another became pedestals, tables, easels, even rocking-chairs!

The carnival, peepshow atmosphere, like Peggy Guggenheim herself, was both gay and serious. One saw Marcel Duchamp's *Valise* (*La Boîte*), within which was ironically packed in reproductions the lifework of this calm traveler through life. Glimpsed through a peephole, like the naughty moving-picture cards of another generation, they spiraled up into view: the *Nude Descending a Staircase* and the *Sad Young Man on a Train*, the *Bottle Rack* and the privy joke of the *Fountain*, the optical, whirling disks, the painted panes, and the mustached *Mona Lisa*—all the meaningful paraphernalia of a great and playful mind. To describe them in their opulent and bewildering profusion one might borrow Chirico's title for one of his own paintings: *Toys of a Philosopher*.

Here, indeed, on every hand in Peggy Guggenheim's sublimated dollhouse, we saw the noble toys of a whole generation: the cubism of Braque and Picasso; Delaunay's orphism and Léger's earthy poems of the mechanical; the virginal mathematics of Mondrian and Van Doesburg, and the fantastic non-utile constructions of Gabo, Pevsner, and Alexander Calder. In little lighted theaters hung Paul Klee's fantasies of knowing childhood, and with appropriate starkness on the wall hung Malevich's famous, almost blank canvas *White on White*, which unloosed on us an interior decorators' snowstorm of white paint, white upholstery, white draperies, and white carpets.

In Peggy Guggenheim's place you always felt you were being watched. The eyes of a whole generation of artists were on you, just as Peggy herself had felt them. For on each page of the now-famous illustrated catalogue of her gallery, they stare out at you, unblinking. On each page, above each painting or each sculpture, are reproduced the eyes of its creator. Even in photogravure they shock you, so piercing, so omnivorous are they, so far from dreamy.

Beyond these two strange rooms lay two more, with excitements of their own. Here trooped in, with canvases under their arms, a dozen wild youths who had found the doors of other museums closed. They liked Peggy. They found in her a fellow spirit as daring as they. For her, history was no post-mortem: she lived it, as they were doing.

So for five years, from 1942 to 1947, international modern art's newest movement filled those two little rooms with paintings that were scarcely dry and sculptures still warm from their molds. Peggy Guggenheim's museum gave them a haven during the years when the struggle was hardest. Her museum may well be remembered chiefly for those two plain, small rooms where she showed the new and the unknown and argued, cajoled, and persuaded every visitor "just to buy one picture."

15. *Go West, Young Art, Go West*

The Russians claim to have invented everything under the sun. We firmly believe that *we* did. It is no propaganda from Washington, it is just our comfortable illusion. An illusion like the average man's idea that because he lives in a scientific age, he is a scientist. His illusion explodes the first time his new car, automatic transmission and all, breaks down on a deserted highway.

The truth in both cases is a little different. Who invented the steam engine? A Scot. The locomotive? An Englishman. Who first ascended in a balloon? Someone in France. Another Frenchman invented photography. Who invented gunpowder? A Chinese while a fellow citizen was busy with the invention of printing. Egypt had already taken care to provide the paper to print on.

All pretty discouraging until we come to the telegraph, the phonograph, and the electric light. Going on, we find ourselves in a three-cornered argument with the French and the English about both the motion picture and the automobile. As to radio, there is no question: Italy gets the credit. Then there is the trick question of who invented the military tank. Being fair, we have to admit that it was an Italian, too— Leonardo da Vinci.

Although you can get an argument on the airplane, we at least flew the first one. This brings us far enough up to date— without going into the touchy subject of bombs—to show that it is all pretty much a dead heat. Everyone will agree, however, that we are tops when it comes to developing anybody's inventions. Remember that harmless little atom that Einstein found?

With all that, for five hundred years—or maybe twice as many—an overmastering current has been moving west over the Atlantic. It pulled ships and people, the people who, as Thoreau once observed, were planted like seeds in the new hemisphere. It pulled wealth, ideas, strength—a great, inevitable, historic process. Not the Decline of the West, but the Incline Toward the West. A German might well be a little melancholy about that. As for ourselves, we might be a little humble about the lucky accident that we were in the right place at the right time.

We were a long enough time, in all conscience, in spotting the wonderful possibilities in that new invention called modern art. It has taken a lot of doing over four long decades for a very few, very devoted people to pry our eyes open. But little by little we did open them: in 1913 we saw that modern art existed—at least in Europe; during the 1920's we glimpsed that it was apparently here to stay; during the 1930's we found out that artists were real flesh-and-blood people living right here. And during the Great Depression, while we were meek and brought down, the champions of modern art having made us take an un-blindfolded look at all those awful isms, we found them rather fun. During the 1940's we finally discovered that we had some pretty darn good modern artists of our own. We thought about that for a while, and then in the 1950's got up the nerve to compare our own stuff with the imports that carried the glamorous label: MADE IN FRANCE. That was a surprise! At the present moment we still cannot quite believe it.

And so, just past mid-century, we have our own art movement, abstract expressionism. Despite the old arguments as to who invented what, it quite clearly started with our boys. What is more, they have got the Frenchmen doing it. Names seem to be important in cataloguing—as well as talking about

—things. So it is worth noting that Sidney Janis seems to have been the first to apply the adjectives "abstract" and "expressionist" to the new work. He did it early, too—in 1944, when the boys themselves were not yet quite sure what they were doing.[1] For good measure, Janis included another adjective, "surrealist." It is just as well to mention this because since then the strong influence of both the surrealists and surrealism has tended to be overlooked.

A few years later the painter Robert Motherwell, during a meeting at an artists' club, advanced a group of suggested names for the new tendency of his colleagues and himself. Among these was "abstract expressionism." The artists bought that one.

To keep the record completely clear: the term actually had been invented around thirty years before this, in 1919 in fact, in Volume X, Number 2, of the German modernists' publication *Der Sturm*. There, Oswald Herzog applied it (in German, *Der Abstrakte Expressionismus*) to the abstractions of Kandinsky. The term, however, did not achieve currency, though Alfred Barr revived it in his foreword to the catalogue of the Museum of Modern Art's opening exhibition in 1929.

The young American abstract expressionists show scarcely the slightest direct influence of Kandinsky. They are more directly indebted to Hans Hofmann, whose painting in America became both expressionist and abstract. As teacher, painter, and friend, he deeply influenced many of this generation of American artists, and Sidney Janis came very close to calling him the original American abstract expressionist.[2]

Our abstract expressionists are too diverse a brood to

---

[1] Sidney Janis: *Abstract and Surrealist Art in America* (New York, 1944).
[2] Ibid.

have one common father. Their work is less an ism, systematized and dogma-ridden, than any preceding one, even surrealism, has been. The name is a convenient label, no more. The most salient thing about abstract expressionism is the free rein that it gives to the individual. These younger painters—like Picasso throughout all his mature career—move freely back and forth between different degrees of the abstract and the representational. Avoiding classification and dogma, they also avoid mannerism—the apish painting "in the manner of." They assimilate various points of view discovered in our century into one point of view, which thus is new and their own.

In 1913, American modernists could nearly be numbered on the fingers of two hands. Thirty years later the roll had become impressively long. The older generation lived on, variously aged and honored: from Marin, already venerable at seventy-two, Feininger only a year younger, and Stella and Hartley each sixty-six, on down to Weber, sixty-two.

This younger generation could have jammed a New York subway train in the old accustomed way. And it would have endlessly confused anyone being introduced to its members. First he might have met the Western cowboy abstractionist C. S. Price, nearly seventy years old, and next Theodoros Stamos, a mere twenty-one. The criterion of youth in this instance was one of ideas, not of years. However, generally speaking, artists mature somewhat later than baseball-players. The average age of the generation that claimed the abstract expressionists was thirty-six in the year 1943.

Artists, on the other hand, remain lively far longer than baseball-players do. So these young-oldsters were stirring up quite a storm at the time when Peggy Guggenheim's new museum was just gathering steam. In 1944 Peggy introduced Motherwell, Pollock, Baziotes, and, one year later, Rothko. Novelty and marked individuality were the first impressions of their work. Not yet evident were the concordances of spirit which within three more years would clearly indicate that a new style was forming.

The art critics, notoriously uncertain as to anything new, positive, and native, fumbled among their adjectives. The artists, as artists should be, were belligerent. Only one of the critics was brave enough to be frank. In 1943 the late Edward Alden Jewell of the *New York Times* confessed "befuddlement" at the paintings of Rothko and Adolph Gottlieb. The two artists dashed off a letter to his paper which was a manifesto in the grand old style:

We feel that our pictures demonstrate our esthetic beliefs, some of which we, therefore, list:

1. To us art is an unknown world which can be explored only by those willing to take risks.

2. This world of the imagination is fancy-free and violently opposed to common sense.

3. It is our function as artists to make the spectator see the world our way—not his way.

4. We favor the simple expression of the complex thought. We are for the large shape because it has the impact of the unequivocal. We wish to reassert the picture plane. We are for flat forms because they destroy illusion and reveal truth.

5. It is a widely accepted notion among painters that it does not matter what one paints as long as it is well painted. This is the essence of academism. There is no

such thing as good painting about nothing. We assert that the subject is crucial and only that subject-matter is valid which is tragic and timeless. That is why we profess kinship with primitive and archaic art.

At that moment, and then only, Rothko and Gottlieb were partners in painting, as Picasso and Braque had been for the few early years of cubism. Both Rothko and Gottlieb were painting a species of pictographs, full of symbols like those in ancient stone-carving and frescoes. In the pictograph Gottlieb found "its own internal logic"; Rothko found "the Spirit of Myth, which is generic to all myths at all times." [3] Picasso and Braque had gone for inspiration to African Negro sculpture; Gottlieb and Rothko went to the even earlier art of cliffs and caves. Each pair of artists was looking for a modern truth in ancient magic.

By 1945 new art dealers were appearing, to join Peggy Guggenheim in sponsoring the coming generation. Older dealers joined in, too. Marian Willard, of course, had introduced the Northwest Painters, Mark Tobey and Morris Graves, as well as the sculptor David Smith, who had been hammering away in a foundry on the Brooklyn waterfront. J. B. Neumann showed Lee Gatch, Karl Knaths, and others.

Chief among the new dealers were Betty Parsons and Samuel M. Kootz. Betty Parsons, in a sense a protégée of Peggy Guggenheim, concentrated on Americans, propagandizing for Ad Reinhardt, Boris Margo, and Clyfford Still. Then, when Peggy flew away to the Adriatic, she took over Pollock, Rothko, and others of what everyone by then called the Guggenheim stable.

[3] Ibid., quoted by Janis.

Sam Kootz combined enthusiasm for art with a press agent's imagination. In 1947 he gave the first post-war show of the work that Picasso had done right under the Nazi eyes. Occasional reports had leaked out during the Occupation: Picasso had refused to leave Paris, and the invaders, afraid of an international scandal, had kept a careful hands-off. By simply staying home and painting, Picasso became a symbol of the Resistance. There was the greatest curiosity as to what his work was now like. Would it be a series of greater *Guernicas*, a climactic *J'accuse?* Sidney Janis dashed to Paris in the spring of 1946, saw Picasso, had his new work photographed, returned, and kept mum. By the year's end, *Picasso: The Recent Years*, by Harriet and Sidney Janis, was published. It contained accounts of Picasso's war life and reproductions galore.

There was no *Guernica* among the paintings—only Picasso's usual violence, somewhat intensified, perhaps, in the portraits and still-lifes. War's fever, nevertheless, was there: death in a bleached, omnipresent ram's skull; hunger as symbolized in a tomato vine that Picasso had faithfully tended all through that time, and that twines throughout the still-lifes; freedom, perhaps, or the light of truth in an oil lamp painted over and over. Of direct allusions: only one unfinished canvas, *The Charnel House*, black and gray like the *Guernica*—a somber record of the grisly ovens of Dachau.[4]

Kootz immediately raced to Paris with the Janis book under his arm, got the paintings, and unveiled them in New York. The town buzzed. Even taxi-drivers, forgetting baseball, lectured to their captive audiences on Picasso, pronouncing the second syllable as in the name of the well-known beast of burden. Alfred Barr was moved to remark that the great

[4] Now in the Walter P. Chrysler, Jr., collection.

Pablo was better known in Manhattan than in Paris, which was probably true. The exhibition was sold out in the first few days.

In the main, however, Kootz concentrated on American artists, exhibiting Baziotes, Motherwell, Fritz Glarner, and others. Between times he worked on the architects, inducing them to employ his artists as muralists, mosaicists, stained-glass window designers, and sculptors. And some time during this period Kootz, oppressed by a moment of leisure, dashed off a whodunit in which the corpse is found in a gallery of modern art.

Dealers were seizing the dynamic, pioneering role that the contemporary museums still failed to fill even after Peggy Guggenheim had shown them clearly how to do it. Everybody pioneered with somebody. Charles Egan introduced De Kooning, in 1948 and the Norlyst Gallery had presented Jimmy Ernst in 1943. The Artists' Gallery had discovered Pousette-Dart in 1941 and then followed up with Ad Reinhardt, while Betty Parsons, in the tiny room in the Wakefield Book Shop which preceded her 57th Street galleries, announced Stamos. Rose Fried's Pinacoteca gave Evsa Model his first show. A wonderful, rosy jag of discovery was going on everywhere. Howard Putzel, genial, nervous, and rotund, who had pioneered in San Francisco and Hollywood and then had come east to assist Peggy Guggenheim, carried on in her stead until his untimely death. Downtown in Greenwhich Village, little galleries like Peridot and the Jane Street, newest sproutings of a continuous crop, gave audience to artists younger still but already stepping on the heels of this generation just arrived.

Lively years, the 1940's! America was getting the exciting

feel of modern art at last. The older art periodicals grew more and more friendly. Dali was issuing his eccentric personal newspaper, a new issue with each annual exhibition. New little "mags" like *VVV*, the *Tiger's Eye*, and older ones like *Partisan Review* gave Harold Rosenberg, Clement Greenberg, and other rising critics of the new American art their first innings in linotype.

The *New Masses* and the *Daily Worker* regularly and enthusiastically "liquidated" abstractionism and surrealism as callously unconcerned with man's higher destiny: Communism. In his lectures at Columbia University and the New School for Social Research, the veteran Meyer Shapiro was starting to evaluate the new phenomenon.

Most widely influential of the magazines, Editor Charles Henri Ford's quarterly *View*, got its shove from surrealism. It lasted from September 1940 to March 1947, and was consistently amusing and informative, occasionally startling. Its back issues, particularly special issues like those devoted to Marcel Duchamp and Max Ernst, are standard reference material nowadays.

Provincial museums everywhere were sending for the Museum of Modern Art's circulating exhibitions. Where no museum existed, women's clubs, libraries, and other organizations were sending for the exhibits. Frankly surprised at the kind of shows that went to the unlikeliest places, the Museum commented that small, isolated, and relatively poor communities were going to the expense of bringing the most controversial art to their people. The prestige of the Museum was growing by leaps and bounds, and it was finding that its circulating program was more effective than its one and only direct attempt to establish a branch. This, as already noted, had been in Boston in 1936; within two years the Beacon Hill luminaries had staged a new Tea Party, taking over the branch office, lock, stock, and abstraction.

In separate regions, even in individual states, cultural circuits were set up and shows of modern art were scheduled as vaudeville acts had once been booked. The Virginia Museum of Fine Arts, for example, instituted "America's first state-wide visual arts system," with several score art exhibits, and lantern slides and films as well, available to any club, school, museum, or non-commercial society for a nominal fee. The Richmond institution, in addition, sent its Artmobile, a traveling art gallery in a huge trailer truck, into remote areas no longer visited even by the country circuses. Meanwhile, the museum directors of the Pacific Coast and adjoining states banded together to share expenses and extend their facilities.

The west coast, in fact, basked in its own modernistic sunshine. In Los Angeles various people were hammering away at that notoriously backward and reactionary neighborhood. Galka Scheyer had been there for many years, propagandizing German expressionism and the Blue Four, whom she is credited with having named. In latter years she had operated from her eyrie, a mountaintop modern house designed by Richard Neutra and Gregory Ain. Miss Scheyer died just as the new generation of American artists was beginning to be heard from. It found other champions willing to put their necks out. Earl Stendahl and Dalzell Hatfield helped with their dealer galleries, and John Entenza lent his progressive magazine *Arts and Architecture* to the cause. The tendency was to favor the local west-coast talent from Charles Eames and Harry Bertoia on, while placing the heavier bets safely on the established French moderns.

The movie colony began dabbling in collecting, but, with one or two exceptions, no major collections resulted. Movie stars, as a rule, hunt the cheapest of bargains with which to establish reputations as big spenders. Edward G. Robinson's collection is a major one, of course, although its main emphasis is on the proto-modern nineteenth century: Renoir, Cézanne, Gauguin, and Van Gogh.

Motion-picture director Albert Lewin's interest materialized both in motion pictures about art and in his own strongly personal collection. Having directed Somerset Maugham's novel of Gauguin's life, *The Moon and Sixpence*, he next produced *The Picture of Dorian Gray*, starring Hurd Hatfield as Dorian. The gruesome Jekyll-and-Hyde transformation of Dorian's portrait, as originally described by Oscar Wilde, was shown by actual paintings commissioned by Lewin. The famous Chicago painter twins Ivan LeLorraine Albright and Zsissly—plain Zsissly—were the artists chosen. Albright is the real family name, and Zsissly, who was Malvin Albright, took a name, telephone-book style, at the other end of the alphabet lest someone mistake him for Ivan. Actually, there was slight chance of this, artwise, because two men could not paint in styles more different. Zsissly did the smooth, pretty, academic portrait of the young Dorian Gray; Ivan, master of "the iridescence of putrescence"—the horrid phosphorescence of decay—painted the degenerated older Dorian in a way that still haunts those who saw the film.

In Lewin's next, *The Private Affairs of Bel Ami*, adapted from Maupassant, his art interest combined with Hollywood press agentry in an international art contest with prizes by courtesy of the movie magnates. The theme assigned to the painters was the classic Temptation of St. Anthony, and the large purchase prize mainly expressed Lewin's personal enthusiasm, because in *Bel Ami* the painting was little more than an extravagant part of the set-dressing. A preponderance of surrealists was invited to submit: Dali, Eugene Berman, Paul Delvaux, Max Ernst, Stanley Spencer, Leonore Carrington. Louise Guglielmi, Dorothea Tanning, the American Negro primitive painter Horace Pippin, and, once more, Ivan Albright. The judges, Alfred Barr, Marcel Duchamp, and Sidney Janis, awarded the prize to Max Ernst, who thus won over two women who have figured strongly in his life—Leonore Carrington and his present wife, Dorothea Tanning.

Five hundred miles north of Hollywood as the starlet flies, at the San Francisco Museum of Art, Dr. Morley, at an incredible rate of one hundred shows a year, was peppering the bay region with modern art like a machine gun with an endless ammunition belt. Then the MacAgys sprang into action.

Dr. Jermayne MacAgy, known far and wide as "Jerry," began a series of sensationally original exhibitions. Jerry then was Curator at the California Palace of the Legion of Honor, which is directed by Thomas Carr Howe, Jr., and is a piece of Gallic gingerbread frosted with some of the Spreckels' golden sugar, stuck on a cliff where the Lincoln Highway ends at the Golden Gate and the Pacific Ocean. Her dramatically installed "theme shows"—like that of *trompe l'oeil* ("fool the eye") painting, and a wonderful one of sundials, watches, and water clocks tolling off the story of time and man—have been second, in their way, to no exhibitions anywhere. In 1955 Dr. MacAgy went to Houston to assume the Directorship of the Contemporary Arts Association.

Douglas MacAgy, a wildly and poetically erudite young man from Toronto, Dr. Morley's Curator during the early 1940's, introduced jazz music as a modern art by organizing lectures and concerts and advertising them on the fronts of the streetcars and cable cars. The San Francisco Museum of Art, accustomed to crowds that had culminated at the historic Van Gogh Retrospective, was literally swamped. The brassy fanfares, knifing through the granite museum walls like Buddy Bolden's legendary New Orleans trumpet, summoned throngs that mounted to ten thousand people at the last Sunday bash.

MacAgy then became Director of the California School of Fine Arts, an academic nest that for some seventy-five years had successfully resisted anything new and was housed in pink California-Spanish stucco on the Chestnut Street hillside. MacAgy raced up and down the vaulted halls with his directorial broom, sweeping out the cobwebs and dust. When he had finished, San Francisco had the most modern and progressive art school in America, where art history was taught, not as graphs of periods or catalogues of styles, but as the biographies of artists, and where famous artists themselves, from Mark Rothko, Evsa Model, and Clyfford Still all the way to Duchamp the Olympian, were brought in to teach.

MacAgy found his school famous overnight. Like a magnet, it pulled the young from everywhere, including platoons of ex-soldiers who came on the G.I. Bill of Rights. Soon its students were winning prizes up and down the coast; that earnest but quixotic Hollywood collector, the late Fanny Brice, was buying their work; and within ten years some, like Sam Francis and John Hultberg, were achieving world-wide fame.

At the decade's end MacAgy conceived a giant symposium, the Western Round Table on Modern Art, on which for three days a distinguished panel considered the subject in its widest range, from "Science and Art" to "Art as Magic," from the artist to the critic, and from the collector to the museum. The San Francisco Art Association was sponsor; Johns Hopkins philosopher George Boas was moderator; and Duchamp, Mark Tobey, Frank Lloyd Wright, the Museum of Modern Art's Andrew Ritchie, critics Kenneth Burke, Robert Goldwater, and Alfred Frankenstein, anthropologist Gregory Bateson, and composers Arnold Schoenberg and Darius Milhaud made up the panel.[5]

By then, Douglas MacAgy was about ready to leave for New York to become assistant to the Museum of Modern Art's Director, René d'Harnoncourt. With his departure, the arch-conservatives promptly moved into his school, turned back the clock, and ended up with an empty till.

For the strong rise of modernism in the 1940's was inevitably crystallizing the forces of opposition. The Milwaukee Art Institute had already weathered a 1940 attack by reactionary groups that were currently called "as ignorant as Hitler and showing many of his prejudices." The Milwaukee Institute, through showing controversial exhibitions from the Museum of Modern Art, was "so vehemently assaulted that [its] very existence was threatened." But its Board of Trustees stood firm for "freedom of expression in art." [6]

There were rather sinister outbursts here and there. Then, in 1946, the United States government made a generous ges-

---

[5] Held on April 8, 9, and 10, 1949. MacAgy's "Digest of Proceedings" is included in *Modern Artists in America*, Volume I, edited by Robert Motherwell, Ad Reinhardt, and Bernard Karpel (New York, 1952).

[6] Quotations are from the *Museum of Modern Art Bulletin*, Vol. VII, No. 5 (September 1940).

ture to American art which only two years later would deto-
nate a blockbuster. The State Department bought and
assembled a large panoramic exhibition of our contemporary
art to send to foreign capitals "in response to requests for
examples of work by the modern school in America." [7] The
plan was immediately hailed as the "first step toward ex-
panding the 'public relations level' for American paintings to
include the entire world." [8]

Congratulations proved premature. Anti-modernists tick
like Geiger counters at an abstraction hanging on a wall forty-
three hundred miles away—for the exhibit was already on
view in Czechoslovakia's capital city, Prague. Someone arose
in Congress and yelled: "Modern art!" which is always spelled
in the *Congressional Record* as one four-letter word. On July 5,
1948, *Newsweek* commented: "The final chapter was written
last week on one of the most controversial art stories of recent
times. What was once called 'Advancing American Art'—the
collection of 79 oil paintings and 38 watercolors which the
State Department had bought and planned to exhibit abroad
—was finally disposed of by the War Assets Administration."

Newsweek erred: it was not the final chapter. The new art
critics in Congress crowed that the work was proved worthless
by the bankrupt prices it fetched. What they did not mention
was that it had been assigned to public institutions at five per
cent of its cost as a matter of a fixed government policy that
Congress itself had insisted upon during the operations of the
WPA. But facts never deter demagogues. Within less than one
year, the 81st Congress rang with ranting about this "Commu-

[7] From a letter of transmissal from the American Embassy in Prague,
Czechoslovakia (1947 or 1948), as quoted in *Modern Artists in America*, Volume
1, op. cit.

[8] John D. Morse: "Americans Abroad," *Magazine of Art*, January 1947.

nist art in government hospitals," charges that modern art was "shackled to Communism," and dire predictions that the Commies were maneuvering to "control art in the United States." [9] Alfred Barr was saying with genuine apprehension: "It can happen here." [1] Barr or any other well-informed person could have told our lawmakers that the Comintern bid to seize our art had been beaten down by American artists themselves during the WPA and that, further, the Soviets themselves had long since closed their modern museums in Moscow and Leningrad, and thereby, like Hitler, had outlawed modern art.

The strong feeling of reaction produced some strange minor results. Leo Stein, in what was all but a deathbed conversion, publicly renounced the modern art he had so strongly abetted nearly forty years earlier and called Picasso a destroyer of art.

It was a world-wide backsliding. The grim race between mind and muscle, which has filled our time with uncertainty and foreboding, had begun. At the Paris *salon d'automne* in 1944, a crowd shouting: *"Expliquez! Expliquez!"* tore fifteen Picassos off the walls. Andre Lhôte reported in *Tricolor* that "Into the ashcan with Matisse!" and "To the booby hatch with Picasso!" were the new slogans of the moment. The strong-arm boys were joined in France by the mouthers of the Big Lie, accusing the defenders of modern art as "perverters of youth." Confusing the issue completely—or perhaps clarifying it—the Communists joined the attack against their new comrade, Picasso.

Those were the lively 1940's. In America all this stir and

---

[9] *Congressional Record*, March 11, 1949, pp. 2364–5.
[1] Alfred H. Barr, Jr.: a letter in the *Art Digest*, August 1, 1949.

bustle of the art world came, in the last analysis, from the artists themselves. It had begun with the WPA's fraternity of friendship and fights. Now our young painters and sculptors were disproving Max Ernst and the various foreign artists, who were busily boarding return boats to Paris. An artists' world *could* exist here. So it came, typically American, a cafeteria Bohemia. It was not afternoon *aperitifs* in a sidewalk café, but the last nickel coffee in New York drunk at midnight in a white-tiled lunchroom.

Low rents were still to be found in the Village: a large commercial loft for $25 a month or a walk-up, "cold water," railroad flat for as little as $15. The lofts were good as studios, but only a few of them had plumbing. Nevertheless, some of the young artists lived in them in violation of Manhattan's housing codes.

A railroad flat, of course, is one in which the tiny rooms are strung out in line like a train of cars. Almost invariably the bathtub, added later in the century-old brick buildings, stands on claw feet in the center of the kitchen. With planks on top, it makes a good dining-table. When the planks are off, an artist or his model, an artist's wife or a guest from a bathless loft can bathe while a gay party goes on all around. In midwinter the heat comes from the gas range, a kerosene heater, or a second-hand electric one that is always short-circuiting and blowing out the fuses. Then candles are lit and the party goes on.

The elite who can afford $40 a month live in hot-water flats with small fireplaces fed with packing-cases salvaged in the streets and broken up. Lacking this flotsam from the concrete beaches of New York or the fireplace for it, the hot water is run continuously through the tub, furnishing a primitive form of steam heat not unlike a Finnish bath. If the house superintendent runs upstairs to protest the waste, the planks are hastily put back to attempt to hide the steaming water before he is admitted.

The beachcombers sally out after dark to prowl the dark, littered streets. Dodging the piles of cat-infested garbage flung out of upper tenement windows, the artists plunder an already plundered metropolis. An hour later they are back with firewood, discarded plywood panels for painting, scraps of iron for sculpture.

Once the Bohemia of the 1920's, Greenwhich Village is Bohemia again, but with a difference most profound. The earlier Eden was, on the whole, the escapist haven of the dilettantes and the ungifted whose only gift was a bitter but picturesque rebellion. It all seems a long time ago, but a ghost or two still hangs around the Minetta Tavern, the Jumble Shop, and the other old haunts. There is bearded Joe Gould, for example, forever scribbling overheard talk on scraps of paper to add to his "oral history of the world," which, rumor insists, has already reached ten million words. And until recently there was Maxwell Bodenheim, seedy and distraught, dredging the dregs of a traduced past for doggerel in trade for drinks. Suddenly one night poor Bodenheim lay sordidly slaughtered in a disreputable Bowery hotel. Faded images— Bodenheim, Gould, and the rest—memos to yesterday.

The present crew is a different bunch altogether, wild but purposeful iconoclasts assembling their new image from the broken bits of old ones. The talk, the arguments, the discussions are endless, all hammering away at art from its shining, unknowable core to all the petty fretfulness around its edges: poverty, lack of recognition, the perpetual, unequal battle with those in power.

Then someone discovers a little cafeteria where coffee is still a nickel a cup and lingering customers are not regularly swept out along with an endless sweeping of the tiled floor. It is an obscure branch of the Waldorf chain located almost directly over the stairs that lead down to the subway. Scarcely a Café du Dôme or a Deux Magots, this "one-arm lunchery" where the dinnerware clatters with each train that thunders beneath, but it serves very well. The Waldorf was already a club when the artists found it, and they had to fit their time to gather there into an already crowded schedule of meetings in order to avoid the conventions of taxi-drivers idling between shifts or the gamblers and touts just back from the race tracks.

The new American Bohemia has found its first clubroom. It is just off 8th Street, Greenwich Village's main stem, and around the corner from Hans Hofmann's art school. Its big plate-glass windows look out on the heavy traffic of Sixth Avenue, which Fiorello La Guardia rechristened "Avenue of the Americas."

16. *Arriving*

Among the shoddy Greenwich Village purlieus of 8th Street milled this new Bohemia, boiling with rebellion, frothing with hope—in the young artist it is often difficult to distinguish between the two. Having found a café, they were looking for a bar. Their lack of money and their troublesome ways brought cold welcomes wherever they went. They were always loudly airing opinions that sounded vaguely subversive to the bartender and the regular habitués, or objecting to the television programs being shown on the screen high on the wall at the end of the bar.

Not that their rebelliousness was out of place. By midnight or before, every drinker there was voicing his own personal mutiny. But the artists' rebellions were incomprehensible—not directed at low wages and high rents, for instance, or the shape-up on the waterfront, or the mysterious and perpetually unjust behavior of the opposite sex. These loud-voiced newcomers were grumbling about art dealers and museums, about abstraction or representation, or, most often, about some guy by the strange name of Picasso.

So from gin mill after gin mill the young artists were shunted more or less gently outside. Finally, working east along 8th Street, they came to University Place and, a little north, to the Cedar Bar. Not enjoying the sure patronage of the joints nearer Sixth Avenue, the Cedar Bar grudgingly accepted them with an overt hostility that gradually softened to tolerance. In the years that have passed since this first invasion, many of these unkempt young men have become famous and well-off. They have moved to better parts of town, but they still come back to the Cedar Bar. For some years, the head bartender, "George," has been regularly attending the openings of "Bill" de Kooning's exhibitions.

It was a Bohemia against odds—or, rather, two Bohemias. Straight across the Village on Hudson Street near the waterfront was the Mermaid of the literati. The new poets and writers gathered at the White Horse Tavern. Here in 1953 Dylan Thomas, tossing down one last fatal potion, fled into that long black tunnel of his coma where, at the far end, stood death—raggedly friendly, sordid and grand. But, for whatever reasons, these two Bohemias remained more or less separate, unlike Paris, where poets and painters have always fraternized and made a common front. Who knows? Perhaps in overspecialized America even the creative spirit must be specialized.

No matter how the saloons felt about artists, Peggy Guggenheim made them welcome. At her Art of This Century on 57th Street they daily formed an argumentative and faintly shabby knot amid the gallery-goers. Peggy, whose office was a small desk in the middle of one of the galleries, found it not at all confusing to be director one moment, lecturer or sales woman the next, and then to turn easily to her perpetual salon.

It was all buoyant with a confidence that American artists had never fully known before. There was, as Thomas B. Hess has written, "cheerful optimism . . . self-reliant re-examination of the past . . . a feeling of arrival and an ability to cope with crises." [1]

At almost precisely this same time the new Americans found another powerful friend in Sidney Janis, who was instrumental in getting them their first national showing. This was four years before Janis opened his own gallery. His book,

[1] Thomas B. Hess: *Abstract Painting—Background and American phase* (New York, 1951).

Abstract and Surrealist Art in America, which came out in 1944, called attention to the whole exciting current scene: the foreign artists then in America and their work done here, and the new American artists and styles, from out-and-out surrealism all the way to complete non-objectivism.

Dr. Grace Morley of the San Francisco Museum of Art promptly arranged a national tour for an exhibit of the paintings illustrated in the Janis book and timed to be co-ordinated with its publication. Thus many of the younger men were launched outside New York.

In a few years more the new Bohemia had its own clubrooms. Largely through the efforts of Robert Motherwell, one of the youngest of the group—he was then about thirty-three —upstairs rooms at 35 West 8th Street were rented. Here, slightly formalized and a little self-conscious, things became very much like Paris. There were weekly evening meetings; Baziotes, Gottlieb, Rothko, Barney Newman, and many others were active; there were lectures and concerts that ranged from "bashes" of disked jazz to live performances of John Cage's "longhair" percussion music. Museum directors and dealers began to attend, and there was even a three-day symposium with both the eggheads and the hotheads participating. Almost immediately the club became known as Studio 35, and finally just as "35."

"35" was a bit on the decline when a rival club sprang up a few doors west at Number 39. Its adherents, however, claim that the newer club was not intended as competition. It was avowedly social and not exclusively avant-garde. Word was sent out that artists of every kind—regardless of abstraction—were welcome. The evenings at The Club, as Number 39 came to be called, were highbrow in a most all-inclusive

way: William Barrett expounded existentialism; Harold
Rosenberg, a little like an American Apollinaire, flowed with
ideas and encouragement; Jesuit Father Lynch from Fordham
gave "the priest's point of view on art"; John Myers per-
formed with his puppets; and Kiesler talked on design. There
was music that went on from jazz and Cage and Henry
Cowell to Bartók and Webern as played by the Juilliard
String Quartet. Everyone came—Max Ernst, Hans Arp,
"Sandy" Calder, Joseph Cornell, museum people like Barr,
Cahill, and Sweeney, and many more, as well as the Waldorf
Cafeteria Alumni including, one by one, the adherents of the
older club.

A little kitchen dispensed coffee. For liquor, the Cedar
Bar was near by. As Leo Castelli, who helped to found The
Club, remarks: "The big thing we had in mind was to create
a friendly group of artists above and beyond all the isms."

The Club was set up in 1949 by a group of twenty. There
was one empty place at The Club which no one could ever
fill. That was the place of that wild, lovable Armenian,
Wostanig Adoyan, who had taken the fanciful name of
Arshile Gorky when he came to America. Gorky, who had
been proud of the fact that three art schools had "canned"
him, who had endured the most abject poverty in order to
paint, who all through the terrible 1920's and on to the end of
his life had fought tigerishly for modernism, was only forty-
four when he died in 1948. But his influence had been tremendous with the other men: he spoke their language both
in paint and in words—that soaring, poetic word-imagery
which painters will not tolerate from critics, but themselves
love to employ. Gorky was gone, and, as Lloyd Goodrich,
Director of the Whitney Museum, was moved to say, it "was

Jackson Pollock at work, 1951.
John Hultberg at work, 1951.

Franz Kline.
Clyfford Still.

a tragic loss to the art of America and the world." [2] Gorky's going was then so recent as to be not quite believable. As De Kooning says, "He was there every evening. You could feel him there."

Meanwhile, the work of the best of these newer men was maturing. Profoundly individual from artist to artist, it nevertheless had certain qualities in common. Most of these men, like Gorky, had once embraced Picasso and then, to save themselves, had rejected him as too overbearing a father image. The marks of both embrace and rejection remained in the new work. It was De Kooning's wife, Elaine, herself a painter, who had once called Picasso the "Great Flame Thrower." De Kooning quotes her. "General Sherman!" she said. "He only burned the country behind him. Picasso burns both the past and the future." Thus she described the almost superhuman avidity with which the Spaniard has assimilated everything he needed out of the past, from Negro sculpture to Ingres. And also his uncanny gift of prophecy: no matter what you do, someone can say: "What the hell? Picasso did that in nineteen-hundred and so-and-so."

Most of all, there was the lesson that the surrealists had taught these men. Not the dream landscapes or the erotic fantasies—all the Freudian furniture—but that basic way of releasing the creative energies so that they come through neither shackled to allusion nor hobbled by theories of style. Through the surrealists these Americans, being men of inquiring minds, found their way back to those two creatures of obsessive release, Van Gogh and Soutine, in whom compulsiveness overpowered reason.

[2] Lloyd Goodrich: biographical note in catalogue of the Whitney "Arshile Gorky Memorial Exhibition" (1951).

The new American abstract expressionists welcomed compulsion as a friend. So, finally, there it is, the new thing about abstract expressionism. Harmony, technique, composition, "finish"—all of the academic formulas—have nothing to do with it. These paintings, whether of landscape, figure, or still-life, are not paintings *about* these things; they are paintings of and about the act of creation itself. They are autobiographical in the purest and most direct sense. As Hess observes, "they stand at the extremes where the spirit of the painter and the body of his paint become indistinguishable." [3]

Peggy Guggenheim had closed her museum-gallery before the full flowering of this new movement. Now the dealers were showing the individual men in one-man shows where the strong group character was not indicated. The museums picked a man here and there to include in sprawling, unselective group shows in which their paintings and sculptures were either submerged or stood out as mere oddities in the tamer general scene.

A big show, everyone felt, was needed. Isolation had to be fought: the public must have a look at the gang as a whole. There was, too, the general preoccupation with work from Paris which in their eyes constituted a new academism. That had to be fought also. "Why don't we make a show?" someone asked, in a spirit very much like that which so many years before had animated Arnold Friedman and his friends in 1908 and The Eight in 1910. Everybody got to work.

On 9th Street, where a block was being torn down, someone found a vacated store. In another month it, too, would be gone. Its condition was horrible, but it could be rented for next to nothing. The bunch moved in, and overnight it was

[3] Hess, op. cit.

swept, mopped, and painted. Franz Kline, meanwhile, had cut a linoleum block and printed catalogues in the massive black on white which was already his trademark. The paintings and sculptures were already there and being hung. About ninety artists were shown, one work to each. At the last moment a few artists were forced to withdraw because of objections by their dealers. Others, like Motherwell and Hans Hofmann, defied their agents and submitted pictures anyway.

Leo Castelli installed the exhibition. "Hung the show!" he says. "I hung it twenty times. Each time it was done, an artist would come in and raise hell about the placing of his painting."

The 9th Street show was in 1951. It was the climactic effort of The Club, which later moved to Broadway and at present is on East 14th Street. The exhibition went far toward proving that modern art in America had at last come of age. As diverse in quality and character as any *salon d'automne*, it, too, had its focal points of authority—American counterparts, in this sense, of Picasso, Matisse, and Braque. Like the *salon*, it was a wave, not a final event. There would be more waves to follow.

Now the museums would begin to take serious note of these men: De Kooning, Pollock, Rothko, Baziotes, Kline, and the rest. But they were part of one wave, and the surf keeps coming in. The museums seldom wade into the water. Generally they are content to pick up whatever is safely deposited on the sand.

A dealer, however, had anticipated not only the museums, but even the artists' own showing of themselves. Sidney Janis, opening his gallery's third year, saluted the new generation and even compared them with their Paris contemporaries. Janis was abetted by Leo Castelli in his exhibit "Young Painters in U.S. & France," which opened in October 1950. Side by side hung fifteen of the new Americans and their foreign counterparts.

The catalogue, as can be seen, was a simple card without blurb or essay. The paintings spoke for themselves. Late the following year, a few months after the artists' own 9th Street Show, Janis, again with Castelli's help, went a step further. He assembled a group show called "American Vanguard Art for Paris Exhibition," previewed it in New York, and then shipped it to Paris, where it was shown during February 1952 at the Galerie de France. It is indicative both of the novelty of the new American work and the strong interest in it abroad among artists and art-lovers alike that the French gallery asked Janis to prepare the exhibition. Paris saw the carefully selected work of a full score of painters of the new American generation. The controversy was intense, most of the French critics assailing the work with violent defensiveness. But it was observed that the younger French painters crowded the gallery daily.

Janis had the co-operation that his fellow dealers had usually reserved for the museums. And for good reason: he was shouldering work, they felt, that the museums might well have done. So, one way or another, the work gets done. In this case, certainly, the job was done thoroughly. The show was brought back and then circulated, with its foreign press clippings, among a number of American museums.

It would be more than three years after the Janis comparative show before the young Europeans and Americans would be compared in an American museum, and then it would be in separate exhibitions nearly three months apart.

Young Painters in

Brooks	**1**	Wols
Cavallon	**2**	Coulon
de Kooning	**3**	Dubuffet
Ferren	**4**	Goebel
Ernst	**5**	Singier
Gatch	**6**	Pallut
Gorky	**7**	Matta

U.S. & France

Graves	**8**	Manessier
Kline	**9**	Soulages
Pollock	**10**	Lanskoy
Reinhardt	**11**	Nejad
Rothko	**12**	de Stael
Sterne	**13**	da Silva
Tobey	**14**	Bazaine
Tomlin	**15**	Ubac

Preview **4-6** Monday **23** October **1950**
SIDNEY JANIS GALLERY . 15 E 57

James Johnson Sweeney, Director of the Guggenheim Museum, personally toured America and Europe to choose both the artists and their work. His show "Younger European Painters" opened on December 2, 1953, and its companion show, "Younger American Painters," opened May 12, 1954.

Finally, in 1955, the Museum of Modern Art and the Whitney Museum got around to the subject with large shows that ran simultaneously. At the Whitney: "The New Decade—35 American Painters and Sculptors"; at the Modern: "The New Decade—22 European Painters and Sculptors." After the New York showings, the twin exhibitions went on national tour for the balance of that year and a considerable part of 1956. Due to unsynchronized scheduling, the shows would not be seen simultaneously anywhere else except in Los Angeles.

The Museum of Modern Art had previously saluted a few of the new Americans, not as abstract expressionists, but in the omnibus surroundings of general shows. Dorothy Miller's 1946 exhibit "14 Americans" included Gorky, David Hare, Motherwell, Noguchi, Roszak, and Tobey. Then, in 1952, Andrew Carnduff Ritchie's "Abstract Painting and Sculpture in America" included a number without specifically recognizing the already obvious emergence of a new style. That same year Dorothy Miller's "15 Americans" showed Baziotes, Pollock, Rothko, and Still in yet another show, one that ran the gamut from extreme abstraction to present-day echoes of the Ash Can School.

As for Sidney Janis, with his varied background of critic, collector, and onetime museum advisor, he has immeasurably raised the general prestige of the art dealer by shows of museum scope and quality. Reviving interest in Fauvism by a timely show, he caught the Museum of Modern Art with scarcely a Fauve canvas in its collection. Other shows of genuine historical importance in Janis's two (later three) small rooms on 57th Street have been "Climax: 1913," shown in 1951, "Dada" in 1953, and the long overdue reprise "Futurism" in 1954. The *Art News* comment on one Janis show would apply to many: "The exhibit . . . would make a worthy addition to the greatest museum."

To single out one Janis show: the "Dada" exhibition consisted of 212 separate original items including manifestoes, posters, books, documents, paintings, objects, collages of waste paper, et cetera—a more complete survey of Dada than may ever again be assembled. The Museum of Modern Art photographed each item on microfilm for its archives.

The exhibit itself, installed by Marcel Duchamp on transparent walls and ceilings and suspended in between, was an apparent shambles that resolved on inspection into a complex but logical ordering of the diverse material, an aspect of the installation that expressed well the serious core within Dada's nonsense. The installation was, in addition, a new work of art by Duchamp, the non-painter.

The Janis "Dada" catalogue, 24½ inches by 37½ inches, was on thin tissue paper. Duchamp arranged its four forewords, written especially by Huelsenbeck, Tzara, Levesque, and Arp (Duchamp studiously refrained from written comment), as a series of steps like those which the *Nude* is forever descending, and surrounded these texts with the numbered items. It was an example of typography that the Bauhaus might have envied. This catalogue was sent out to the gallery's mailing list crumpled into a ball like a discarded thing, and at the entry to the exhibit, similarly crumpled catalogues were offered in a wastebasket. Crumpled or uncrumpled, they are now collector's items.

But to return to the abstract expressionists. There was only one 9th Street Show, but inevitably something has taken its place. As no museum has shouldered the obvious—and, one would think, welcome—task of showing all the younger people each year, it has fallen to the lot of the Stable Gallery. Every year since the 9th Street Show there have been round-ups at the stable (for the gallery is just that: a stable from which equestrians used to sally forth for a canter in near-by Central Park). Dealers now gladly co-operate, but the annuals remain the artists' own selections of their work, one example to each. At the Stable, in theory at least, the darkest of dark horses can always find a stall.

But of late there are mutterings among those younger still. Another annual may be coming up, newer and still more independent. If so, space will be found and crowds will come. The bars are finally down, and the frustrations, timidities, and hesitations have been left behind. And here and there, on those newer walls, will be a painting that, as Marcel Duchamp has said, "lives by itself"—a painting that has won the "race between the artist and the work of art." [4]

Gorky, Pollock, and De Kooning were the acknowledged leaders of the generation of the 9th Street Show, the abstract expressionists of today. Jackson Pollock emerged earlier than many of his fellows. His 1944 show at Peggy Guggenheim's came four years after he had launched into abstraction and thirteen after he had become a professional painter. De Kooning, although Pollock's senior in age and professional activity, waited until 1948 for his first show at the Egan Gallery.

[4] At the Western Round Table on Modern Art (see note 4, Chapter 11).

Phoenix, *1951*,
by Hans Hofmann.
Oil, 60¾″ x 40½″.

Painting, 1951, *by Franz Kline. Collection: Mr. and Mrs. A. Neuman.*

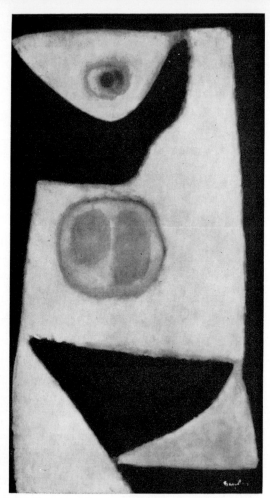

Sleepwalker, *1949*,
by William Baziotes.
Oil, 40" x 22".
Collection: Erle Ludgin.

William Baziotes at work.

During those years both men were a strong influence. Younger painters as well as some of their own generation kept gravitating to one or the other without affecting the unassailable prestige that was Gorky's. Within this new Bohemia the triumvirate was almost like Old Masters before the outside world had even heard their names. Amazingly, in an intensely personal and factional world, they remained good friends.

Jackson Pollock was born in Cody, Wyoming, in 1912. He studied at the Art Students League in New York with Thomas Benton, and thereafter made no less than twelve sketching trips across the United States. It is evident that he was not looking for subject matter: he was looking for himself. Not having found what he sought in Iowa or Nebraska, in the Northwest, the Middle West, or the Southwest, he came home and sat down. Suddenly there was an explosion. When the smoke cleared, Pollock saw a man standing in his studio. It was himself. Pollock ever since has been a series of explosions.

Tall and rugged, partially bald, awkwardly sure in his movements, Jackson Pollock looks like a pessimistic cowhand or a pugilist seriously considering quitting the ring. Hard living has eroded him like a rock. Prevailingly moody—almost surly—he is vastly withdrawn. At his most genial he is perpetually preoccupied, speaking grudgingly, as though with each word he lost something of himself. The canvas is his cattle range, his roped ring, his auditorium. His words are deeds, deeds of an incredible violence done with paint.

With the deepest admiration and with no little historical sense, De Kooning says: "Every so often, a painter has to destroy painting. Cézanne did it. Picasso did it with cubism.

Then Pollock did it. He busted our idea of a picture all to hell. Then there could be *new* paintings again."

At twenty-eight, after almost ten years of nondescript work, Pollock suddenly found himself in a series of explosive releases. There were several years of obsessive paintings in which recognizable images—she-wolves, birds, chimeras, tortured human faces—half appear and half dissolve in a wilderness of encrusted paranoid paint.

Then the moment came—it would be sometime in 1948 —when Jackson Pollock made a picture of the very explosion itself. He threw his easel out into the yard, spread a vast canvas on the floor, and began throwing paint at it. He raced around it with pails, hurling gushes of violent hues to splash and flow, to gut and to congeal. Clots and rivulets, freshets of excitement, layer after layer of blot and blob and of weaving, tangled lines. Hours went by before the pails were empty and the fury over. Pollock squatted on his heels in a corner, trembling and spent, looking out over the exultant, screaming chaos that lay on the floor.

Jackson Pollock was looking at a totally new way of painting as if someone else had done it and he had just happened on the scene. Everyone had been talking about a "way to get the explosive moment of creation on the canvas." Someone had just done it: simply turned the paint loose in the air without a parachute. A violent Duchamp, not gravely accepting the "laws of chance," but flinging the door open to chaos.

Almost all night Pollock sat looking at that picture, and slowly before his eyes it changed: order marshaled itself in all that wilderness. Those violent forces—the whirls, the plunges, the thrusts—began to float in an equilibrium of violence against violence. It was a miracle, like deadly explosives held inert in a chemical compound, a miracle like the atom-loaded galaxies orbiting themselves. It was as miraculous, even, as the burned forest hiding its wounds with the thousand green spears of its new pines.

Those first paintings of a new, released Pollock slapped the public in the face. It took a lot of looking to let their miracle work. But other artists got the idea right away. A canvas or two got to France. The young Frenchmen got the idea, too. By 1949, when Leo Castelli saw the now-famous Georges Mathieu, the latter, working with a shipping line, was collecting every American periodical showing Pollock's new work which he could lay his hands on. Soon Mathieu, putting on a grim face and donning bits of armor, was inviting audiences in to watch him as he sprinted around throwing paint on canvases to make what he calls battle scenes. By 1954 the French were unanimously claiming "simultaneity" —it happened at the same time. But there is the strongest evidence that the man finally bit the dog.

Almost immediately Bill de Kooning came along and took another bite. It was no case of standing in order until Pollock had done snapping. De Kooning had been sharpening his teeth for a long time: his abstract work dates from as early as 1934. But his big bite consisted of a series of paintings he began in 1949, called, in general, *The Women*. This series of utterly horrifying demolitions of the woman image—mother-wife-sister—scarcely takes second place to Picasso's lifelong painted assault on the form divine.

The De Kooning *Woman*—any one of them—actually does not resemble her counterpart in Picasso's work except in the general nightmare air of horror in the boudoir. They do, however, remind one of Walkowitz's classic remark about a very famous woman, one rather battered and totally without arms. This is the Louvre's prize *Venus de Milo.* In the very early days in Paris, Walkowitz was defending the distortion in modern art: "When I see the shape that poor Venus is in," he said, "I wonder, now how could Picasso possibly do anything more awful to a woman?"

It cannot be said that Picasso and De Kooning have not tried. De Kooning evidently felt that he had succeeded, because, after painting a dozen large canvases, he desisted and the *Woman* series was complete. Every one of them has already found its way into a museum or a private collection.

Except for the fact that he was born in Rotterdam in 1904 and lived in Holland until 1926, Willem de Kooning, though he looks the part, is the exact opposite of what we expect in a Dutchman. He is of medium height, and his slight huskiness conceals a physique of iron. With his neat, conservative dress, his iron-gray hair, scrubbed, shining cheeks, and china-blue eyes, he looks the quiet burgher of Rotterdam. There the resemblance ends. He is mercurial, not calm, and actually loathes the clean and tidy. He seems to be concerned with proving that the ideal Dutch orderliness is a spiritual chaos while actual chaos is a new kind of order. Above all, he is neither smug nor serious, though he is profound. His slashing wit would horrify a compatriot. Nowhere in all bovine and pastoral Holland is to be heard the typical sound of his paintings: the horselaugh.

De Kooning studied the immaculate rectangularities of the *de Stijl* abstractionists, and loved that serious arch-priest of purity, his countryman Piet Mondrian—whom he called "that great merciless artist." Yet his own paintings have the purity and the tidiness of a deserted junkyard. From his rejections fully as much as his acceptances, De Kooning's present masterful art has come.

He rejected Holland and accepted America when, in 1926, he stowed away on an English coal boat bound for Newport News. When the stokers found him "swimming in sweat" above the boiler room, they were so afraid he was going to die that they fed him, hid him from the officers, and let him slip ashore. Here he has remained ever since, an illegal entry long since officially legalized.

De Kooning looked for the America all the Rotterdam youths were dreaming of: "broad clean streets in a glare of white light and everywhere the sound of Louis Armstrong's trumpet." "The streets and the light," he now says, "were only in the Hollywood films. The jazz you could find, if you could get away from the squares to look for it."

Here, anyway, you could be anything you wanted to be: house-painter, window-trimmer, commercial artist ("I was never a good one, thank God!"), and finally—with WPA help—an artist. And here you could make friends so easily: Alajalov, Anton Refregier, Misha Reznikoff, and, through Misha, Gorky. Not love at first sight. Gorky was insulting: "You're just a truck-driver," he said.

"But there was something about that guy," De Kooning recalls. The next time they met, the volatile Armenian was friendly, even let De Kooning see his paintings, which were cubist in that period. In his broken English, Gorky was a spellbinder of wild and extravagant phrases. Yet he constantly hit the mark.

De Kooning adored Gorky and, despite their similar ages, deferred to his seniority as a modernist. Every night through those early 1930's Gorky's Union Square studio was crowded with his friends. Modern art was still being discovered, and the air seemed to surge with the surf of discussion. Then Gorky would wind up his phonograph and sing and dance while he played Georgian and Armenian records. Through it all he interspersed a running, never ending tale of his childhood on the farm near Lake Van in Turkish Armenia. All evening De Kooning would sit unnoticed in a corner, never speaking, silently drinking it all in. To him it was the magic core of America, and Gorky's rich, husky voice, he thought, commanded everything like Armstrong's trumpet. Then De Kooning met Stuart Davis, and Davis, hepcat from the ragtime days, took him to jazz.

Like Pollock, De Kooning the artist matured slowly like fruit ripening in cold weather. America, no Paris then, had to change to let her artists change. By 1940 or earlier, De Kooning was painting strange, bare, ungracious abstractions full of equivocal shapes tantalizingly like and unlike natural things, pictures in which solids become space and space is fitted with trapdoors leading into unknown depths. Already De Kooning's art was his own, though the fury and the disorder were yet to come.

Gorky and De Kooning were inseparable, but now their relationship was more nearly that of equals. Gorky's art, slow-maturing too, was ripening into a harvest of complex pictures full of Oriental color and beautifully drawn calligraphic forms. Then, without warning, came the first of Gorky's catastrophes: in 1946 his studio, full of paintings, burned to the ground. He set to work determinedly, eclipsing the destroyed canvases with a new series. But disaster followed fresh disaster. In the midst of the creative orgy (in one summer, 292 drawings alone), Gorky fell prey to cancer and underwent an operation. In 1948 an automobile accident broke his neck and temporarily paralyzed his painting arm. The giant Armenian, who believed in the lake gods of his childhood, must have thought that they had turned upon him. Three weeks after the accident, at the very height of his creative powers, he hanged himself.

Plunged in grief at Gorky's death, De Kooning was nevertheless released. A hand—even if only that of friendship—was taken forever from his arm. From his mouth, almost like a medium's, began to issue wild metaphors full of insight. They reminded one of Gorky himself, except that the poetry was more sardonic. The horselaugh had drowned out the shepherd's tune.

De Kooning's paintings suddenly became prolix and violent. Like those of Pollock, they are anti-art—no classic ordering of disorder into significant form, no picturesque detail vignetted out of chaos, but the very disorder, the very chaos. No longer painting about anything—just painting. And yet an artist is an artist. Here, too, as with Pollock, order comes uninvited like the stranger at the feast. Silence settles over it all at last.

De Kooning now paints and ceaselessly repaints, layer upon layer, with the earlier strata still showing through. His paintings are never finished. Left with the artist, they would go on evolving forever, or at least for as long as he lives. Into them are coming at last the two Americas, the one sought and the one found: the clean streets and the white lights, the dirty streets and the darkness—the order and the dishevelment. And through it all, Satchmo's golden horn is weaving those never ending variations on a simple song of the people.

De Kooning began pouring out huge canvases like *Excavation*, in which cubism, which had already exploded natural form, itself explodes. Then, when his followers had their feet comfortably planted in his abstract footsteps, Picasso-like he suddenly veered back to representation and into his savage assault upon womanhood.

De Kooning is irrepressible. He is the mocking muted horn of the jam session. Over the whole scene echoes his gigantic, monstrous horselaugh.

He laughs at art: "Art never seems to make me peaceful or pure. I always seem to be wrapped in the melodrama of vulgarity." [5]

Or at any idea that art should serve a noble or useful purpose: "It is exactly in its uselessness that it is free."

He laughs at all the art movements. Personally, he says, he does not need them. Yet in the next breath he hails one of the gods of modern art: "And then there is that one-man movement, Marcel Duchamp—for me a truly modern movement because it implies that each artist can do what he thinks he ought to—a movement for each person and open for everybody."

Then De Kooning turns with a withering bray on the museums: "So goddam historical minded that they put us in pigeon holes. Who the hell ever said we were pigeons?" [6]

At education, De Kooning's mouth flies open like the horse in Picasso's *Guernica*. "The one thing a teacher can never say is those three little words, 'I don't know.' And yet give

[5] This and the two quotations immediately succeeding are from "What Abstract Art Means to Me," a symposium of six artist speakers, in the *Museum of Modern Art Bulletin*, Vol. XVIII, No. 3 (Spring 1951).

[6] This and the succeeding quotation are from conversations with the author.

any Joe four years at college and he thinks that wisdom sticks to his ass."

De Kooning can even unloose that shattering laugh at our demigods, the solemn scientists: "That space of science . . . I am truly bored with it now. Their lenses are so thick that seen through them, the space gets more and more melancholy. There seems to be no end to the misery of the scientists' space. All that it contains is billions and billions of hunks of matter, hot or cold, floating around in darkness according to a great design of aimlessness. The stars *I* think about, if I could fly, I could reach in a few old-fashioned days. But physicists' stars I use as buttons, buttoning up curtains of emptiness. If I stretch my arms . . . and wonder where my fingers are —that is all the space I need as a painter." [7]

[7] *Museum of Modern Art Bulletin,* op. cit.

Toughness, both physical and mental, is perhaps the most striking thing about the abstract expressionists. Without swaggering, most of them impress you as men who could take good care of themselves in a free-for-all, and could do it singly. For they are certainly not a close-welded brotherhood. When they band together, it is for social and tactical reasons, but in art and everything else they fight alone. The title "abstract expressionism" is a garment that fits because it is loose. Far less united than were the Fauves, the early cubists, or the *de Stijl* geometricists, they want no part of conformity or the dictatorships of theory and style.

Expect no mass standing vote from this group. You have to call the roll separately.

First is short, stocky Hans Hofmann, florid and white-haired, approaching eighty, yet overflowing with the vitality and the optimism of youth. Hofmann, born in Germany in 1880, belongs in the generation of Picasso, Braque, and Léger. Yet he takes his stand here, though old enough to be De Kooning's father and Stamos's, or even Motherwell's, grandfather.

Hofmann was reared among the German expressionists and then came here, where he has taught and painted since 1932. Hans is overpoweringly likable; he made many friends. The young accepted him as one of themselves, and his strong convictions, so magnetically conveyed, made him an early influence, particularly in the basic way that he insisted painting should be approached. The freed imagination, he has said, must create life in the picture. He believes that color by itself creates form, and he paints spontaneously with fury that is a real fury even if it is cheerful rather than grim.

Fervor, rather than fury, belongs to Mark Tobey, who,

by virtue of age, comes next. Tobey was born in Wisconsin in 1890, but his modernism begins with this generation. One of the original Greenwich Village Bohemia of World War I, he moved his charcoal portraits from Washington Square to Knoedler's, where they became fashionable oils. Then Tobey began wandering: to Paris, to the Near East, and to England, to Mexico, and then to Seattle, where he first felt the Sino-Japanese influences that are so strong on the Pacific Coast. These pulled him on to China in 1934. There he studied with the artist Teng Kwei, learning the Oriental's active magic with brush as well as the magic of memory that lives on in Chinese calligraphy and art.

Here was method. Returning to Seattle, he embraced Bahaism and found his material: light. "Light," Tobey says, "is a unifying idea." He began painting cities and "figures caught in light." One almost says "writing" cities because the pictures are multiple interlacings of calligraphic writing as mysterious yet authoritative as undeciphered hieroglyphs. Lyonel and Julia Feininger credited Mark Tobey with the invention of calligraphic painting—in our culture, at least: "a new convention of his own, one not yet included in the history of painting."

Extraordinarily quiet and noble, these networks of paint —more sober-colored even than cubism—and yet they are the end product of a life that began on Main Street, U.S.A. "My gods were in the beginning American gods: Harrison Fisher, Christy, . . . Gibson.

"Then . . . the Armory Show came as a powerful blight. . . . The 'Nude Descending a Staircase' looked to me like an explosion in a shingle mill, which I thought would settle it for all time. But later, after the blaze of Bellows and Henri,

I saw it again . . . thinking this time what a wonderful abstraction.

"Many times my ship has almost foundered. . . . The 1920's were enough to turn any creative heart into an organ without blood. Then I saw the 'Nude' again. It seemed full of the sorrows of the Son of Man. It's the Crucifixion, I thought."

Today, Mark Tobey is Europe's great new discovery. He and Pollock dominated the Bern Kunsthalle in its 1955 exhibit, "*Tendances Actuelles.*" *Art News* reports from Paris: "All eyes are now on Tobey, who has just had a one-man show." [1] One can imagine Tobey's pictures there, like Duchamp's immortal *Nude*, quiet, never changing, while, all about them, time changes and people change.

For a number of reasons the name of Morris Graves is generally associated with that of Tobey. Both live in the state of Washington. Graves, twenty years younger than Tobey, for a long time painted under the older man's acknowledged influence. Then, when Marian Willard introduced them in New York, they became popularly known as the Northwest Painters. Now French critics place them in a "Pacific School," linked with younger men who trained at the California School of Fine Arts during the MacAgy renaissance. Morris Graves, like Tobey, is obsessed with light, but his personages are birds, not men. He, too, is a poet and a mystic, but not so much a philosopher.

Next is a formidable man, Mark Rothko, whose gentleness is only a little less terrifying than his anger. A Russian Jew (born in Dwinsk in 1903), he has lived here since he was ten. Rothko's many angers are those of a Jeremiah; his wit

[1] *Art News*, Summer 1955.

has the ancient folk-tale grotesqueness, the humanity and the awareness of human frailty, of real Hebrew humor. Rothko is a one-man Report on Israel: the anger, the love, the passion, the apocalyptic vision, the poetry of warm flesh, the morbid, aggressive sensitiveness bred by historic injustice.

Rothko hulks large physically, and his canvases are room size—"Eight feet high," says Hess, "is not an unusual dimension in Rothko's œuvre." [2] He himself is variable. Outgoing, he fills a room or the street where he stops you to talk. Indrawn and brooding, he shrinks like the echo of a cry. But, whatever may be said of his excesses, Mark Rothko is never piddling.

He has been painting a long time, and never gently, though he studied briefly with gentle Max Weber. He was a muscular and fervent expressionist until 1939, and then, as noted, briefly joined Gottlieb in a pictograph or, at least, primitive symbolism phase. Then, while Peggy Guggenheim was showing him in the mid-1940's, Rothko entered a biological-zoological period in which the large canvases are like microscopic close-ups of the creatures in a steaming, primordial swamp.

Then all at once, as it had hit Tobey, light hit Rothko. But Rothko's light is not the light of cities like a nimbus around man, but the light of time and space, unconcerned even with man's existence. It was light and silence seen and heard as one and the same thing. As George Heard Hamilton, Director of the Yale University Art Gallery, has written, "In

[2] Thomas B. Hess: *Abstract Painting—Background and American phase* (New York, 1951). In 1955, reviewing a Rothko exhibit, Hess wrote in *Art News* of "twelve paintings—the best one taking up a whole wall, several others stretching from floor to ceiling."

Rothko's measured space movement and silence turn into themselves." [3]

The canvases that Rothko now paints stun almost everyone with their simplicity, their great muted rectangles of colored light, their vast size that reaches out and pulls the spectator into the picture. It is possible to be violently for or violently against them—it is impossible not to be involved. Hubert Crehan writes: "I have heard one painter speak of 'Rothko's roomful of light.' Another . . . has said, 'You can warm your hands in front of them.' " [4]

Rothko yesterday was one of the "17 Irascibles," the abstract artists whom *Life* photographed in 1951 when they jointly refused to take part in a Metropolitan Museum exhibition of contemporary American art. He has boiled and fumed and sulked ever since. But a different Rothko is to be found in his paintings, wherein all the torments, great and little but abiding, have fused together into one bright, silent flame. So today he amazes Americans, amazes even the Parisians. Only Rothko, being finally himself, is not amazed.

For well over ten years Adolph Gottlieb quietly explored the comparatively narrow confines of his pictograph world. His pictures, with their symbols and signs compartmented in rude rectangles, ovals, and arches, all painted with a deliberate clumsiness, look as archaic as prehistoric paintings on stone. He says that he was projecting images that seemed vital to him, "disinterred relics." In the general view, Gottlieb held letters-patent on the pictograph idea, which came to be associated exclusively with his name. In point of fact, a

[3] George Heard Hamilton: "Object and Image," *Art News*, May 1954.
[4] Hubert Crehan: "Rothko's Wall of Light," *Arts Digest*, November 1, 1954.

Uruguayan, the late Joaquín Torres-García, who lived in Paris, had explored this vein a number of years earlier than Gottlieb.

Within the last few years Gottlieb has turned to the painting of vast pictures (*Labyrinth*, 1954, is twelve feet wide) that seem to magnify the late Bradley Walker Tomlin's over-laid mazes of calligraphy—"bands, pot-hooks, boomerangs, letters, dots, rectangles, zigzags" [5]—into gigantic brushstrokes. It remains to be seen whether this new departure of Gottlieb's will lead to a more personal expression.

Tomlin died in 1953 at the age of fifty-four. He had painted for more than twenty-five years; had turned to ab-stract work in the early 1940's. Yet the exhibit of 1950 at Betty Parsons's was his first one-man show in the modern vein. Like the work of certain contemporary Parisians—Alfred Manessier, for example—Tomlin's abstract work somehow seems to lack conviction.

Pollock roamed the country to find himself. Baziotes went to West Nyack, New York. He made his discovery—partly, at least—in a garbage dump there.

William Baziotes was born in Pittsburgh in 1912, and had orthodox training at the National Academy of Design. At twenty-four he was painting like Cézanne. That palled soon enough, and then he began painting figures and still-lifes from memory. "What I saw insulted me," he says. "I tried to escape it by doing it somewhere else." He was bored and frustrated. A whole year followed during which he "worked and worked and couldn't finish one picture."

Right after this year Baziotes rented a cottage in the

[5] Edward W. Root in the catalogue of the Museum of Modern Art exhibit "15 Americans" (1952).

little Hudson River village of West Nyack for a honeymoon summer. A young architect shared the cottage with the newlyweds.

"There was a sixty-foot porch," Baziotes recalls. "This guy, being a Bauhaus man, couldn't let that porch wall alone. It made him sad. He kept after me—'There's got to be a mural there.'

"At last I gave in. At the garbage dump we found some old weatherbeaten doors, yanked out the panels, and I got some pastels and went to work. There was nothing in my mind, you see, so every crack and every mildewed spot suggested something—I developed it and ran wild, just played with the shapes. First automatic stuff I ever did.

"The whole porch was done in one afternoon. I felt like someone unexpectedly let out of jail."

Baziotes, essentially, has painted like that ever since. He has said that each of his paintings is an excursion into the unknown. They are also excursions into the night. Short but square-shouldered, well-muscled but gentle-mannered, he conceals a strong mystical strain that comes out in his work. Night is his obsession—night and its creatures—and it is night that shimmers in the half-lights.

His character comes clear when he talks of Picasso. "Cubism," Baziotes says, "never interested me. But when that big Picasso show went on in 1939 at the Museum of Modern Art, I went every day. Now, something happens: you look at a man long enough and you sort of digest him and when it comes out it's not him, it's you.

"Well, I looked at Picasso until I could smell his armpits and the cigarette smoke on his breath. Finally, in front of one picture—a bone figure on a beach—I got it. I saw that the

Mark Rothko, 1954.

Abraham Walkowitz, New York, January 1908.

Abraham Walkowitz,
New York, c. 1950.

*The U.S. & France Exhibit, 1950, Sidney Janis Gallery, New York.
Left: Dubuffet and De Kooning. Right: Rothko and De Stael.*

The 9th Street Show, New York, 1951.

figure was not his real subject. The plasticity wasn't either—although the plasticity was great. No. Picasso has uncovered a feverishness in himself and is painting it—a feverishness of death and beauty."

Robert Motherwell and Baziotes were friends before even Peggy Guggenheim discovered them. But Motherwell knew the French surrealists who were here before he met Baziotes or any other American painter. At the surrealists' urging, Motherwell began editing a series of art books for Wittenborn, a series that has since grown into the dozen volumes called *Documents of Modern Art*. Mixing with the surrealists, Motherwell was bound to meet Peggy. This was in the early days of her gallery. She was busy planning an all-collage exhibition that Motherwell believes was the first such exhibit ever done by a museum.

Peggy got Motherwell, Baziotes, and Pollock together—this was even before she had given them shows. "I want you to get some paper and scissors and paste," she told them, "and make some collages for my show." The three snipped and pasted away, and their work was hung together with the early and later collage masters: Picasso and Braque, Ernst and Masson.

"I had never seen a collage in my life," says Motherwell. "But I was excited with the three I made. Naturally: the Baltimore Museum bought one, the Museum of Modern Art bought one, and Peggy bought the other."

Before that, however, Motherwell and Baziotes had already had a public showing of one work each. This was at Marcel Duchamp's surrealist exhibit in the Whitelaw Reid house, in which they were the only younger Americans represented. Baziotes, who had met Matta, had become friendly with the surrealists, too. Both of the men were deeply impressed by the surrealist attitude, which Baziotes sums up in a remark of Matta's: "There are many roads but painting must be an adventure concerning yourself."

Of the three artists who clipped and pasted for Peggy Guggenheim, only Motherwell has continued with collage. In it he found his abstract medium, and he has come to be identified with it.

So far, as can easily be seen, this is a generation of tough-minded individualists who are not yes-men even to Picasso and who will throw not so much as a bone to the meek dogs of conformity. Clyfford Still is one of the toughest of them all. He kicks the hungry dogs, then goes on to kick the museums, the dealers, the collectors, and the whole public. He is an embittered and embattled martyr determined that society must at all costs burn him at the stake. He encounters vast difficulties in achieving this goal because his paintings are original and fine. The public crowns him not with thorns, but with controversy that is the envy of other painters; younger artists acknowledge his authority. Still's answer to all this is to burrow deeper than ever into his molehill of self-immolation. He frequently refuses to have exhibitions, will not lend pictures to the museums, hoards his canvases in secret. With each would-be destructive move, Still's legend grows; instead of achieving martyrdom, he only grows more frustrated. Now, despite his best efforts, collectors show signs of wanting his large, expensive pictures. Soon Still may face a new crisis.

He grants interviews with the freedom of a Capone; trapped in conversation, he gives with the autobiography like the Sphinx of Gizeh. All students of the life of Clyfford Still

must be referred to a certain Museum of Modern Art catalogue, that of the exhibit "15 Americans," published in 1952.
Therein are to be found two collectors' items: a biographical
note, and (a real rarity) the artist talking about himself.
History is indebted to Dorothy Miller, who arranged the
exhibition and compiled the catalogue.

Referring to the note, we find that Clyfford Still was born
in Grandin, North Dakota, in 1904, and grew up in Canada,
"alternating farm work with schooling in Alberta and in
Spokane." There follow graduation from Spokane University, an advanced degree from Washington State College, and
teaching. We next find Still working in war plants in San
Francisco. Soon he is putting in a four-year stint, 1946–50,
teaching at the California School of Fine Arts.

Peggy Guggenheim introduced his work in a one-man
show in 1946.[6] Clyfford Still's notably difficult paintings attracted little attention until the early 1950's, when Betty
Parsons cornered him for two successive exhibitions. It was
then that the Still legend began to grow.

Still's sprawling canvases are almost indescribable. Huge
areas of uncompromising color lie like the land and sea masses
on maps or in aerial photography. Yet they do not lie—they
move like threatening clouds at different altitudes. Altogether
remarkable is the anger that leaps from such abstractly non-
committal elements. George Heard Hamilton is moved to
point out "how with Still the anger *is* the pigment, the
corruscated surface, the aching color." [7]

With it all there is none of the unabashed frankness of

---

[6] The catalogue of "15 Americans" states that the San Francisco Museum
of Art gave Still a one-man show in 1941. This is an error.

[7] George Heard Hamilton, op. cit.

Pollock or De Kooning. Still's paintings are peripheral, and the greatest violence is likely to occur furtively at the very edges, half on and half off the canvas, like a man exploding in anger when he is safely around the corner. From whatever private torments, nevertheless, Clyfford Still has wrung authority, and from the dregs of bitterness has distilled a startling originality.

Franz Kline is the same age as Baziotes and from the same state. Kline was born in Wilkes-Barre. He was the last of the present-day leaders to emerge. After general education at Girard College in Philadelphia, he entered a protracted phase of academic art study: Boston University and then Heatherley's School in London. Kline was twenty-eight years old when he returned to New York to begin exhibiting at the traditional Washington Square outdoor shows and then at the National Academy.

During all this time Kline gradually, almost timidly, gravitated toward the modern. He has told of his interest in such varying kinds and degrees of modernism as that of Marsden Hartley, Milton Avery, Tomlin, and De Kooning. He struggled vainly, as Henri and The Eight had done so long before, to be modern without changing his point of view. It was evident, despite awards by the National Academy, that Kline was getting nowhere in particular.

The 8th Street Club's non-sectarian welcome to artists regardless of their style attracted Kline, who joined. He was popular immediately, an elbow-bender second to none at the Cedar Bar; he drew closer to De Kooning; he worked harder, worried more, wrestled with the stubborn paint as a New England farmer wrestles with the rocky soil. It developed into crisis: it would be a nervous breakdown for Kline or a modern

style of his own. Franz Kline is another man of strong physique, oaken independence, and stubborn pride. As De Kooning says, "a real all-or-nothing guy."

If De Kooning asked him what he was searching for,
Kline could only say: "For clarity, for the statement that can
be read only one way." The nights and days blurred in a
whirling scroll of struggle—dark nights, bright days—and
then he had it: black and white! When De Kooning came in
and saw the first new canvas, he was flabbergasted. Kline
could only point at the canvas, saying nothing. In fact, Kline
has been inarticulate about his own work ever since—"I find
it impossible to make a direct statement about the paintings
in black and white." [8] No wonder: Kline at last is speaking
as a painter, through his paint.

The night before, Kline had looked at a blank white
canvas almost in complete despair. "I was thinking of a
woman." A real woman, a woman of warm, desired flesh,
but in his confusion she merged with all the claptrap dead
symbolism of the academicians: she was Leda. She was already in his mind's eye, pinkly voluptuous, entwined with the
swan in all the antique foliage. And there on the palette were
heaped all the sumptuous colors of Boucher and Titian ready
for another tinsel allegory.

Symbols! Symbols!

And then *the* symbol had loomed, stark black on the
white canvas, like an after-image of the tired eye or brain: a
great black hieroglyph, a letter from an alphabet that never
was. Kline seized a huge brush, lathered it with the pure,
unctuous ivory black, tore at the canvas. A dozen sure, swift

[8] Biographical article in the catalogue of the Whitney exhibit "The New
Decade: 35 American Painters and Sculptors" (1955).

slashes and the painting had been done.

"Well, for Chrissake, does it have a name?" De Kooning was saying.

"Oh," said Kline. "Leda."

This was in 1949. One year later Charles Egan gave Kline a one-man show. There was no question about the newness of the work. Yet so "inevitably 'right' and even familiar" were these canvases, as Hess observes,[9] that they delighted rather than shocked. They seemed always to have been there.

They are not really black on white, they are black *and* white. A painting may take minutes or months. The moment of "clarity" must come. There is no room in these bare structures for denial or the lie. Franz Kline, as his friend De Kooning says, is as much an absolutist as Mondrian. As for Kline himself, he knows he is as isolated as a man on the edge of a cliff. "These paintings!" he says. "I object like hell to every one of them. But I'm stuck with 'em."

Japan, land of calligraphy, was the first foreign country to hail Kline. Japan's artists had been rebelling against an academism imposed by MacArthur's General Headquarters, which, as Ray Falk reported in the *New York Times* (April 24, 1955), was "critical of . . . 'imitations of Western painters' and suggested instead a return to the very traditional." American sculptor Noguchi introduced Kline's work to his parental homeland. Now Kline is a cult there, his work spread through the art journals. In *Bokubi*, the calligrapher Shiryū Morita writes:

> I have seldom felt so keenly that the character of a work can be made through the harmony of the outside

[9] Thomas B. Hess, op. cit.

and the inside . . . the outside being the combination of
the lines and the inside the quality of these lines.

. . . the painter's deeper consciousness of the beauty
of blank space must be noticed. He modestly pays attention to and makes use of the beauty of white as well as that
of black. . . . It is my greatest pleasure to find—not in
the East but in America . . . the same beauty as in the
calligraphy.

As for France, black-and-white calligraphy appears and,
as far as the French are concerned, it is "simultaneity" again.
Having steamrollered the league for fifty years, they are now
content with a tie score. Kline was in the vanguard American
group that Sidney Janis chose for the 1951 Paris showing.
Soon France's Pierre Soulages was slashing away with black
on a broad brush. It's easy, once you know how. For Soulages,
anyway. Kline still has to struggle to reach that "clarity"
which to him is vital.

The woods, where artists once were scarce, are full of
artists nowadays. Without a WPA, they get along. Our abstract-expressionist generation abounds in painters who might
have been leaders a generation ago, but are consigned to
secondary roles today.

There is Ad Reinhardt, for example, a competent and
assured fixture in the exhibition world through many phases:
a Malevitch sparseness, a *de Stijl* geometricism, an amorphi-
cism of melting forms. One cannot safely categorize Reinhardt
as a taster of styles. Too many of his generation have searched
for years and then flared into their own particular incan-
descence.

The same might be true of Jimmy Ernst. In his early

abstract surrealist canvases, deep conviction made a then uncertain technique come to life. As restless a technical inventor as his father, Jimmy lately has been painting pictures that seem more and more to be virtuoso pieces in what *Art News* calls his "language of . . . needley crystals." Thrown off by this cold fragmentation, *Art Digest* feels that his "respect for his materials and forms has not lessened but he is not interested in saying anything with them at the moment."

If this is so—the critics by no means agree—it might be because Jimmy Ernst is interested elsewhere. His paintings hanging in the museums and his annual one-man shows may seem ivory-tower stuff and their audiences pretty slim pickings.

The tower that interests Jimmy Ernst now is a slim 222-foot mast that soars 1,472 feet in the air on top of the Empire State Building. His newest abstractions are disintegrated, then transported bodilessly through space to be reassembled, finally, and set up in something like thirty million American living-rooms. The number of actual people in Jimmy's new art audience, at a recent maximum, has been estimated at from sixty to sixty-five million.[1]

For Jimmy Ernst is pioneering in a completely new field for the abstract painter: television. He chose not to wait for the museums, which so far have not cottoned to what television really means. In view of the fact that at least half of our total population has already repeatedly seen them, it seems scarcely necessary to describe the novel works of art which Jimmy has created as "visual signatures" for NBC's two gigantic "spectaculars," Fred Coe's "Producer's Showcase"

[1] The total number of viewers of NBC's telecast of *Peter Pan* was estimated at the higher figure by *Time* (August 22, 1955) and at the lower figure by NBC.

and his "Pontiac Theatre."

The television people affectionately call the intricate construction of abstract paintings on plastic used on "Showcase" "the gizmo." Before and after and at intervals during the program, as everyone knows, the gizmo fills the screen, slowly revolving while a musical theme is played. It is Jimmy Ernst's perpetual one-man show unfolding in the biggest museum ever dreamed up. The "abstract modulator" for Pontiac is something else again, a mobile sculpture. It defines space by its motion and declares light in equal measure by the flash of its forms and by their shadows. To build it, Jimmy Ernst sought the collaboration of the young sculptor-in-steel Al Terris. In 1942 Ernst built two disconcerting Dada pictures, run by the works of an alarm clock, which changed appearance when you were not looking. Now they have come of age in gizmos and modulators.

It is interesting to note that, while the producers give Jimmy a free hand, the unions have started to raise hell. "One of them," says Jimmy, "is the Screen Cartoonists Guild. I may have to join them yet."

It came to a crisis forty-eight hours before the Pontiac *première*. Union officials and NBC executives huddled and wrangled. The teamsters refused to haul the modulator to the studio; if the teamsters gave in, the electricians would not plug it in; the carpenters, property men, and "cartoonists" were in full cry. After many hours, compromise: picked men from the five embattled unions took the modulator apart and then put it together again. Only that and nothing more—at overtime pay, of course. Then they affixed to it the necessary union labels.

The abstract expressionists by no means have the scene

completely to themselves. There is room for non-objectivists like Fritz Glarner, Harry Holtzman, and Burgoyne Diller, and one of international stature like Josef Albers, as well as for followers of a personal cubism like Byron Browne, Karl Knaths, and Lee Gatch.

America being America, there is ample room, too, for individualists so individual that they cannot be classified even in the most general way. They are solitary voyagers without crew or followers. Some may become leaders like Homer and Eakins, after they themselves are no longer on the scene.

There is Milton Avery, who, though his painting is grounded on the free drawing of Matisse, has painted in a most personal way for thirty years, for nearly the first twenty of them in poverty and obscurity. There are American overtones to Avery: allusions, however slight, to the playful distortions of our chief present-day folk art, the comic strip. These allusions, rather than diminishing the validity of his art, add to it. Avery's color, too, is personal, completely un-French.

There are American women, too, who fit none of the art world's tailored suits. One is Loren MacIver. She starts, as she has often said, with simple things—a clown's face, a puddle on the pavement, the sidewalk chalk marks of a children's game, lighted candles in colored cups—the material, in a sense, of a Paul Klee. Seeking to make "something permanent out of the transitory," [2] Loren MacIver makes a poem in slowly shifting grays and muted tones strongly akin to a Whistler *Nocturne*.

The painter known simply as Lucia (Mrs. Roger Wilcox)

[2] Loren MacIver, quoted in Alfred H. Barr, Jr.: *Masters of Modern Art* (New York, 1954).

is so complex and original that she has had to find her own language. Although she knew Léger and everyone else worth knowing in Paris—where she was a jewelry- and fabric-designer—there are only the slightest traces, if any, of their work in hers. In America, Lucia began to paint, first as a delightful primitive, latterly as a knowing craftsman. Half French, half Syrian, Lucia is an Oriental modernist, painter of cities in the sky with temples as tenements and common folk who are winged beings. Her mysticism, like that of the true Oriental, is sensuous and magnificent, her holiness is lit with delight, her angels are odalisques with pinions.

Evsa Model, born in Siberia, is a chronicler of the American city without the remotest ties to our own Ash Can School or its present-day descendants. Model does not speak in prose. Mondrian gave him only the vertical-horizontal framework; the rest is all his own. The city (to Model, all America is a city) spreads across his big canvases in almost fluorescent hues, in an unperspectived pattern without depth, building over building as if pasted on in collage fashion. The colors are gay, and the cities sparkle cleanly. But the loneliness and anguish of a Chirico float in their clear air. Each building has windows, but never a door—you are either inside it forever or forever outside. Each treeless street is a blind alley at both ends, and no streets ever intersect. In one hermetic square the American flag will be stiffly flying and one lonely figure will be walking nowhere. Sometimes he is the only inhabitant or, in another picture, he walks alone, separated by the whole picture's length from The Woman. It no longer makes any difference if he is Mayor or peddler or she secretary or prostitute—they are the last of the race.

More than most, Evsa Model has paid the price of

uniqueness. His fellow painters scorned him even while some of them borrowed his ideas. He even quit painting once in despair. Rose Fried premiered him and then assiduously exhibited him at her Pinacoteca Gallery. Sidney Janis showed him later. But still Model has not caught on.

And of course there is that strange Ivan LeLorraine Albright of Chicago, who paints as if looking through a microscope that will register only decay. He did surgical drawings of wounds for the AEF in France in World War I, returned, and soon was showing with the Pennsylvania Academy. There is no describing an Albright painting. Everything is recognizable: he does men and women, and he does things to them that shouldn't happen to a dog. His realism is a jungle of flesh and fabric and wood, over which play the grisly blues and greens of phosphorescence. No sentence from Poe can pack more horror than one square inch of Albright. And yet Ivan Albright, as the Janises report, "is a simple and engaging person" who "speaks most casually with an almost continuous play of humor." [3]

Albright has not had the fate of Evsa Model. Although the public—quite understandably—does not exactly eat him up, he is constantly receiving cash prizes, medals, and honorable mentions. In December 1942, for example, his painting *That Which I Should Have Done and Did Not Do* won first prize in the Artists for Victory exhibition at the Metropolitan Museum, and as recently as 1955 he took second prize at the Corcoran Biennial in Washington. It would be quite an experience, all the same, to live with an Albright painting.

And we are left with still another man whom it is almost

[3] Harriet and Sidney Janis: "Albright: Compulsive Painter," *View*, Series III, No. 1.

impossible to categorize—Charles Howard, now living in England. Never understood by his fellow painters, he has never been popular here. With Howard, surrealism becomes abstraction in thinly brushed pictures that deny the gratification of pigment while the artist's exact and exacting intellect holds the erotic with a tight rein.

Charles Howard's small pictures, though darkly mysterious and recessively introvert, breathe a painter's true authority. Hung in today's shouting company of colossal extroverts, they are tight little islands, uninvaded, unencroachable. His paintings, like the man, are not to be slapped on the back. You have to be introduced to Charles Howard. Some who have known him for years do not yet dare to call him "Charlie." One result: he has not had a New York dealer for a number of years.

For all of our "New Vision," we seem to make some misses. There is a lot of fun left for our children when they begin discovering the artists we have passed by.

And this leaves us with the sculptors. In all modern art chronicles, they are the ones left over. Sculpture's great day— recently speaking—was the nineteenth century and the early twentieth, when Canova and Thorwaldsen, Barye, Carpeaux and Rodin, Augustus Saint-Gaudens, Gutzon Borglum and Daniel Chester French loomed large in all the collections, public and private.

But in our time the heavy emphasis has gone to painting. After city traffic had forbidden cluttering up the streets with statues, the bareness of the new architecture began wiping out the sculptor's last refuge. It almost seems as though sculptors survive only because of some vague feeling that, after all, there should be some statues, or where would we all be?

Extreme plasticity has entered painting to a degree virtually unknown since Tiepolo and the other giants of the baroque. Augmented by the forces of distortion, it functions with a more compressed violence in the shallow, almost depthless space of the modern canvas than it ever did in the old deep perspective. It pushes against the confines of picture space like Samson against the pillars, growing in fury, immediacy, and even agony.

It has quite taken the play away from sculpture. Transferring these trapped tensions into our real, three-dimensional space, the sculptor is likely to find the gestures remaining but the agony either gone or else cheapened into a banal melodrama. Our own space—however sublimated in the physicists' dreams—is sooty with the mundane.

Some sculptors, true, found the strategies to avoid the dilemma. Hans Arp stayed within the painters' space, gluing his witty, band-sawn, punning forms on a flat surface. "Bah!-

relief," someone once called them during Arp's Dada days. Brancusi, bolder, invaded space and defeated it by denying tensions, portraying the slow or never-moving, by polishing surfaces until no soot could cling. Giacometti, the surrealist, by some magic of his own, sets up a private space within the public space, to use Bertrand Russell's terms. It is like those entertaining science-fiction stories in which beings from the fourth dimension move unseen in our world, quietly walking through walls or doors. Then, too, there was the early Archipenko, who went as far as anyone could in trying to release cubism from the bonds that the cubists themselves had chosen. Perhaps Archipenko found himself in a blind alley. After a while, anyway, he gave it up.

Perhaps the most successful strategists of all were the Russian constructivists, Lissitzky, Tatlin, and the brothers Gabo and Pevsner. Like mad scientists devoted, not to the fictional sadism, but to pure odd-ball research, they built constructions. They wanted no part of marble or bronze— used wire, string, and plastics. They succeeded—most signally —by translating the psychological tensions of modern painting into their counterparts in physics; their featureless sculptures are almost ominous, awing us with their look of being diagrams of cosmic forces. Not only are the constructivists' constructions perhaps the most modern of all sculptures; they are out of this world altogether.

Here in America, where the skyscraper grew on a steel skeleton and the machine brought its own beauty with it, we plodded along without even seeing these things. The Russian constructivists beat us to it a third of a century ago at a time when their own country was almost wholly unindustrialized, while here Henry Ford was already running mass production down his long assembly lines. The Russians built machine-like structures that are not machines—ones that, motionless yet poised for motion, symbolized not only the Machine but also Science itself.

Painters as sculptors are something else again. Not since Michelangelo have we had so many of them, beginning with Degas and Renoir and coming on down to Matisse and Picasso. Degas's and Renoir's sculptures are as modern as their paintings, neither more so nor less. Matisse and Picasso, however, are special cases.

Matisse's most powerful sculptures, beyond a doubt, are the three great bronze bas-reliefs of *The Back*, now owned by the Museum of Modern Art. These are three related versions of a standing female nude seen from the back. They grow in abstraction in the order of their approximate dates: 1909, 1914, 1929. The force of this triptych is immense, but again it is trapped force. The figures are half buried in the prison of their own plaques, drowning in their native element, bronze.

Or take Picasso's great bronze *Man with a Goat*, in the Museum at Antibes. This heroic, free-standing figure is powerful and affecting. But it is so in large part, perhaps, because it denies its own period. With its look of hoary antiquity, it invokes all the force of the remembered past.

In America for the first twenty-five years of modernism we had two sculptors of reputation—Robert Laurent and William Zorach—and two of genuine originality—Elie Nadelman and Gaston Lachaise. Then along came Alexander "Sandy" Calder to usher in a sculpture both new in concept and utilizing a new technique: the moving sculpture or mobile.

Two kinds of sculpture are honored by ancient custom. Two are new, the children of industrialism and its technologies. Traditional are the hewers and carvers, on the one hand, and the modelers, on the other. New are the machinists, the hammerers, and the welders.

Rodin was at different times hewer or modeler. He cajoled the marble to the velvety flesh-softness the Greeks had once given it, in which the obdurate stone would seemingly yield to the press of a fingertip. When he modeled clay to be cast in bronze, he paradoxically roughened the soft mud into the erosions of weathered stone crags.

Brancusi's works appear both in hewn stone and in polished cast bronze that retains the character of stone hewn and then polished, not to softness but to a granitic hardness. Many of them, like *Maïastra*, the mythical Romanian bird, and the famous *Bird in Space*, appeared first in marble, later in metal. They seem conceived by stone and born of stone, as if hatched from that veritable stone egg, the Brancusi *New-born* of 1915. And as if to prove that metal can gestate in stone —as indeed it does in ore—the stone egg in 1922 hatched its bronze identical progeny, now in the Museum of Modern Art. Enough of human physiognomy remained in the celebrated head of *Mlle Pogany* to shock Armory Show visitors. The ultimate blankness of the *Bird* or the *New-born* might have been less shocking, strangely more acceptable.

Elie Nadelman was in Paris before World War I, but his subsequent sculpture, done here, used the folk art of our own Early American woodcarvers and metalsmiths as the vocabulary of a thoroughly contemporary satiric wit. At the same time, William Zorach was hewing static stone figures full of those symbolisms of maternity, fertility, and so forth, which, when explicitly stated, so easily become pretentious.

Gaston Lachaise, using subject matter similar to that of Zorach, was something else altogether. His great full-blown bronze women float on tiptoe as if the air supported them as water supports the swimmer. There is no sententiousness or any attempt to be abstract—no direct reference, in fact, to any other sculpture past or present. Lachaise's look is a straight look at naked woman, as direct, as devouring, and as naïve as Adam's first look at Eve. Lachaise seems somehow to have grasped timelessness. Clothed only in a prehistoric purity, his *Standing Woman*, all the seven and one-half feet of her assured presence, dominates the sculpture in the Museum of Modern Art garden.

In 1926–7 Alexander Calder was building his wire *Circus* "peopled by diminutive caricature performers whom he sent perilously and enchantingly through familiar circus routine."[1] By 1931 he was using the new techniques of the welder, and there, finally reflected in our art, was the technological change long since made from handicraft to the machine-made. Calder then added that which was implicit in constructivism and so typical of our time: motion. Not that he was first to do so: Duchamp's *Bicycle Wheel* of 1913 could be turned by hand; Nahum Gabo's *Kinetic Sculpture* of 1922, "a metal band with a small weight at the head . . . was operated by a clockspring, producing torsion in an intense, sustained movement"; and Duchamp in 1925 had used a motor to rotate a spiral optical disk. Duchamp, as Barr relates, even gave Calder's new moving sculptures their name of "mobiles."[2]

---

[1] This and the succeeding quotation are from Harriet Janis: "Mobiles," *Arts and Architecture*, February 1948.

[2] Alfred H. Barr, Jr.: *Masters of Modern Art* (New York, 1954).

Calder occasionally uses motors, but in general his intricate, suspended galaxies are free sheet-metal forms propelled by the wind. In any event, Calder has thoroughly explored the possibilities of motion—so thoroughly, in fact, that a stroboscopic photograph of the performance of a Calder mobile is as complex as almost any modern painting.

With their contemporary aptness—joining industrial process with art, and scientifically ordered movement with the "laws of chance"—the Calder mobiles have become one of the most widely known of modern art forms. "How to Do It" magazines publish patterns and instructions; drugstores sell "mobile kits"; people who literally have never heard of the Museum of Modern Art make mobiles at home. Perhaps there is an unnoticed kinship between a Calder mobile and the traditional wrought-iron weathervane or the carved Early American "whirligig" on the barn.

Julio Gonzalez adopted iron sculpture in Paris in 1930, and Calder popularized it at about the same time here. For all the furor in that decade over the newly discovered vinylacetate plastics, good old iron was the timely thing. Americans, on the whole, took to it more readily than the French, who let go of elegance most grudgingly. Within a few years the American welder-sculptors were coming on in force. They liked iron and the sizzling acetylene welding torch, and all the captivating metals—cadmium, copper, silver, brass, and bronze—that can be welded or brazed. But Calder seems to them to have exhausted the practical calculus of motion so conclusively that to a man they have avoided making moving sculpture.

Into their work has gone the influence of Calder and, more overtly, of Gonzalez. The Spaniard, who taught iron-working to Picasso, was first shown at the Museum of Modern Art in 1937. His grotesquely abstract and imaginative *Head* of wrought iron had an immediate appeal for the new American sculptors. Into the work of most of them has gone, too, the strange alphabet of surrealism—chiefly through the work of Giacometti—and much of that space which De Kooning calls "melancholy." Their work has opened up to reveal gaping empty holes that often are intended to be the most significant "forms" in their work.

Dean of this sculptural generation is Isamu Noguchi, born in Los Angeles in 1904, bred in Japan, but American to the bone. In Paris in 1927–8 he was assistant to Brancusi. Returning here, he exhibited his metal constructions in New York in 1929 at the Eugene Schoen Gallery. Iron, however, has not held Noguchi's interest. In the 1940's he worked in stone, interlocking flat, free-formed slabs in a geometrical relationship of support. Having gone back to Japan to master the ceramic art, he is now producing unglazed pieces of notable size, considering the technical limitations to be faced when baking clay.

The rest are metal men.

David Smith had an early *première* in 1938 at Marian Willard's East River Gallery. His work is rugged and massive. Sometimes, as in *Blackburn: Song of an Irish Blacksmith*, it has faraway echoes of the work of Duchamp's sculptor brother, Raymond Duchamp-Villon, a casualty of World War I. Duchamp-Villon's bronze *The Horse*, which Barr has said "is conceived as a great animal-machine," [3] stands in the Museum of Modern Art garden. So bright had been the promise of Duchamp-Villon that, Walter Pach commented bitterly,

[3] Ibid.

"he could have been replaced by numberless men among the millions who fought; in his own field he was the greatest man of his time." [4]

Seymour Lipton, actually, is a year older than Noguchi, but he came into sculpture later and did not work abstractly until 1944 or show extensively until four years later still. He works characteristically in thin, concave forms of sheet metal which combine like growing forms. In one piece Gonzalez can be seen, or in another, Duchamp-Villon.

Herbert Ferber, like Lipton, is a dentist and, again like Lipton, is a comparative latecomer in abstract sculpture, which he began about 1942. There is much of Gonzalez in Ferber's work, in the spiky forms and the spiky resulting spaces. His first museum sale was to the Metropolitan in 1943.

By contrast with Ferber, Peter Grippe's work in metal tends to be visceral like that of one phase of the School of Paris sculptor Lipchitz, and placed in cages like some of the pieces that Ossip Zadkine did in Greenwich Village while exiled here during the last war.

Ibram Lassaw, born in Egypt in 1913, works with lumpily welded lines of metal sometimes geometrically joined, at other times growing in the upward articulations of plant or flame.

Theodore J. Roszak is Polish-born. From 1935 to the mid-1940's he made rather dry constructions of wire, wood, and plastic, somewhat in the Russian vein. Of late he hammers and welds steel encrusted with bronze and brass into veritable apparitions and monsters of metal.

Another Japanese sculptor—now American—is Leo Amino, who works with slabs of mahogany as Noguchi had worked with stone. Amino's most interesting work seems to be

[4] Walter Pach: *Queer Thing, Painting* (New York, 1938).

in his hollow transparent plastic forms filled with liquid wherein floating objects circulate.

One of the brightest talents of the 1940's was David Hare, first shown by Peggy Guggenheim in 1945. His early alphabet was largely that of Giacometti, but his message was different. Taking another page from the surrealist credo, Hare expressed overtones of a cruel sadism. The characteristic works of that period are in white plaster, and occasionally in bronze cast from the plaster originals. Apart from plaster's fragility, its ghostly white seemed best to express Hare's intention. Hare at present seems to be in transition, working, like the others, in steel.

Richard Lippold, who did not show until 1947 at Marian Willard's, is a man with something quite his own to say, even though it certainly is the exact opposite of the abstract-expressionist idea. Lippold works with tempered wires of different gauges and metals. Lacking evidence to the contrary, one feels that his are the most delicate sculptures in human history. They are certainly the most fragile-looking. The tiny wires drawn in space as if etched with the engraver's finest burin would seemingly yield to a breath of air. That Lippold's wire sculptures should actually have so considerable a strength and that, almost weightless, they should carry so much weight as statements, should not be so surprising as it seems. Lippold approaches the daring art of the arachnids. The hand of the human artist has perhaps never come closer to the miracle of the spider's web.

If, on the whole, the sculptors of the abstract-expressionist generation fail to fire unqualified enthusiasm, this, after all, is painting's day. The painters have said it. If you find in them the fury of Van Gogh and Soutine and whatever other elements from cubism to surrealism, these are no more than the automatic inheritance of any painter of mid-century. Out of old words and new they have found something of their own to say.

They will be long remembered as a remarkably rugged lot, with minds as well muscled as their bodies (*Time* calls Pollock "The Champ"). They are built like athletes, and some of them, like Pollock and De Kooning, paint like athletes. If pictures could explode, theirs would, so grimly by the force of their wills have they compressed their dual muscularity onto the canvas.

Physical power lends their rebelliousness the primitive weight that it carries in the lumber camps; their tough-mindedness dispels the slightest suspicion of querulousness. They are a strange breed of esthetes completely unlike the old notion of painters as a wan fraternity of daydreamers. They live their art. It took this generation to give us the center of the stage. If any group can ever force our museums and collectors to accept American modernism, this is surely the bunch to do it.

Best of all, hard on the heels of the Pollocks and the De Koonings, the Klines and the Rothkos, there pound the eager feet of a new generation. Already to the oncomers these are not the titles of gods, but slightly old-fashioned names. They have found new leaders of their own.

One of these, remarkably enough, is a woman: Joan Mitchell. Rosa Bonheur and Mary Cassatt must surely be turning in their graves with joy. The other is an older painter, Philip Guston, of whom one has just suddenly heard, though he was vastly successful, it seems, in the world of conservative art. Guston was a Woodstock painter, enjoying great financial success and painting murals everywhere, when suddenly the bug bit him. In 1948 he had his first abstract show. Things move so swiftly today that no sooner is a new painter established than he becomes a force to react against. Thus, Philip Guston becomes a leader of this still newer generation.

New dealers spring up to water the new crop, in lofts or obsolete offices in the low-rent areas of downtown New York. At this precise moment the Stable is inheriting the artists who sprouted in the Hansa Gallery and particularly in the Tanager, an artists' co-operative that in four years showed nearly one hundred and fifty painters and sculptors of the youngest generation. By tomorrow there will be galleries newer still.

The names of the new generation have begun to emerge: Joan Mitchell, Wolf Kahn, and Ernest Briggs, as well as Robert Goodnough, Paul Brach, and John Grillo, all in New York; Richard Diebenkorn of the Pacific Coast, and his fellow Californian, Sam Francis, who at the moment is wowing Paris. Then there is a sculptor named Richard Stankiewicz, a welder who disdains bright new metal to assemble rusty iron junk into personages that might have been spawned by our sad and wasteful time. What a truly modern art school can accomplish is shown by the large number of artists from Douglas MacAgy's California School of Fine Arts, among them Briggs, Laurence Calcagno, Diebenkorn, and Francis.

And then, suddenly, fame's veering spotlight picks out the first of the newcomers. John Hultberg, of California and MacAgy's school, wins the Corcoran grand prize in 1955. Almost immediately thereafter he is the only American prizewinner in Rome in an International Exhibition for Artists under Thirty-Five. Then, while *Time* and *Life* are taking him up and the Whitney, the Albright, and even the Metropolitan are adding Hultbergs to their collections, he takes an honorable mention at the Pittsburgh International, which in 1955 awarded no prizes to Americans.

Credit goes to the Museum of Modern Art's Andrew Carnduff Ritchie for originally discovering this artist. Ritchie showed him in 1952 at the Museum's New Talent Show at a time when John Hultberg was a completely unknown name.

Here, then, is some of the newest new art. We look at young Hultberg's paintings and are reassured. No aping of success—or obeisance, even, to complete abstraction—in these extraordinary visions of ruined cities, broken houses, shattered ships. Nightmare lives in these pictures that are not quite like any pictures ever painted before. The private nightmare of surrealism and Chirico becomes the general nightmare of our time.[5]

Then we look at Hultberg himself and are re-reassured. He has the hulking build and the modesty coupled with quiet truculence which we have come to expect of our American modern painters. Then, to increase our gratification, we learn that John Hultberg went it alone—against the public, the critics, and his fellow artists—before he made it. Finally, we discover that most of the critics and most other artists still reject him. Good. Art needs such rebels.

Something of the wild grandeur of these kids—space men of the brush and canvas—is conveyed in *Time*'s quote of a remark by one of Hultberg's former San Francisco art school-

[5] A critic asked Hultberg: "Do these show New York after the atom bomb?" Hultberg grunted a curt "No," and then added: "The cities are already ruined."

mates. Sam Francis, who is built like a wingback, is "the hottest American painter in Paris," says *Time*, one who "has caused even palette-jaded Parisians to perk up." His gigantic canvases—one recently bought by the Kunsthalle at Basel measures fourteen by ten feet—are galaxies of light. But Sam Francis dreams of canvases incalculably larger, and he expects science to help him to paint them.

"I'd like"—*Time* quotes him—"to buy one of those flying platforms they've just designed. Gosh, with one of those, you could hover any place you wanted, and you could make 40-ft. brush strokes."

So there is no let-up in sight.

Already the great pioneer group of the early days of our century are departing from the scene that they made so lively. In 1955 both Matisse and Léger died. Picasso, the seemingly indestructible, lives on, nearing eighty, apparently destined to fructify art until at last he drops his brush. Here in America, Lyonel Feininger, the artist who came back to his country, at eighty-four has just put the last brushstroke on his final canvas, leaving to the world his long, serene mastery of light and air. John Marin is dead. Snowy-haired Walkowitz is blind. Only Max Weber still works. But their statements have been made. Even those of Marcel Duchamp, who, as Georges Hugnet has written, has "left on the period the magnificent mark of his disinterestedness." Duchamp, who believes in time and its work as others believe in God, can calmly wait until we unravel his meanings.

They have made their statements. Or rather, one should say, they have asked the questions that were crying out to be asked. For half a century modern art has been one great question shouted at the world. Like Jericho's walls, the dead thought of centuries, all the moldy masonry of absolutism, have fallen in a heap of rubble, leveled by the shattering sound. The essence of the modern spirit, as our time has known it, has been not so much in its answers as in its questions.

It is a great thing to be able to ask questions. What is this thing called fire that can warm our bodies or can destroy us? Is our earth really flat? What is truth? What is the good? What is the act of seeing? What is it that is seen?

Man is the only animal that asks questions. These questions move mankind as mankind moves. What a long affirmation of man as Man they have been!

We are not going to stop asking them.

Index

v

A Note on the Type

The text of this book was set on the Monotype in a face called Baskerville, named for John Baskerville (1706–75), of Birmingham, England, who was a writing master with a special renown for cutting inscriptions in stone. About 1750 he began experimenting with punch-cutting and making typographical material, which led, in 1757, to the publication of his first work, a Virgil in royal quarto, with great primer letters, in which the types throughout had been designed by him. This was followed by his famous editions of Milton, the Bible, the Book of Common Prayer, and several Latin classic authors. His types foreshadowed what we know today as the "modern" group of type faces, and these and his printing became greatly admired. After his death Baskerville's widow sold all his punches and matrices to the SOCIÉTÉ PHILOSOPHIQUE, LITTÉRAIRE ET TYPOGRAPHIQUE (totally embodied in the person of Beaumarchais, author of THE MARRIAGE OF FIGARO and THE BARBER OF SEVILLE), which used some of the types to print the seventy volume edition, at Kehl, of Voltaire's works. After a checkered career on the Continent, where they dropped out of sight for some years, the punches and matrices finally came into the possession of the distinguished Paris type-founders, Deberny & Peignot, who, in singularly generous fashion, returned them to the Cambridge University Press in 1953.

Composed, printed, and bound by KINGSPORT PRESS, INC., Kingsport, Tennessee. Paper manufactured by S. D. WARREN COMPANY, Boston, Massachusetts. Designed by HARRY FORD.